D1352969

Schreber's Law

EDINBURGH CRITICAL STUDIES IN LAW, LITERATURE AND THE HUMANITIES
Series Editor: William MacNeil, Southern Cross University
Senior Deputy Editor: Shaun McVeigh, University of Melbourne
Deputy Editor: Daniel Hourigan, University of Southern Queensland

With a global reach, this innovative series critically reimagines the interdisciplinary relationship between legal and literary (or other aesthetic) texts through the most advanced conceptual frameworks and interpretive methods of contemporary theory available in the humanities and jurisprudence.

Editorial Board
Dr Maria Aristodemou (Birkbeck, University of London)
Associate Professor Fatou Kine Camara (Université Cheikh Anka Diop de Dakar)
Professor Daniela Carpi (University of Verona)
Dr Susan Chaplin (Leeds Beckett University)
Professor Andrew Clarke (Victoria University)
Dr Stella Clarke (University of Melbourne)
Professor Penny Fielding (University of Edinburgh)
Mme Justice Hon Jeanne Gaakeer (Erasmus University Rotterdam)
Professor Peter Goodrich (Cardozo School of Law, Yeshiva University)
Professor Elizabeth Hanson (Queen's University at Kingston)
Associate Professor Susan Sage Heinzelman (University of Texas at Austin)
Professor Bonnie Honig (Brown University)
Professor Rebecca Johnson (University of Victoria)
Dr Orit Kamir (Hebrew Union College)
Associate Professor Lissa Lincoln (American University Paris)
Professor Desmond Manderson (Australian National University)
Professor Panu Minkkenen (University of Helsinki)
Dr Anat Rosenberg (IDC Herzliya)
Professor Renata Salecl (Ljubljana/Birkbeck, University of London)
Professor Austin Sarat (Amherst College)
Dr Jan Melissa Schram (University of Cambridge)
Professor Karin Van Marle (University of Pretoria)
Dr Marco Wan (University of Hong Kong)
Professor Ian Ward (University of Newcastle)
Professor Alison Young (University of Melbourne)

Available or forthcoming titles
Schreber's Law: Jurisprudence and Judgment in Transition
Peter Goodrich

Living in Technical Legality: Science Fiction and Law as Technology
Kieran Tranter

Schreber's Law

Jurisprudence and Judgment in Transition

Peter Goodrich

EDINBURGH
University Press

Edinburgh University Press is one of the leading university presses in the UK. We publish academic books and journals in our selected subject areas across the humanities and social sciences, combining cutting-edge scholarship with high editorial and production values to produce academic works of lasting importance. For more information visit our website: edinburghuniversitypress.com

© Peter Goodrich, 2018, 2020

Edinburgh University Press Ltd
The Tun – Holyrood Road
12 (2f) Jackson's Entry
Edinburgh EH8 8PJ

First published in hardback by Edinburgh University Press 2018

Typeset in 11/13pt Adobe Garamond Pro by
Servis Filmsetting Ltd, Stockport, Cheshire
and printed and bound in Great Britain by
CPI Group (UK) Ltd, Croydon, CR0 4YY

A CIP record for this book is available from the British Library

ISBN 978 1 4744 2656 5 (hardback)
ISBN 978 1 4744 2657 2 (paperback)
ISBN 978 1 4744 2658 9 (webready PDF)
ISBN 978 1 4744 2659 6 (epub)

The right of Peter Goodrich to be identified as author of this work has been asserted in accordance with the Copyright, Designs and Patents Act 1988 and the Copyright and Related Rights Regulations 2003 (SI No. 2498).

Alternative book cover and frontispiece by Jake Tilson, 2018.

Contents

List of Illustrations   vi
Preface and Credits   vii

Introduction: On the Case   1
1   Miscarriages of Transmission: Body, Text and Method   9
2   Silencing Schreber: Freud, Lacan, Rejection and Foreclosure   32
3   *Morbus Juridicus*: Crisis and Critique of Law   61
4   The Impure Theory of Law: The Metaphysics of Play-With-
    Human-Beings   87
5   The Judge's New Body: Am I That (Woman)?   112
Conclusion: Laughing in the Void   138

Bibliography   151
Index   159

Illustrations

Frontispiece 1   Miss Schreber (composite image from photoportrait
of Daniel Paul, moustache removed, accoutrements
added; by Jake Tilson)   xi

Frontispiece 2   Photoportrait of Daniel Paul Schreber (with thanks
to the Library of Congress, Niederland Collection)   xiii

Figure 1   Schreber, *Memoirs*, 1988 edition   13
Figure 2   Schreber, *Denkwürdigkeiten*, title page, first edition, 1903   17
Figure 3   Schreber, *Memoirs*, cover image, 1988 edition   18
Figure 4   Schreber's dedication of *Denkwürdigkeiten* to his wife   27
Figure 5   Silvestro Pietrasancta, *De Symbolis heroicis*, 1634 edition   146
Figure 6   From James Bramston, *Art of Politics*, 1729   147
Figure 7   Sheet music in Schreber's possession   150

Preface and Credits

I first and fleetingly came across Judge Daniel Paul Schreber's remarkable record of his nervous illness, *Denkwürdigkeiten eines Nervenkranken* (Memorabilia of a Nerve Patient), as a law student.[1] I assumed, in my youthful state, and later as a neophyte academic, that such a unique and candidly graphic work by a senior judge would have been dissected, deliberated upon, argued over and disputed, if not excoriated or anathematised by lawyers, ad infinitum. It transpired, however, that the Judge's *magnum opus* had received no such attention and indeed the medical and psychoanalytic diagnosis of his madness had seemingly put a stop to any attention being paid to his legal discourse and the radical experience of gender dysphoria and transitional theory of sexuality, of creativity and law that he gives vivid vent to in his immaculate text. The recent and comprehensive study of *The Jurists* by James Gordley, for instance, a work I greatly admire, is much within the norm in making no mention of him in its 312 tightly packed pages, and yet by any count he was one of the most interesting, complex and painfully inventive of lawyers.[2] He has been studied, of course, and endlessly, by psychiatrists, psychoanalysts, philosophers, and literary theorists, but neither within the pantheon of the biographical dictionaries of law, nor, as said, among 'the' jurists, is there reference, comment, accolade or critique. Yet, it is hard to claim that the definite article excludes a jurist whose work has had such remarkable longevity and remains in print to this day.

Much later, in the self-confessed moment of 'trans revolution', of testo junkies, hormone hacking, xenofeminism, trans identities of all sorts,

---

[1] The various possible translations of the title are discussed in Chapter 1. For ease of reference, although not without serious reservations, I will cite Ida MacAlpine and Richard Hunter's text, *Memoirs of My Nervous Illness* (Cambridge, MA: Harvard University Press, 1988) and, simultaneously, the German text whose pagination is used in the margins of the translation and will be my point of reference in all moments of disorientation.

[2] James Gordley, *The Jurists* (Oxford: Oxford University Press, 2013) and this despite significant attention to the late nineteenth-century German legal schools of thought.

surgical, chemical and pharmacopornographic, X-passports on the near hori-
zon, Schreber always somewhere at the back of my mind, the silence of all
manner of jurists and jurisprudes, *nomikoi* and jurisconsults, came slowly
to seem ever more deafening and surprising. I experienced, just to reference
Foucault, an inkling of an archaeology of a juridical silence and so I decided
to investigate further and then to reclaim the Judge's lively and discriminat-
ing text as also being of interest and importance for law and lawyers. Here, in
a vivid, emotive and highly critical juristic text can be found the cogent and
thoroughly coherent bellowings, the *bullae*, meaning edicts and legislations of
a senior Judge turned furious forensic orator in the cause, most proleptically,
of transgender sensibilities, of sexual ambiguity, transition and x-status, and
their proper jurisprudential elaboration through a novel metaphysics of law.
Surely this text was too good to be left, to borrow a phrase from Lacan, to
'the little shrunken brains' of modern legal scientists. It needs to be taken
seriously by humanistic lawyers, the *iuris periti* in their artistic intellective
role. They, of all professions, should know the maxim *lux et lex ex tenebris*,
that light and law emerge from darkness, and that the judge's bellowing, and
specifically his supposedly occult book, resonate still, and indeed sound more
in these plural and imaginatively trans times.

In such a vein and mood, I lectured on Schreber at the University of
Turin in Italy, in the faculties of theology and law, in the spring of 2012,
at the invitation of the Italian Association of Aesthetics and Law. Don't
ask – or what better forum for a convention of tested souls and the resurrection of Daniel Paul's text for the benefit of existentially anxious lawyers?
A veritable forum of unsettled identities and mobile personae. The talk was
held in a Renaissance seminar room, on a cool clear morning, in the old part
of the university, with much too much light and too much divinity for my
slides to be visible. I was elaborating, and it must have been about 11am,
on the Judge's bellowing. It was a symptom, I opined, that could be termed
a brontological ailment, the speech of thunder. No sooner had the words
fallen from my lips than there was a single, crystal clear clap of thunder
outside. *Schreber afflavit et dissipati sunt.*[3] It may seem far-fetched, and that
is because it undoubtedly is, my colleague the theologian Professor Heritier
claims not to have heard – Heritier nodded – but in a sentiment of spiritual
apprehension, in a tenor of support and acknowledgement of fellow feeling,
I intuited that Schreber had momentarily manifested, he had bellowed again,
his fleetingly improvised appearance confirming the need I had long felt to
pursue the project of retrieving his text from the historical asylum instituted

---

[3] Schreber bellowed and they were scattered abroad.

by his doctors and hir interpreters.[4] And by way of credit, acknowledgement and due payment of debts, my thanks to many. Anselm Haverkamp, most loyal discussant, helped me initially upon my way with critical percipience and his profound sense of *languor iuris*. Paolo Heritier invited me to Turin and has remained a colleague and friend. Bernie Meyler and Elizabeth Anker organised a symposium at Cornell University in New York where I performed some snippets on Schreber. Hilary Schor offered invaluable intuitions on my method, Julie Stone Peters manifested a wave of support and Bradin Cormack smiled. Connal Parsley and Maria Drakapoulou organised a seminar in Paris where I tried out these ideas again and in more elaborate form. A conference at Cardozo (School of Law, New York) and, in the same week, a mock trial of Schreber's case organised by Scott Von at Analytica provided opportunities and conversations that expanded my thinking. Daniela Gandorfer touched down and meticulously assisted with translation and with many of the finer details of much of the German to be found in the text. Her work was selfless, generous, expansive and fashion conscious. Michelle Castaneda took time out of her oscillating schedule and multiform pendulations to provide feminist criticism but never critique. Vanessa Rüeger helped with references and shared her opinations. Davide Tarizzo, my fellow seminar convener in Paris, was vocal in criticism and enthusiastic in his generously intended encouragement to abandon the work. We agreed eventually to disagree. Mark Sanders provided signal inspiration, invaluable guidance and generosity of time in mind. His scrupulousness is exemplary. Henry (Zvi) Lothane was expansive in conversation and in his willingness to share his own memorabilia, remarkable research and depths of knowledge of Schreber. Linda Mills, *amicus fidelissima*, more than the many, offered her own unique insights and correctives from the very beginning. She understands better than any that the lure of Schreber's text is the madness within.

---

[4] For social, political, moral, legal and pharmaco-technological reasons Schreber's transition was in the main unsuccessful, blocked, and so I have melancholically retained in the main the pronominal he. Occasionally, when Schreber is in vivid moments of transitional acceptance, I have used she, or simply to unsettle the idiocy of binary differences, and elsewhere, in between, I have in some instances used hir. All pronouns are contingent, and can be changed as suits mood and tone.

Schreber's Law

Jurisprudence and Judgment in Transition

Introduction: On the Case

Judge Daniel Paul Schreber, jurist, scholar, self-confessed poetaster, spiritualist and pianist fell famously ill first when, as a junior judge, he stood and failed to get elected to the Reichstag, the German parliament, in the fall of 1884. His ignominious defeat at the poles triggered a nervous breakdown, manifested in insomnia, hypochondria and weight loss. It resulted in a relatively brief stay in the Leipzig clinic run by Professor Flechsig, who on this occasion seems to have cured the judge. Eight years later, soon after his appointment to a senior judicial position, Senatspräsident of one of the three Chambers of the Royal Court of Appeals in Dresden, he suffered a second breakdown marked most notably by gender dysphoria and, to coin a phrase, *Scriptarrhea*, or the drive to write – the Thoth complex, which insists, in good juristic fashion, upon inscription, a record, and in consonance with the Statute of Frauds, is impelled by the postulate of the parol evidence rule, namely that writing is the best proof.

Schreber's uniqueness lies not in his nervous breakdowns, which are common enough in the legal profession, but in the uniquely detailed, extraordinarily candid and paradoxically lucid account of his nervous indisposition, his transitional desire and his critique of law, published in 1903, with a rather early modern length of title as *Denkwürdigkeiten eines Nervenkranken nebst Nachträgen und einem Anhang über die Frage: 'Unter welchen Voraussetzungen darf eine für geisteskrank erachtete Person gegen ihren erklärten Willen in einer Heilanstalt festgehalten werden?'*.[1] A denizen of the late nineteenth century, he

---

[1] Published after Schreber's release from Sonnenstein Asylum, in 1903. The English translation, by Ida Macalpine and Richard Hunter, using the truncated title *Memoirs of My Nervous Illness*, is available from Harvard University Press, and a dual-language edition, to which all page references refer, is available online. For ease of citation, I will use *Memoirs of My Nervous Illness* in the footnotes, with emendations of the English, but will retranslate the title, borrowing from Mark Sanders, as *Memorabilia of a Nerve Patient* in the text. Discussion of this idiosyncratic cry for attention on my part follows later in the introduction.

fell through a mental hole and abandoned his profession for unusual but highly articulate spiritual, libidinal and juristic reasons. It will be argued here that in his unflinchingly forthright description of his gender dysphoria and her transitional experiences, in his delineation of anger and pain, she authored a radically novel and surprisingly visceral critique of the masculine body, and of the law that it manifested, a positive theory of the highly tenuous spiritual grounds of judgement and an engendered conception of justice and right. It is in the manner and method of law, out of respect for the Judge's writings and in honor of their creativity and often judicious insights, that the starting point of any encounter with Schreber must be his frequently ignored and prejudicially labelled text. The silence needs to be broken and voice returned to the transitional judge and to his extra-judicial elaborations and syntagma. The Judge begins the book with a profession of intent: he is persuaded, the Preface announces, to publish this unusual work because of its value for science and 'for the knowledge of religious truths'.[2] All subjective considerations, and especially any reticence in candidly relaying the subject matter of his experience, are overtly dispelled by the drive to knowledge, a radical case of epistemophilia. The initial veracity sought, he continues immediately, is that of the law and of a verdict – a statement of the truth, *vera dictum* – that will allow him to be released from his involuntary tutelage in the asylum at Sonnenstein and the wardship of its director, Dr Weber. He then acknowledges that his litigation for release was successful, 'my legal capacity was thereby acknowledged' and he has in his possession, at the time of writing, the record of the authority for his liberty, the instrument and juridical writing that entitles him to freedom and recognition. He is able now to change some of what he had earlier inscribed, he can write with greater range, but he decides to leave the text largely within its previous scope to retain its 'freshness' or, perhaps better, its virginity. More than that, his account of God's relationship to him, 'contrary to the Order of the World', is of secondary importance in a work of theological and so permanent significance. Again, personal considerations and subjective experiences are to be read only in the context of the ideas, juristic and metaphysical, that they witness, exemplify and convey. The Preface, even though it introduces the text, is written last. It is the prelude, the *prae-ludium* or foreplay that prepares the reader for the encounter and here begins the disclosure of a double struggle, the *agon* of the asylum and the antagonism of the law. In the 'Open Letter to Professor Flechsig', who was the immediate cause of Schreber's involuntary commitment to the Sonnenstein Asylum, it is a combination of the two antinomies

---

[2] *Memoirs* at iv.

that gains expression. Law, both in the letter and in the litigation of the Judge, here confronts psychiatry and gently yet firmly accuses Flechsig of playing God and doing Schreber harm. Despite the threat of legal action being taken against him, and undeterred by any personal affront that may be occasioned, the Judge insists in a crucial and proleptic manner that even though Flechsig and others – Dr Weber, Sigmund Freud, Professor Lacan, Gilles Deleuze, Elias Canetti, Colin MacCabe and Davide Tarizzo all spring to mind – will be tempted to read the book that follows 'as nothing more than a pathological offspring of my imagination', he insists upon its truth, the justness and veracity (*Richtigkeit*) of his experience. Here, introducing the concept of the 'tested soul', meaning the impure, full of faults and mislocated being, the grounded, undeparted, trapped soul, Schreber portrays Professor Dr Flechsig, and by association the psychiatric profession, as the instigator of hir injuries. Dr Flechsig may have had good intentions, morally pure purposes, but the effects of his practice were interference and injury. Far from treating the Judge, it is Schreber's assertion that the Doctor had with ruthless lust for power followed his own interests and drives. Rather than providing an appropriate therapy he had fallen prey to the temptation 'of using a patient in . . . [his] care *as an object for scientific experiments* apart from the real purpose of cure'.[3] Schreber terms this scientific play with the patient medical malpractice and, for additional emphasis, soul murder – *Seelenmord*.[4] His appeal in the letter is not, however, an attack on the Doctor so much as it is a request for support, and specifically, in so far as such was possible, for affirmation of the Judge's experiences. Schreber's primary concern is that of building a case, advocating his own sanity and proposing that his text be read not as madness but as theory, as that mixture of philosophy and law that bears the inelegant name of jurisprudence. The juristic impetus of the *Memorabilia*, the legal fight against medical malpractice and misdiagnosis, is reasserted straight off in the introduction. Page 1, opening line, Schreber announces that he has applied for release from the asylum, to live again among civilised people and to be understood. This may be ambitious, but it is certainly clearly stated that this 'is the purpose of this manuscript', namely to explain his apparent oddities (*Absonderlichkeiten*) of behavior, and peculiarities of religious belief, as founded in experience and rationally presented. There is nothing dogmatic in this. He admits that he cannot maintain that 'everything is irrefutably certain even for me: much remains only presumption and probability'.[5] More honest than most of us. What the Judge offers is modestly depicted as 'approximately correct', and he

---

[3] Ibid. at x; emphasis in the original.

[4] Ibid. at x–xi.

[5] Ibid. at 1–2

circumspectly proposes an appropriately limited approach to questions of
theology, of the eternal and infinite, of nature and the supernatural, of creation, the void and the soul. It is with a relative freedom from dogmatics, liber-
ated from legal science and the strictures of pure theory and positivism, that
the Judge announces a malaise, an ailment (*Krankheit*) that propelled his
entry into 'peculiar relations with God – which I hasten to add were contrary
to the Order of the World'.[6] What follows, by way of setting the scene and
preparing the ground for Schreber's account of his own transformation, is
self-consciously predicated upon axioms – tenets – that cannot be proven, as
to the nature of the divine, the definition of nerves, the role of miracles and
particularly the equilibrium that the Judge believes to be proper for the Order
of the World. The drives propel from outside, an alien will within that is both
familiar and peculiarly explicable in terms of an era devoted to categorical
imperatives that are legislated a priori. So we read. The noumenal is unknowable, according to Kant, whose 'Nebular Hypothesis' Schreber briefly references. Belief should therefore be separated from knowledge, theology from
science and metaphysics from law. There are indeed for Schreber 'forecourts
of heaven', spaces of pre-law or *arche* institution that separate the living from
the dead, the body from the corpse and so too the pure from the tested soul.
The concept of the *Vorhof*, is that of an atrium, a foundational space of
paternity, of tradition, oversight and transmission, the site of the classical
image (*imago*) through which the variegated messages and imaginations of the
collectivity, the *Phantasie* of the psychiatrists and lawyers – the wonderfully
depicted 'fleeting-improvised-men' or sketchy beings – who insisted and continue to presume to judge the Judge as pathological, as mad and as the author,
solely and singly, exclusively of a lunatic discourse. It is the last aspersion that
is the most indicative.

The Judge, confined once in the asylum, is incarcerated again by his
interpreters, by history, by psychiatry and psychoanalysis, and thus emerges
in the contemporary as an author who should not be read prior to his foreclosure, before the judgement of insanity has been pronounced, and the text has
thus pretty much invariably been viewed through the lens of lunacy and the
diagnostic categories whereby those judged insane are excluded and their
voice rendered silent, their tones eviscerated, their affects impounded. Times,
however, have changed and Schreber is indubitably different. He persists. He
won his lawsuit. He carried around the written proof of his legal competence
but never of his sanity, because that cannot be proved against the all too easy
ascriptions upon his corpse, the text. That said and marked, another reading

---

[6] Ibid. at 5.

is increasingly possible and will be pieced together in this book, one that is more sympathetic and literal, less judgemental, less oblivious to the obvious metaphor, and expansive allegorical qualities of the text, not so blind to its humor and its pain, not so determined to determine, in sum, not so decided upon deciding. The law, the verdict of the Royal Court of Appeals, was that Schreber was legally competent and should be released. The fact that the other disciplines refuse to release him deserves a certain attention, a degree of scrutiny. As the Court put it, belief in the spiritual, indeed invocation of the ineffable and all comprehending, is not usually a reason to designate someone as being insane. It seems, in other words, that even if Schreber's readers in the psy-disciplines tend to ignore his prefatory and introductory statements of purpose and methodology, it is the text that follows his overtures that raises the hackles and bends the instruments of science to their unilateral and choral diagnosis. What should be treated as description, the empirical basis of his legal critique and the theory of free law, are rather confined for the somewhat implausible purpose of an aetiology and diagnosis aimed at curing the dead judge. But that is not Schreber's purpose. He does not need a cure. He is well. The text that flows from the preface offers an account of a slow transition, via the forecourts, the pre-law of the heavens, to the visceral description of the improper and resisted intrusion of the divinity into and on to the Judge. He experiences, as Fernie so well describes, a possession, an alien force within, the disarray of his nerves, the transitional hyper-sensitivity of the body in response to the sudden incursion and drive to identify with the feminine and become, to all appearances, in his own second mirror phase, a woman.[7] It is only on the thirty-fifth page of the *Memorabilia* that Schreber first mentions his nervous breakdown. Prior to that the tone of the text has simply been discursive and concerned with the Judge's confinement and release, his battles and litigations with his various warders, literal, disciplinary, institutional and theoretical. He is first a jurist, an advocate, a logographer of the self who eventually, painfully and ironically represents and wins the case for release by proving that he is fully capable, like any good lawyer, of ignoring his own affects, of making himself ill to the end of maintaining appearances. When the breakdown occurs it immediately portends a shift in sexual sensibility, a reorientation of the nerves, the advent of a lengthy and alternately painful and pleasurable transformative trajectory towards femininity.

---

[7] Ewan Fernie, *The Demonic: Literature and Possession* (London: Routledge, 2013). For recent and valuable memoirs of transition that can provide a radical corrective to the presuppositions of the psy-professionals, see Juliet Jacques, *Trans: A Memoir* (London: Verso, 2015), and the genre-bending metamorphoses of Paul. B. Preciado, *Testo Junkie: Sex, Drugs, and Biopolitics in the Pharmacopornographic Era* (New York: Feminist Press, 2016).

Schreber famously experiences an erotic awakening. This is literally the case in that he has a hypnopompic dream, an awakening reverie that it must feel rather good to be a woman engaging in sexual intercourse. We can note that this libidinal desire, this sensual apprehension of the imagined feminine, comes immediately upon the breakdown occasioned by the Judge's failure to get elected to the Reichstag, which I interpret as his failed attempt to escape law. It is as if his profession, his juridism, is preventing her creativity and blocking his experience of her desire, meaning the erotic pleasure, the voluptuousness and beauty of the feminine sensibility and erogenous affect within. His immediate refusal of the fantasy certainly suggests as much, but the rejected returns, the repressed repeats and it is with ever greater insistence, in multiple and vivid images, at first equivocally, tentatively and then poetically and performatively that the feminine constantly re-emerges. I want to suggest that slowly, over time, in the face of resistances both intimate and extimate, this desire becomes real. Certainly, by now, well over a century later, however suppressed, tormented, ignored, conflicted or resisted, it deserves recognition. The narrative is lengthy, at times tortured, on occasion sublime, frequently witty and always pressing against the barrier, the censorship and the excitement, of the erotic. The Judge's strange journey continues through a confusion of miracles, a plethora of visions and variegated expressions, his bellowing and incantations, copraphobia, extremes of mood, paranoia, 'pollutions', always towards a changed erotic state and sensibility. Staying with the text, borrowing momentarily from the Italian the concept of '*cherchez la femme*', the next encounter of significance is some ten pages later, when the Judge describes a visit from his wife: 'when after a long time I did see her again at the window of a room opposite mine, such important changes had meanwhile occurred in my environment and in myself that I no longer considered her a living being, but only thought I saw in her a human form produced by miracle in the manner of "the fleeting-improvised-men" . . . during that night I had a quite unusual number of pollutions (perhaps half a dozen)'.[8] As another judge puts it, in a very different context, but allow me this once to digress: 'The question of who is one's wife is at times, under circumstances similar to what we are here considering, a matter of grave concern and genuine dispute.'[9] It is this sense of the illusion of the wife and the accompanying spectre of the feminine, of the pleasure and the risk of covert affects, nocturnal excitations, erogenous phantasm that provides the resistance and the drive towards what comes next, the absorption of the nerves, the changes in the

---

[8] *Memoirs* at 44.
[9] The citation is from *In re Estate of Ira Soper* 264 N.W. 427, at 431 (1935).

body, the unmanning (*Entmannung*) that precedes the image and experience of a feminine sexual sensibility, of the transitional state of becoming a woman. For Schreber, the gender dysphoria that goes under the name unmanning, the transitional state, the becoming woman marks a changeable sensibility. The modes of transformation are complex and mutable, shifting and inter-mingling, at times resisted – for his honor, for his sanity, for moral reasons, for convention – and at other moments embraced, welcomed and enjoyed. It is not easy, then or even now, for a judge to become a sexual being, for 'His Worship' to become or also to be 'Hir Honour' or 'Madam the Bench'. If we consider the law of genre and sexual mores at the end of the nineteenth cen-tury we can recognise fairly immediately that Schreber's struggle was an intensely policed and vigorously excluded experience. The bifurcation of sex was at its Christian height, the 'third sex' a dark and incarcerated spectre in the capitals of Europe. It is, according to Foucault, in about 1870 that psychiatry invented the homosexual as a category of person, a type and exem-plar or 'personage' and perversion.[10] In Germany and England this fabrica-tion of the feminine inside the masculine was the object of vigorous interdiction, and the medical law that classified the sodomite as an aberration continued into the castigation of the homosexual as a character and species. There is, as Murat's historical work details, a visible '*continuity* of the dis-courses of the medical, literary and legal' on the inverted character and per-verse anti-nature of sexual transition.[11] It is one that continues as the convention to this day. To signal ahead, to give a proleptic premonition, let me briefly note the clinical psychoanalytic conclusions of a recent enough study of *Sexual Ambiguities*, where the author observes a psychotic structure of delusion by means of which 'transsexuals manage to convince doctors and psychiatrists that they are not psychotic, and their only misfortune was to have been born into the wrong sex'.[12] No wonder that Schreber continues to weep, still bellows, enunciates and relays again his law. The only point I wish to stress here is the simple and yet diffuse one that the institutional and disci-plinary difficulties that Schreber faced, the social hostility towards the gender dysphoric and transitional, have been significant impediments to the recep-tion and interpretation of his text. The details will follow, the narrative and form will be excoriated, expatiated and elaborated fully enough. It is rather

---

[10] Michel Foucault, *The History of Sexuality. Volume 1* (New York: Vintage Books, 1990 [1978]) at 43.

[11] Laure Murat, *Loi du genre: Une histoire culturelle du 'troisième sexe'* (Paris: Fayard, 2006).at 19; emphasis in the original.

[12] Geneviève Morel, *Sexual Ambiguities: Sexuation and Psychosis* (London: Karnac, 2011) at 192.

here the moment of sexual origin that will be noted by way of anticipatory adumbration, as device and *insignum* of what follows. Schreber was incarcerated as insane and his text was read as a lunatic's utterance, as a discourse emanating from the asylum, as a series of symptoms, a set of keys to a pathology and its diagnosis, within the disciplinary regimes that variously attend to the circumscription of madness as the support and proof of sanity and its sexual mores. Civility, the Judge claimed, was what he sought, and it was civilisation that locked him up and locked him out. The text becomes secondary to the scientific or academic projects that seek to appropriate it. Crucially, the voice, the style and plea, made more than a century ago, to address the feminine in the juridical, the woman interior to the male judge, the creativity and affect immanent in the process of judgement, get wholly lost. It is time, then, to attend to the text, to listen to Schreber anew.

1

Miscarriages of Transmission:
Body, Text and Method

Don't forget that all representing is nonsense.

The remarkable late nineteenth-century case of the bellowing Judge Daniel Paul Schreber is relatively well, if generally indirectly, known. He has been analysed *in absentia* by Freud and Lacan. He has been studied posthumously by psychiatrists, psychologists, intellectual historians, literary critics and cultural theorists. We will arrive at these texts soon enough. His own meticulously judicious record of her time in treatment, first in a university clinic and latterly incarcerated in Sonnenstein Asylum, has been widely translated and the questionable Anglophone version of this extraordinary extra-judicial document has been through two editions with Harvard University Press and has then been reprinted as a 'Classic' by the New York Review of Books, and thus is available, although as we will see less often read than previewed through secondary sources.[1] And then, just to stick to highlights, there is *Schreber* the movie, and more recently the mixed-genre biopic *Shock Head Soul*.[2] His name has long stood as an emblem of anti-psychiatry.[3] A dual-language version of his text is available on the Internet. Schreber has thus, over the century and more since his demise on 14 April 1911, acquired a certain notoriety in psy-circles and beyond. In a more academic vein, by way of final flourish, he is the subject of a monumental defense by Zvi Lothane, as well as being the subject of a bravura interpreta-

---

[1] Daniel Paul Schreber, *Memoirs of My Nervous Illness* (Cambridge, MA: Harvard University Press, 1998 [1955]). The translation is by Ida Macalpine and Richard A. Hunter. The New York Review of Books reprinting in 2000, with a new introduction by Rosemary Dinnage, uses the same translation. It is generally, however, but I will make this point at much greater length, approached or not read through the accounts of those that have diagnosed and frequently also discarded the author and then his text as lunatic prose.

[2] The movies are *Memoirs of My Nervous Illness* (Dir. Julian Hobbs, 2006), with Jefferson Mays playing Schreber, and *Shock Head Soul* (Dir. Simon Pummell, 2011).

[3] Most directly, Thomas Szasz, *Schizophrenia. The Sacred Symbol of Psychiatry* (Syracuse: Syracuse University Press, 1976).

tion of his demonic possession by Ewan Fernie.[4] He has, postmortem, been analysed to death. It is time, and let me repeat the prolegomenal point, to return to Schreber, and in particular to revisit and rescue his text from the various and multiple misappropriations, preclusions and foreclosures that have been perpetrated upon it by analysts obsessed with 'curing' the diseased and deceased author or more usually simply scoring disciplinary points by projecting their theories of psychosis on to the mutable body of the man imagined beyond the text. The tendency, as Lothane has ardently argued, has been to diagnose, explain and symptomise Schreber rather than to stay with what we have, namely the text of the jurist and latterly senior judge who first suffered affective indisposition in 1884 when he tried to escape from the bench and the law by standing unsuccessfully for election to the Reichstag. That moment, the escape attempt, Schreber's failed breakout, is my starting point and basic assumption. He wanted to relinquish the dogma of judging, slip out of the iron cage of legal science, take off the jurist's mask and create a little, write some, make new law. Indicatively, that aspect of Schreber's story, its origin, the genesis and starting point in the juridical has not been treated as important and has not been attended to or interpreted. The legal subject is erased and Schreber becomes *homo sacer*, a version of bare life whose text is simply a symptom of other causes, of a familiar but unresolved homosexual ideation for Freud, of the linguistic unconscious for Lacan at his most opaque, of narcissism for the post-Freudian MacCabe, of delusion for Morel, and of megalomania for Elias Canetti, to name but a few.[5] Schreber the text, the printed discourse, the treatise and testament, needs to be saved from pre-judgement, from that species of theory that sees in advance of reading or seeks through the text the familiar and well-known categories of a discipline, and *mirabile dictu*, finds them there.[6] Such interpretations are

[4] Zvi Lothane, *In Defense of Schreber: Soul Murder and Pscyhiatry* (Hillsdale: The Analytic Press, 1992); Eric Santner, *My Own Private Germany: Daniel Paul Schreber's Secret History of Modernity* (Princeton: Princeton University Press, 1996) at xiv; Ewan Fernie, *The Demonic: Literature and Possession* (London: Routledge, 2013). The other significant defensive text is Louis Sass, *The Paradoxes of Delusion: Wittgenstein, Schreber and the Schizophrenic Mind* (Ithaca: Cornell University Press, 1995).

[5] Sigmund Freud, 'Psychoanalytic Notes on an Autobiographical Account of a Case of Paranoia (Dementia Paranoides)', in James Strachey (ed.), *The Standard Edition of the Complete Psychological Works of Sigmund Freud vol XII* (London: Hogarth Press, 1958 [1911]); Jacques Lacan, *The Seminar of Jacques Lacan Book III: The Psychoses* (New York: Norton, 1993); Colin MacCabe, 'Introduction', in Sigmund Freud, *The Schreber Case* (London: Penguin, 2002); Elias Canetti, *Crowds and Power* (New York: Farrar, Straus, Giroux, 1984).

[6] This point is well-made in Samuel Weber, 'Introduction to the 1988 Edition', in Daniel Paul

decided already, prior to reading, and determined in advance to determine and judge. More patience is needed, more lectoral care, a little time in honour of our distance from this case, now clouded by the myriad intercessions and aspersions under whose auspices the text arrives pre-judged. This means starting with the question of law, as also with the title page of the work, with the frontispiece, the statements of intention, the project, the litigation, rather than with that curious assemblage of exterior inventions, concepts and scribblings, with which so much of the apparatus of interpretation is generated ahead of any actual scrutiny of the text. So, an initial curiosity. Lawyers have not addressed the case of Schreber, and this despite his elevated status as the equivalent of a Supreme Court judge in what was then the independent dominion of Saxony. This despite the fact that his text played a crucial role in his successful *pro se* appeal of the Court Order that, unbeknownst to him, had in 1894 incarcerated him as incompetent to manage his own affairs. This, finally, despite the quite unprecedented determination of the Royal Court of Appeals that while the former Judge and erstwhile member of their own body was without question mad (*geisteskrank*), his insanity was merely religious or, as they put it, a species of spiritualism, and so it was determined at the same time that he was legally competent. Mad, but entirely rational. A paradox that led to judgment for the plaintiff. He was judicially determined, at the very highest level, to be fit for release, and so also amenable to a re-reading. A recent study of the political history of madness notes early on that the proper term for the documentation of madness, the registers and records of the nineteenth-century asylums, was the books of the law – *livres de la loi* – 'slumbering in often empty libraries'.[7] It is against these law books, these *faux* edicts of 'scientific psychiatry' that Schreber was most exercised. He was determined not to be judged and sentenced for his opinions merely on the strength of the 'subjective' views of non-lawyers.[8] He resorts to law, which in the civil law tradition is technically and explicitly *ratio scripta*, written reason, so as to successfully bring the case for his release, against the lengthily expressed views of his attending physician, Dr Weber, superintendent of the asylum. Schreber eventually wins the case and in the process answers for himself Kant's *quaestio quid iuris*, namely that as between the psychiatric books of the law, the records of the keepers of the asylum, and his law, that of the jurist and now also jurisprude and legal theorist, it is the judicial determination,

Schreber, *Memoirs of My Nervous Illness* (Cambridge, MA: Harvard University Press, 1988) at xiv, who cites Hegel – 'the well-known, just because it is familiar, is not known well'.

[7] Laure Murat, *The Man Who Thought he was Napoleon: Toward a Political History of Madness* (Chicago: Chicago University Press, 2014) at 9.

[8] *Memoirs*, 365 referring to 'the mere subjective opinion of the chief physician'.

the court ordering his freedom that is the appropriate jurisdiction, power and dominion. It is, ironically, Schreber's theory of law as tellurian and independent of theistic influences, his impure and corporeal jurisprudence, that is mirrored in the extraordinary decision of the Court, his former *corpus iuris*, his erstwhile judicial body, that allows him free, and permits him to return to the fold of law. Clearly, there is a story of law, of litigation and legality that has yet to be excised and examined. While there is substantive work on the conflict of these two laws, the competition and animosity between the two institutions and jurisdictions in the late nineteenth century, Schreber's own theory and corporeal inscription of law has gained zero recognition. Take, as the most egregious instance of this exclusion, the English translation of the Judge's treatise. It is highly symptomatic in its own right. Lacan, in his introduction to the French translation, alerts us perhaps to a problem with the translation when he remarks that Ida Macalpine had been in his seminar, had needed the help of her son and had taken her time: 'a delay so scarcely justified warrants one keeping it under scrutiny for long, or else coming back to it'.[9] He seems to signal that something is odd, wrong or out of joint with the translation, and that is without question the case, but the remark is elliptical and is not pursued. So, consider the title page, the threshold and entrance to the work, the emblem of the book, and see what it lacks (Fig. 1).

The most striking aspect of the translation is not simply what is reproduced in English, but what is omitted. Lothane makes the first salient point that the translators quite simply do not bother to translate the lengthy subtitle of the Judge's treatise. What we get is *Memoirs of My Nervous Illness* – Daniel Paul Schreber, and then the names of the mother and child team that translated. What Lothane dubs the forensic essay, the title of the juristic analysis of the legal grounds upon which an individual can be incarcerated in an asylum, forms the rest of the title that reads, and the translation is not here particularly complicated: *with Postscripts and an Addendum Concerning the Question: 'Under what Premises Can a Person Considered Insane be Detained in an Asylum Against His Own Declared Will?'*[10] This extraordinary *aposiopesis*, the simple exclusion of the longer part of the title, the unremarked and unjustified truncation of the nomination, the excision of the appellation, immediately signals translation in its older etymological sense of betrayal and of traducing of the text to be relayed. If not even the title gains more than a

[9] Jacques Lacan, 'Presentation of the *Mémoires* of President Schreber in French Translation' 38 *Ornicar?, revue du Champ freudien* 5 (1986).

[10] In full: *Denkwürdigkeiten eines Nervenkranken nebst Nachträgen und einem Anhang über die Frage: 'Unter welchen Voraussetzungen darf eine für geisteskrank erachtete Person gegen ihren erklärten Willen in einer Heilanstalt festgehalten werden?'*

Memoirs of My Nervous Illness

DANIEL PAUL SCHREBER

Translated and edited by

IDA MACALPINE

and

RICHARD A. HUNTER

With a new introduction by

SAMUEL M. WEBER

Harvard University Press
Cambridge, Massachusetts
London, England
1988

Figure 1 Schreber, *Memoirs*, 1988 edition. Photograph P. Goodrich.

very partial expression in English, what hope for the rest of the work?[11] The misprision, or I prefer miscarriage, of the title is symptomatic of the interpretation that underpins the translation. It is one in which the author, as already designated to be a lunatic, paranoid, and delusional, is stripped of his status of authorship. It is as though the diagnosis of his psychosis, which the translators will have been very aware of from the 1995–6 seminar of Lacan's that they attended, and from the texts that they read for that course, starting with Freud's lengthy essay on Schreber as a case of *dementia paranoides*, have already overdetermined the meaning of the work to be translated. It is not, it would seem, in any sense, a juristic text. It is taken to be the opposite of law, simple chaos, mental disorder. But as the Royal Court of Appeals correctly and cautiously points out, 'Because the medical expert calls the illness which is manifested by the plaintiff's delusions paranoia, one might be tempted to regard the question *sub judice* as thereby already decided.'[12] Sage words of caution, useful procedural cautels from a Court that was on this occasion willing, at Schreber's instigation, to separate law from religion and by association from the spiritualism of the psychiatric institution. The observation is sound. It seems that for the reason of diagnosis prior to scrutiny of the text, the interpreters have not even been willing to address the work as being also a work on the legal criteria for incarceration against one's will for insanity and this despite the fact that the Royal Court of Appeals in Dresden vindicated Schreber and released him from the asylum, in large measure on the strength of this text as a judicially recognised legal pleading. It should also be noted that with the exception of Lothane's *Defense*, later works that address the case almost universally restrict themselves to citing the five-word main title alone. The erasure of the legal essay is successfully conducted by means of leaving it off the title page, signaling not only the demotion of the subtitle to no title but also the stripping of the jurist of his office and persona, that of a lawyer and more than that, of a retired senior judge. The legal essay is lacking, it would seem, in symptoms and so is not conducive to the theory of the Judge that the interpreters seek to peddle. Continuing down the title page, matters only get worse. After Schreber's name, in the English edition, come the names of the translators. Return, however, to the German edition and there is another and massive exclusion operative here. It is not Daniel Paul Schreber in the original, but rather and significantly, it is Dr. jur. Daniel Paul Schreber Formerly *Senatspräsident* of the Royal Superior Appellate Court in Dresden.

[11] The German title page is reproduced eighty-two pages into the text, after introduction to the 1988 edition by Samuel Weber, and then the translators' introduction. Hardly a frontispiece or first impression.

[12] *Memoirs* at 496.

It was not enough, it transpires, for the translators to truncate the title of the work, they also needed to strip the Judge of his doctorate in law and remove any mention of his previous dignity and high legal office. This cannot be viewed as innocent, nor as simple translation. It is an interpretative excision and a radical exclusion of what the Judge wrote. The translators have elevated themselves into co-authors, they have rewritten the emblematic text of the title page and, most significantly of all, they have taken away the Judge's credentials, even to the point of refusing to translate twenty-four of the twenty-seven words of the German title of the book to hand and truncating his name and credentials from ten to three words. A surprising apostrophe, of superiority, a literary castration. While Schreber could doubtless have with-stood the insult, he was after all used to being called mad, the text suffers the greater travesty of being interpreted before it is even read. It is by implication not the work of a lawyer, not an extra-judicial publication, nor a work in any sense of doctrine and juristic principle, even though it advertises itself as such. The translators have supplanted the Judge and they have erased both his cre-dentials and his words. *Aposiopesis* is by definition a histrionic figure. The removal of the end of a statement is a mode of dramatising the message, and here the putative or presupposed insanity of the Judge is theatricalised prior to, or more properly as the opening of the text itself. Schreber is stripped of titles and qualifications. He becomes a bare name, an actor without a mask, so as to pave the way and also to soften the threat of the work being deemed obscene, blasphemous, improper or unreadable because of the extremity of his views, and particularly that he wanted to become a woman, and that he imagined sex with God. The truncation and caesura of the title places the emphasis on *Nervous Illness*, which in the English edition of 1988 is printed on the cover in red letters and in a bold font that is four times the size of the black typeface of the initial three words.[13] The cover also adds three vertical red bars at the top and the bottom of the titular details, as if to signify incar-ceration, an author and message behind bars, confined and dangerous. In subtle and not so subtle form, the already determined madness of the bare author is being signalled ahead, as if to say, along with the psy-professionals, that he is insane, and at the same time that it is alright to read the work, as a medical case study, as an instance of insanity. It is equally legitimate, this set up suggests, to not take the work on its own terms but rather to read it as a symptom of illness rather than as an expression of legal, philosophical or religious views. The theatre of the titular truncation has one further

---

[13] The 1955 edition is somewhat less histrionic, as was the way with dust jackets prior to the 1960s, but the lettering is again sanguine red, and pitched for emphasis against carceral grey.

typographic dimension that bears allusion. The German title page, reproduced in Figure 2, not only provides the full title and credentials of the
author but is also set in a bold blackletter, Gothic, typeface (Fig. 2). This
again has been ignored and treated as impertinent and immaterial to the
matter, the narrative and reminiscences of a lunatic, to be translated and
conveyed. Once more, however, the change in typography, in layout, emphasis and font is an arrogation of meaning and intention, an imposition of a
new law upon the text that Schreber had overseen with great care and published after lengthy deliberation. The red letters on the cover fairly obviously
mark an extreme significance to the letters that are thus sanguinated (Fig. 3).
Historically, red was used as the font color for signalling augmented importance, and the rules of law, the *regulae iuris*, of Book 50 of the *Digest* were
frequently printed in red precisely so as to mark their universal and enduring
significance. Here is it not the memoirs that matter, they are in pedestrian
black font, it is the NERVOUS ILLNESS, in enlarged font and bleeding red
that demands attention and states significance or acts as the first heavy signifier of the cover. The red lettering of the translation is thus less juristic than
histrionic, a mottled crimson, red seeping and splattered like blood on the
walls of a cell, prison writings, screed that has escaped the asylum. There is
unquestionably an element of dramatisation in the outlined lettering with its
seemingly bloody interior. Add to this the thin red bars at the top and bottom
of the cover, signalling confinement, Gotham, bedlam, the jaws of madness
and descent even into the viscera of demonic possession. Case closed, as it
were, before it is opened.

For Schreber, however, there are no red letters to the title, no drama,
mad or otherwise, of nervous illness or of nomination beyond the arguments
and explanations that he proposes at length in the body of the work. So,
if we return to his font, the Gothic blackletter of the title page, this is the
standard lettering for legal texts of the period and earlier, which commonly
gains expression in the phrase blackletter law. This means, ironically in this
context, a text that cannot be changed, a message whose parameters and
words are set immutable and permanent, a language of law that is distinct
from the evanescent and mutable print of other texts. In erasing the font,
innocent though it may seem, a mutation has occurred, a change of meaning,
a different drama and secularisation of the judge's text has been enacted. The
subdued stamped lettering on the cloth cover of the first edition becomes
the suggestive and sanguinated figuration of the anglophone translation of
the work, which in its paperback version emblematises a new and erroneous
threshold and point of entry into a text already weighed down by prefatory,
introductory, essayistic and glossatorial apparatuses as if it were incapable of
speaking for itself, incomprehensible without clinical guidance.

Denkwürdigkeiten

eines

Nervenkranken

nebst Nachträgen

und einem Anhang über die Frage:

„Unter welchen Voraussetzungen darf eine für geisteskrank erachtete Person gegen ihren erklärten Willen
in einer Heilanstalt festgehalten werden?"

von

Dr. jur. Daniel Paul Schreber,
Senatspräsident beim Kgl. Oberlandesgericht Dresden a. D.

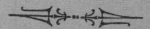

Figure 2 Schreber, *Denkwürdigkeiten*, title page, first edition, 1903.
Photo P. Goodrich.

This leads then, finally, by way of methodological introduction, to
the question of the translation of the main title, *Denkwürdigkeiten eines
Nervenkranken*. This should be attempted only after the substantive work
has been addressed in detail, and in Freud's account, read at least once. It is

Figure 3 Schreber, *Memoirs*, cover image, 1988 edition. Photograph P. Goodrich.

polysemic, as the semioticians used to like to say, and offers multiple possibilities. Lothane in his *Defense* renders this as *Great Thoughts of a Nervous Patient*
and this provides a reasonable, although not a grammatical corrective, in two
senses.[14] First, these were not memoirs, because this was not autobiography,
but rather a highly motivated record of a religious system and philosophy, as
well as being a meticulous account and register of a subjective itinerary and
trajectory of what Schreber would likely have formulated as affective indisposition and periods of depression that accompanied ecstatic insights, epiphanic
intuitions and moments of spiritual vision. The Judge may have intimated
that he planned to 'submit my *Denkwürdigkeiten* for examination to special-
ists from other fields of experience, particularly theologians and philosophers'
but that remark comes at the end of the work that begins, first sentence for
content, page 1, opening line, worth repeating: 'I have decided to apply for
my release from the Asylum in the near future in order to live once again
among civilized people and at home with my wife.'[15] For his application to
be successful, Schreber believes that those who will judge his application will
need an 'approximate idea at least of my religious conceptions . . . even if they
do not fully understand [the] apparent' oddities of his behaviour.[16]

The reference to apparent oddities, as opposed to the controversial terms
'delusion', 'hallucination', 'lunacy', 'dementia' and 'insanity', can alert the
translator and the reader alike to the fact that Schreber maintains not only his
legal competence, his facility with doctrine and principle, his fully rational
capacities, but also his acumen and authorship of a novel theory of religion
in its separation from law. What is most important here, in interpreting
the title, is that Schreber is adamant that he is not in any sense paranoid,
demented or otherwise to be excluded for being delusional. Thus, in his
extensive argument to the Royal Court of Appeals, he states: 'I contest (*bestre-
ite*) absolutely that I am mentally ill (*geisteskrank*) or ever have been.'[17] He
expands on this theme at various points, refusing to accept that his intellect
has in any way been clouded, or his mental functioning been anything other
than uniformly incisive. He takes pride in his rational capacities, going so far
as to conclude: 'I trust I have proved that I am not only not "controlled by
fixed and previously formed ideas", but that I also possess in full measure the
"capacity to evaluate critically the content of consciousness with the help of
judgment and deduction"'.[18]

[14] Lothane, *Defense* at 7.
[15] *Memoirs* at 422, and at 1 respectively.
[16] Ibid. at 1.
[17] Ibid. at 406.
[18] Ibid. at 78 fn. 42.

Schreber is not concerned to deny his eccentricity, novelty, peculiarity or a certain outré bent. There is no question that he is aware that he has mood swings, depression, affective indisposition and thus is unwell, sick at times, that he is anxious, ill at ease and has often felt persecuted, interfered with and imposed upon both by spiritual forces and at certain junctures by the attendants at the asylum. That all goes, as one says, without saying. The question now, preliminary though it may be, is how to best capture this in the translation of the main title. *Great Thoughts* works reasonably well, but the connotation is not simply of greatness, but also of worthy and remarkable thoughts, even of the exotic, of cabinets of curiosities. Thus, *Peculiar Thoughts* or *Remarkable Thoughts* are perhaps closer to what the jurist intended, as he was well aware throughout the text of the idiosyncrasy of his views and the eccentricity of his perceptions, while at the same time being confident that he had good grounds for his elaborations and that time would vindicate his reasons. Thus, illness is perhaps too strong, his *Thoughts* are in his perception and interpretation valuable and rationally motivated and while they may be peculiar this is mainly a reference to their extreme novelty and universality. These *Remarkable Thoughts* and theorems thus are to be related not to illness as we would now understand and diagnose it, but on the Judge's terms the thoughts relate rather to nervous indisposition, to affective disruptions and overall to the process that he went through, the nervous collapse and recovery, rather than to any intransigent state of affairs, or disequilibriated state of mind. Lothane's rendering of *Nervenkranken* as *Nervous Patient* is workable, and one could even go further and, taking account of the enormous importance of music, of playing the piano, of rhyme and rhythm in Schreber's process and progression, the *Remarkable Thoughts of an Unsound Mind* could capture the further reaches of the Judge's self-consciousness and the battles that it experimented with and the dysphoria he experienced over time. *A Nervous Mind* may also play upon certain of the more disturbing visions that Schreber underwent. At all events, and we can leave this open here, the title of the translation is not simply, strikingly and immorally incomplete but also rather less than elegant in its blunt ascription of illness acknowledged and recollected. There is something more and more fluid and evocative and so *Memorabilia of a Nerve Patient* is perhaps closest to the poetic inspirations and quizzical philosophical bent of the treatise.

* * *

The institutional conflicts, the late nineteenth-century rise of the psychiatric profession, the invention of the unconscious and the codification of German civil law may help to explain but do not justify the refusal to attend to the nuances of Schreber's expression. The new skein of disciplines and institutions does not exonerate analysts from thinking or specialisms from dialogue. That the legal dimension of the Judge's text is lost from the outset, expunged from the title page, as also are his juristic credentials, is an attempt, conscious or otherwise, at anathematisation. It will come as little surprise that there are further excisions and failures to translate, other infelicities of expression and a tin ear is directed at the legal connotations of terms that occur later in the text. Just to signal ahead slightly, the crucial philosophical and jurisprudential term *als ob* – as if – which was the subject of a lengthy philosophical treatise contemporary with Schreber, and which became juristically important in the work of the Austrian legal philosopher Hans Kelsen, is used on eighteen occasions in the text but is simply in the bulk of instances not translated.[19] I will here note only that the concept of 'as if' is a crucial signal of invention, of an awareness of fiction and of an ability to distinguish the real and the imaginary, fact and fiction, *fictio iuris*, as lawyers like to put it. So again, the lapse is likely significant and symptomatic of pre-judgement and thus bears reconstruction. If a key term is simply not translated, the implications for the manner of translation of the terms that are noticed and relayed, the soul murder, the voluptuousness, the fleeting improvisations and miracles, to take but a few, is equally perturbing but that will have to await the explication of the *ipsissima verba* of the text in subsequent chapters.

All of this, the presences and absences, inventions and omissions, will be examined later as part of the endeavour of providing a description and account of Schreber's juridical theology, his metaphysics and philosophy of law. I will argue that he offers a radical critique of law and proposes a novel account and inchoate or at least nascent theory of the governance of intimacy, a profoundly and presciently impure philosophy of legality, together with an oppositional account of the theology of *oikonomia* and its practices and dispositions or administration of interiority. To set the stage for this rescue attempt, for the recovery of the text, it is necessary, I have argued, to approach Schreber on his own terms and in his own words. This means insisting on the primacy of the text, the printed discourse being all that we have, and it deserves attention before any attempt is made to categorise, stigmatise, diagnose or judge the Judge. If the author is dead, both literally, which is to say corporeally, and then again conceptually, according to the structuralist thesis that the text speaks through the author, rather than the author through

---

[19] Most notably Hans Vaihinger, *The Philosophy of 'As If'. A System of the Theoretical, Practical and Religious Fictions of Mankind*, trans. C. K. Ogden (London: Kegan Paul, 1924); Hans Kelsen, *The Pure Theory of Law* (Berkeley and Los Angeles: California University Press, 1960).

the text, then credit should be given initially much less to who wrote it than to what was written.

The initial question is not that of madness but of thought and its inscription and so, by the same token, it should not be the reports of the director of the asylum that are the initial focus, as they were for Freud, nor the concepts of psychosis and foreclosure (*Verwerfung*) that occupy the first twenty pages of Lacan's book on Schreber, but rather the opinion, as lawyers say, meaning the judicial text, the pronouncement and edict of the jurist that should be addressed. Thus, I have dealt at length with the title page, the frontispiece and opening, the threshold of the work, the immediate paralipomena. This is because it is the point of entry, the initial image of the opus, the first impression and mark of what is to be approached through the window of the title. The substantive analysis of the work will have to await but a synoptic overview of Schreber's perspective, from inside the text, can act as a cautionary introduction and paving of the way.

The primary object of the *Memorabilia*, as signalled by the main title, is affective disorder and the inspirations and adventures, the conflict and confinement, the insights and the sufferings that a nervous ailment occasioned. The book begins with a Preface and an 'Open Letter to Professor Flechsig', both preceding the Table of Contents. The Preface, which is brief, indicates the history of a case and the purposes of the work, in retrospect. The *Memorabilia* and their postscripts relay a medical and a legal aetiology. The author was imprisoned in an asylum and at first kept away from the world, although later and gradually gained more freedom until finally, after the successful conclusion of his lawsuit, he is judged competent and is free to be released. That said, the book is then presented as a work of metaphysics and 'of value both for science and the knowledge of religious truths'. In the face of this heuristic and accompanying claim to scientific value, Schreber adds, correctively, that 'all personal issues must recede'.[20] The court case and successful final appeal are justifications, in Schreber's view, for ignoring the judgements of psychobabble or the subjective opinions of psychiatrists and attending, as I also propose we should, to the text, the substantive work and doctrine. If the nerve patient doesn't need to be cured, diagnoses, symptomologies and other counter-factual prognoses are beside the point. He made his choices, unsettled his identity, experienced ecstasy and dysphoria, laughed and suffered, lived and died. What remains is what he wrote, an extra-judicial text, a pleading, records of a cause of action. Schreber, in other words, made a case, a law suit, and won, and now wishes the reader to attend seriously to the philosophical

---

[20] *Memoirs* at iii.

and religious case that he is presenting, after the adjudication in favour of his legal competence, in a bid to have his views taken seriously. He does not here say directly that he became a woman, or that he identified with the feminine, but he does state a belief that 'expert examination of my body' would provide useful and probative results for his views. Beyond that he introduces the work in the more abstract terms of his struggle with the divinity and his attempt to restore the Order of the World (*Weltordnung*). He indicates, finally, that the experiences that he has undergone were subjective and personal rather than objective and shared and should be understood as such, a theme that runs throughout the book and is crucial to his assertion of the validity of his lawsuit as well as to his juridical theology. What the Preface also indicates is a grasp of time and change, if not cure. Schreber recognises different perspectives and experiences at different times. He is acknowledging his disorder, its misdiagnosis as madness, and asserts the value of his perceptions as well as adverting to the history of his nervous indisposition and its amelioration.

The open letter to Flechsig, the first physician to treat Schreber, is also predominantly epistemic in intention. It is again a justification of the publication of the work and, after apologising to the recipient for any pain that the work may occasion, in effect accuses the Professor of Psychiatry of playing God and of interfering with the patient: 'I have not the least doubt that the first impetus to what my doctors always considered mere hallucinations but which to me signified communication with supernatural powers, consisted of influences on my nervous system emanating from your nervous system.'[21] Flechsig is then described as a 'tested soul', meaning an impure soul rejected from the forecourts of heaven, and he is in effect accused of 'soul murder' and, in much more easily recognised legal terminology, of medical 'malpractice'.[22] All of this is excused by Schreber in the interests of having Flechsig validate his experiences and provide an external proof of the visions that he experienced, perhaps, by dint of hypnosis. Flechsig, however, never responds and so we move from the unanswered letter to the misread text.

The *Memorabilia* commences as a work of theology with an account of the creation of the world and the provenance of human being. The nature of God is discussed and defined in terms of invisible nerves, vibrations and rays, the fashioning and movements of the soul are discussed and then Schreber's own 'peculiar relations with God' are expounded. In the face of God's interference with humanity and with Schreber in particular, contrary to the Order of the World, the Judge then spells out both his experiences of the proximity

---

[21] Ibid. at ix.
[22] Ibid. at xi. Lothane, *Defense* at 356.

of the divine, his personal struggle with and against a bifurcated God and the theological implications of this untoward behavior. In the following chapter, Schreber spells out both the conflict and the dogmatics that constitute his particular theology and he elaborates on a number of the terms of art that will be used, such as tested or impure souls and their transmigration, the mode of action of the nerves, the diverse states of the soul, and its goal of voluptuousness and the state of eternal blessedness.

For Schreber the Order of the World requires the removal of God from all human affairs and this is his basic struggle. God is cognisant of corpses only. God does not understand human beings and, most interestingly for juridical purposes, God cannot judge. The inoperative divinity requires that Schreber step up and judge or at least become in Shelley's phrase an unacknowledged legislator, an author, a poet, a maker of worlds. Judge Schreber, who abandoned his judicial position, makes it his theological and political mission to confront God, to fight his representatives, and in particular, initially at least, Professor Flechsig, along with the other manifestations of God's nerves, the tested souls, the diverse beings produced by miracles, the fleeting-improvised-beings, who include at certain points his wife, and all other expressions of a world beyond that should only ever act at a great distance from human being and belonging. Schreber stands up for the human playthings – the 'play-with-human-beings' – of the divine.[23]

Schreber is insistent in the account of his theology and of his spiritual experiences generally that he is presenting hypotheses, that he is not always certain, that others may well question or simply not share his perceptions, and that much of what he has witnessed is unfathomable and deeply enigmatic. In discussing the divine rays, for example, Schreber spells out a method: 'This is naturally only a hypothesis, but as in scientific research it has to be adhered to until a better explanation for the events under investigation is found.'[24] There is a degree of modesty, a spirit of enquiry and a mood of tentativeness that carries along the narrative of divine intrusions, soul murder and clashes between higher and lower forces. Schreber is also interested in challenging the institutional and disciplinary claims to a monopoly on knowledge of matters relating to spiritual life and the human soul. He presents elements of a history of madness and specifically stresses the novelty of asylums and of the modern (and contestable) profession of psychiatry of which Professor Flechsig is in his view a dubious and inglorious representative. All of which summons the personal turn and history that explicitly starts in Chapter IV.

[23] *Memoirs* at 212.
[24] Ibid. at 25.

The first nervous illness occurred in the autumn of 1894 when Schreber was chairman of the County Court at Leipzig. He was admitted to the University of Leipzig Psychiatric Clinic under the directorship of Professor Flechsig and was 'fully cured' by the end of 1885. He comments, at this point, with regard to the first treatment, that 'some mistakes may have been made'. He goes on to clarify: 'I believe I could have been more rapidly cured of certain hypochondriacal ideas with which I was preoccupied at the time, particularly concern over loss of weight if I had been allowed to operate the scales which served to weigh patients a few times myself; the scales . . . were of a construction unfamiliar to me.' He then explains that it would be unreasonable to expect the director of a large asylum 'to concern himself in such detail with the mental state of a single patient'.[25] He goes on to say, and here the translation again has to be corrected, that this is a minor point 'on which I do not put great weight (*Gewicht*)'. The pun is undoubtedly intentional, and marks a facet of the work that has escaped consideration and comment, namely its humour, its alleviation of depression with wit and hence also the function of writing, but for the moment it is the surface rather than the metaphor that requires attention.[26] As Mark Sanders points out in an insightful analysis of this seemingly incidental detail, it is precisely in the marginal and overlooked that psychoanalysis finds significance.[27] Adopting that approach, Sanders shows how the scales are a perfect metaphor for Schreber's judicial unease, the inability to weigh and balance cases that afflict the Judge later, and also limit the relevance of God to human affairs: 'the scales that he chooses to mention . . . are also a symbol of justice, a reminder of his métier as judge', and as such condense several significant facets of his condition and cause, his exodus from his judicial position and from the virile identity and settled masculine office of the law.[28]

What is generally ignored, and I have neither qualm nor scruple in emphasising the point, is that Schreber's inaugural affective disorder is occasioned by law and an attempt to escape it. He wanted to change profession, to go into politics, and this thwarting of his exit oriented attitude to his legal office occasioned his depression, his mood imbalance as he would doubtless

---

[25] Ibid. at 35.

[26] Weber, 'Introduction' at xi cites this passage but indicatively enough interprets it simply as a sign of Schreber's illness, his hypochondria fixating on weight.

[27] Mark Sanders, 'Psychoanalysis, Mourning, and the Law: Schreber's Paranoia as Crisis of Judging,' in Austin Sarat and Martha Merrill Umphrey (eds), *Law and Mourning* (Amherst: University of Massachusetts Press, 2017).

[28] Sanders, 'Psychoanalysis, Mourning, and the Law' at 131.

term it. It is crucial to note the importance of law in the original nervous breakdown, because the theme returns, and specifically the farewell to law as profession and contemporary practice in the second illness. Here it is even more marked. It is, as is reasonably well acknowledged, his appointment as Senatspräsident of the Royal Court of Appeal in Dresden that triggers the relapse and the much more virulent disorder of bellowing, as well as innumerable auditory and visual hallucinations, or in the terminology that Schreber would prefer, as being less judgemental, visions. These were the famous and rather wonderful fleeting-improvised-people, the sketchy beings, that designated departed souls who had returned temporarily to earth in impromptu human forms. These included, significantly, his wife, but in the main the figures of ghosts were those of lawyers, councillors and judges who had dealings with Schreber but for him no longer seemed either interesting or real. As the virile masculine world of law receded from view, as the legal became spectral for the now defrocked judge, there came into view the proper object of his affections, the desire to become a woman.

There are several features of Schreber's identification with the feminine that deserve attention here. The first, as Freud correctly instances, is the hyp-nopompic dream that preceded the second disorder: 'I had a feeling which, thinking about it later when fully awake, struck me as highly peculiar. It was the idea that it really must be rather beautiful to be a woman succumbing to intercourse.'[29] Predictably enough, the Judge immediately rejects the idea as utterly foreign to his nature but acknowledges at the same time that 'external influences were at work to implant this idea in me'. The extimacy of the feminine is a theme that persists until Schreber later and temporar-ily embraces and gains pleasure from his desire to be a woman. Initially, however, there is an understandable resistance to the urge both from fear of sexual abuse, and because of its implications for his current identity as judge, husband and lawyer. Later, however, the allure of the feminine has wholly changed Schreber's stance towards law and the social. He states that he has 'wholeheartedly' or, better, because the German is *mit vollem Bewusstsein*, 'with full awareness inscribed the cultivation of the feminine on my banner, and I will continue to do so as far as consideration of my environment allows, whatever other people who are ignorant of the supernatural reasons may think'.[30] To this we should add another cost, which Schreber also immediately recognises, namely that '[t]he pursuit of my previous profes-sion, which I loved with all my soul (*mit ganzer Seele*), every other aim of

---

[29] *Memoirs* at 36.
[30] Ibid. at 178.

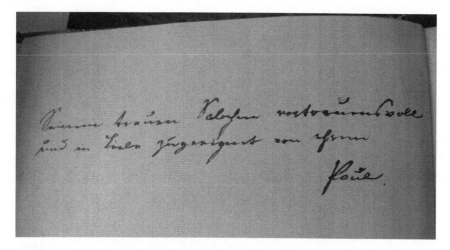

Figure 4 Schreber's dedication of *Denkwürdigkeiten* to his wife.
Photograph P. Goodrich with thanks to Henry [Zvi] Lothane.

manly ambition . . . are now closed to me'. Here, in his banner, Schreber
declares his love and signals his cause and camp. The love of his profession
is in fact the only express mention of love in the entire text, although he
expresses love for his wife, characteristically enough in a footnote, although
also in his dedicatory inscription of a copy of the *Memorabilia* to his wife,
in trust and admiration (Fig. 4). The German, because this is interesting
and strange, reads *Seinem trauen Sabchen vetrauensvoll und in Liebe zugee-
ignet von ihrem Paul,* and translates as 'to his faithful Sabchen in trust and
love dedicated by her Paul'. Nothing mad about the inscription, trust and
admiration extended to the feminine, the diminutive Sabchen, the woman
that man lacks, that Paul wants to be. And then again, the forward tilt of the
chirography, the gnostic leaning forward, a sense of futurity. The signature.
God would sign like this. The rectitude of the P also a partial crucifix, p tied
to a stake, for our sins, for what is to come. But through all of this, as the
feminine to which Paul is committed in its multiple forms, as ghost, as wife,
as retracted body, as tensile ligament, voluptuous effect and affect, all this
and more in the place of law.

The love of law is transferred to a love of the feminine and voluptuous,
as well as to the cause or mission of sexual transformation. The vexillo-
logical declaration, and elsewhere he cites the crusaders motto *in hoc signo
vinces* – in this fashion you will conquer – clearly marks his radical political identification with the feminine as a reformist project. More than that,
the feminine gives Schreber pleasure: 'I consider it my right (*mein Recht*)
and in a certain sense my obligation (*Verpflichtung*) to cultivate feminine

feelings.'[31] Elsewhere, and in furtherance of this theme, Schreber acknowledges that when he needs mental peace he achieves it, either through music
or by standing in front of the mirror and putting on female accessories
– ribbons, necklaces and the like. Even more strongly, just to enforce the
theme, we read the following plea: 'if only I could always be playing the
woman's part in sexual embrace with myself, always rest my gaze on female
beings, always look at female pictures, etc.'[32] Stronger still, Schreber believes
adamantly that his body is transforming into that of a woman. He has a
woman's buttocks, he develops bosoms, his genitalia retract and with light
pressure 'I can produce a feeling of female sensuous pleasure, particularly if I
think of something feminine'.[33] The truth of these sensations is for Schreber
open to verification by experts: 'because I consider that the transformations
observable on my body may possibly lead to new scientific insights in this
field'.[34] It was real for him, a corporeal change, and he wanted recognition,
affirmation in an age that would only judge and dismiss such affect and
feminine sentiment as misplaced in a male body.

The cultivation of the feminine, the pleasure in 'feminine occupations'
and female attire, the fervent belief and hope that his body is diminishing
and that his organs are feminising, that voluptuousness awaits him in the
eternal feminine, all signify explicitly and directly that Schreber desires to be
a woman. It could hardly be more evident and yet the possibility that this
was actually his wish, that a man may legitimately believe himself to be or be
becoming a woman, is no part of the multifarious diagnoses proffered by the
psychiatrists, analysts and philosophers who have endlessly laboured over the
case. This could be because Schreber was ahead of his time, in advance of
the mores of his contemporaries, and anticipating later sex-change surgeries,
hormone hacking, tersto junkies, trans identities in their variable forms,
but the least that can be said is that it is not obvious today that desiring to
become a woman is simply and unequivocally a sign of madness. Yet again,
Schreber's text is ignored in favour of presuppositions, dogmas and other
prior determinations.

It remains to say that as far as becoming a woman is concerned, Schreber
probably has rather more insight than his analysts. He is fully aware that
it is socially undesirable, that he will be judged, that it is hard for his wife,
but he concludes that he must follow 'a healthy egoism, unperturbed by the

---

[31] Ibid. at 281.
[32] Ibid. at 285.
[33] Ibid. at 277.
[34] Ibid. at 276. And at 274: 'I would at all times be prepared to submit my body to medical examination.'

judgment of other people . . . In this way only am I able to make my physical condition bearable.'[35] The right to his own identifications, the legitimacy
of female expression and dress, the sensation of being a woman in a man's
body, and of bodily transformation into the performative roles and physical
routines of the feminine all place Schreber inside his body and in consonance with his text. It is the others, the analysts who could not recognise,
let alone accept his identifications and desires, his feminine corporeality
and pleasures. In short, at the time that the *Memorabilia* were published,
the medical profession could not accept either Schreber's performance of
gender or his desire to change sex. These were simply and immediately
taken as signs of madness and that diagnosis has continued pretty much
to the present day. There was no 'outside mental health', no mad rights,
no Argonauts or trans-identities in the Teutonic domains and laws of his
environment. The die was cast when Schreber came out. The psychiatric
Rubicon was crossed and there has been as yet no full returning, no chance
to continue exploring and in the end to arrive at the same place and know
it for the first time.

Schreber's law, his novel *oikonomia*, meaning his avowed disposition to
perform gynaecocratic roles, conflicts directly with the contemporary conceptions of public and masculine polity and the profession of law. As he
puts it: 'particularly helpful for my bodily well-being are those jobs which
count as feminine occupations, for instance sewing, dusting, making beds,
washing up, and so on'.[36] What this inclination suggests is an identification
directly opposed to those of law and lawyering, of bench and judgment in
their designated, and in the jurisprudence of his day, scientific forms. It was
Schreber who declares that he can no longer practice law, it is the Judge
who decides his own abdication from the judicial throne, but who then, in a
paradox of circumstance, has to litigate the rationality of his femininity and
of his religious beliefs. He appoints lawyers, but of course the lawyers fail
to understand him and bungle his case, leading to the renewal of the order
for his incarceration as an insane person. The voices remind Schreber that
'all representing is nonsense', and certainly his legal representation has been
ineffective, so much so that he fires his lawyers after losing his suit before the
District Court, and thenceforth he argues the case himself and successfully
litigates his own release. It is held, as mentioned earlier, that he is mad but
legally competent.

The Royal Court of Appeals that ordered Schreber's release from the

---

[35] Ibid. at 178.
[36] Ibid. at 271.

asylum recognised that 'one does not usually and without further reason declare the adherents of spiritualism mentally ill'.[37] The Royal Court accepts Schreber's theory that law should be concerned with the human and not the divine, that the order of the world is a tellurian affair, a temporal matter that should remain separate from and uninfluenced by the judgment of God. His religious beliefs were neither probative nor relevant. They were eccentric, but they were also his own and harmless as he neither imposed them on others nor allowed them to dictate his behaviour in any practical, financial or administrative way. Similarly, the Court was of the view that he was perfectly entitled to publish his book. He did so, as we know, and it was immediately diagnosed as an expression of paranoia, of psychosis and as the work of a schizophrenic. I am suggesting here that these are not necessarily the most interesting or valuable of approaches. To read Schreber's discourse as the utterance of madness simply confirms antiquated stereotypes of gender, sex and law. It is a reading that neither opens up the potential of the text nor attends to the declared aspirations and intentions of the author who was well aware that society and law would view him as insane.

I am concerned with taking a different tack and offering a novel interpretation. The Royal Court of Appeals heard Schreber's case and acknowledged his legal right to self-expression and to publication. The highest court validated his theory and acceded to his argument. Taking that decision somewhat further and following the lead of some of the more interesting work on Hölderlin's poetics, I am suggesting that the *Memorabilia* be read not as the expression of madness but as the discourse of law and specifically of critique of law.[38] I have shown, in a preliminary manner, that law is bound up inextricably with the genesis and the development of the Judge's nervous condition. It is the law that causes, or at the very least is the location and prompt of his affective indisposition, his nervous collapse and his subsequent suffering both by virtue of incarceration and by dint of the refusal to acknowledge or accept his identification with the feminine as anything other than a symptom of insanity. What, however, if we start elsewhere, not with the 'Father's No' but with the son's refusal?[39] Schreber is mad of, and mad with law. He wants to

---

[37] Ibid. at 481.

[38] Jean Laplanche, *Hölderlin and the Question of the Father* (Victoria, BC: ELS Editions, 2007) at 14: 'This project should be seen as both a preface and an introduction to investigations that would aim not at interpreting the oeuvre according to a certain conception of psychosis, but at listening to and making more explicit the poetic utterance of madness.'

[39] Michel Foucault, 'The Father's No', in Foucault, *Language, Counter-Memory, Practice: Selected Essays and Interviews* (Ithaca: Cornell University Press, 1977) at 80: 'Any discourse which seeks to attain the fundamental dimensions of a work must, at least implicitly, examine its relation to madness: not only because of the resemblances between the themes of

escape the iron cage of the juridical and the strictures of the masculine and so he starts to dream and then to inscribe an alternative juridical theology, a new body and a new law. His *ars iuris* or art of law has yet to be rescued from the clamour of warring physicians.[40]

lyricism and psychosis . . . but more fundamentally, because the work poses and transgresses the limit which creates, threatens and completes it.'

[40] A comparable point is well made in relation to artistic experience, by Chelsea Haines, 'Beyond the Schreber Principle' 35 *Mousse* 264, at 267 (2012), 'if Schreber was alive today he would be a social media sensation rather than a case study in psychoanalytic theory'.

2

Silencing Schreber: Freud, Lacan, Rejection and Foreclosure

The-human-thought-of-recollection was used to indicate man's automatic need to imprint on his mind by repetition an important thought which had occurred to him.

Schreber was voluble as a scribe of his nervous condition and as an enraged, litigious and bellowing captive, held against his will, in the Sonnenstein Asylum. He voiced and penned his resistance at length, but as I have argued in the previous chapter, it is equally evident that the juridical aspects of his writings hit a blind spot and were scotomised by his translators, while his auditory inventions and bellowing, his anger at his treatment by the psychiatric institution, his rage and his pain, his gender dysphoria, his drive to transition, fell back then, on the petard of form, on deaf ears. Only upon final appeal to the Royal Court did his reason and juristic writing gain a limited acknowledgement, although his theology, philosophy and sexual politics were ignored and have been pretty much dismissed to the present day. His corpus, his text, is treated uniformly as being fit only for autopsy. It would seem that Judge Schreber's oeuvre falls still, and pivotally into Foucault's depiction of an archaeology of a silence: 'The language of psychiatry, which is a monologue by reason *about* madness, could only have come into existence in such a silence.'[1] That censorship, the quietude of his reception, the refusal to attend to the language and speech of the Judge on its own terms, as a discourse in its own right, fully self-aware of its extremity, its fictions and its own alien law, should be understood quite literally. His discourse, his 'running around' as MacCabe puts it, was blocked by the extant powers, both institutional and interpretative, and the prior perception and categorisation of his condition, a malady and madness always known in advance, precluded any candid scrutiny of the thesis, his *ennui* with law, his desire to create, to legislate, and most radical of all, the bodily transformation that he pro-

---

[1] Michel Foucault, *History of Madness* (London: Routledge, 2009) at xxviii; emphasis in the original.

pounded in his *magnum opus*.[2] As my focus begins with the juristic discourse of the Judge I will concentrate on the Freudian impasse, the absence of an oeuvre as constitutive of madness in his and later in Lacan's reading and pathologisation of the *Memorabilia*. The Freudian thesis, and we can note and borrow from Foucault again, is in its way a surprisingly standard one for a nascent and supposedly rebellious psychoanalysis: 'for nineteenth century psychiatry the madman is essentially always someone who takes himself for a king, that is to say, someone who wants to assert his power against and over all established power, whether it be the power of the institution or of the truth'.[3] Freud does not deviate that much from the norm. The founder of the new and still threatened movement, quickly reverts to the patristic metaphor and introduces the figure of the father, Moritz Schreber the spectre of the totem or paternal principle, and so the question of the symbolic law, into his synoptic diagnosis and more importantly his theorisation of the jurist's paranoia. That figure of the father as king, in Freud's account enacted initially, through transference, by Professor Flechsig, and then by God, and by the rays of the sun, comes to dominate and so play the law for all of the later interpretations and so it is to Herr Freud and his errant and extreme disciple Monsieur Lacan that scrutiny must first be paid. I will begin, in the morphological fashion of the historian, with Freud. The introduction, etymologically the leading – *ducere* – to the inside – *intro* – is highly revealing, a genuine sign, I will suggest, of the aporia of the interior, the doubt that is to be travailed throughout the work. Sigmund begins with a statement of inadequacy: 'The analytic investigation of paranoia causes particular kinds of difficulty for physicians, like myself, not working in public institutions. We cannot accept patients suffering from this disorder' because they are not amenable to analytic treatment. They resist, they follow their own desires and rudely ignore those of the psychoanalyst. Freud sounds somewhat resentful both of that deflection of the analytic method, and of the empowerment of psychiatry. He then moves on to say that because 'paranoiacs cannot be forced to overcome their inner resistances and in any case only say what they wish to say . . . the published case history may serve as a substitute for personal acquaintance with the patient'.[4] We can immediately note not simply the tension that

---

[2] Colin MacCabe, 'Discourse', in MacCabe (ed.), *The Talking Cure* (London: Macmillan, 1990). It is of course Barthes, in *A Lover's Discourse*, who makes the point that discourse is etymologically *dis-currere*, to run away or latterly to scamper to and fro. But this, of course, adds little specific insofar as it is also true of MacCabe's linguistic escape attempts.

[3] Michel Foucault, *Abnormal: Lectures at the Collège de France 1974–1975* (London: Verso, 2003) at 120.

[4] Freud, *The Schreber Case* (London: Penguin, 2003) at 3. As John Forrester, *Language and*

produces the leap from analysis of a subject to the printed report, a significant and rapidly passed over substitution, due in part to the psychiatric institution's monopoly on treatment of paranoia but, more perversely, directed at the resistance and willfulness, the pleasure of the paranoiacs who insist that they 'will only say what they wish', and hence express directly a desire to remain within their desire. The passions that resist analysis are unwelcome, just as a sexuality that refuses to conform to Freud's monotheistic and paternalistic law of familial reproduction is an affront to the metapsychological theory of the libido. Schreber begins at a disadvantage because he is already diagnosed as resistant, as paranoid, as the subject of an absurd Latin label, and not to put too fine a point on it, as psychotic. The introduction, the conduction into the interior of the case is formulated, never a good sign, as a double negative: 'I am not therefore inclined to think it inadmissible to attach analytic interpretations to the case history of a paranoiac (one suffering from *dementia paranoides*) whom I have never seen.' In fact three negatives, if the muted lack of encounter with the still living Schreber is tallied, and so in biblical terms an affirmation of the illegitimacy of his method, expressed in a suitably convoluted and tortured manner. As Santner points out, this divagation in style, the recourse to unnecessary, boundary marking, the absurd Latin and the justification of such an extravagantly distanced method of analysing a patient, signal Freud's professional insecurity at that time. He was reacting in part to the rather embattled status of the psychoanalytic movement that was in this period experiencing its first splits and so also a questioning of Freud's own paternal authority as the founder of the school: 'The institution of psychoanalysis was, one could say, in a state of emergency, meaning a state of *emergence*, of coming-into-being, as well as one of *crisis* and endangerment.'[5] Freud is nervous, even somewhat scared of the nervous patient, who is not only *ex officio* resistant to the new method, the talking cure, that Freud has devised and is proselytising, but also belongs to a profession that is profoundly hostile to, and has no uses for the psychoanalytic technique and project.Freud's nervousness manifests itself in a war of books, a paper litigation that most symptomatically and indicatively evades any actual contact with the patient. As Calasso observes cryptically 'it is significant that Freud's great study of paranoia, the paper on Schreber, is the only

---

the *Origins of Psychoanalysis* (London: Macmillan, 1980) at 157 perceptively points out, 'it is quite clear that the method of propositional analysis can be employed completely independently of the direct speech of the analysand'.

5   Santner, *My Own Private Germany* at 24; emphasis in the original. It was a period, Santner continues, when, to use Schreber's terminology, the basic language, 'the *Grundsprache*' of psychoanalysis was 'being hotly and bitterly contested'.

one of his great cases to be based solely on a text'.[6] After bemoaning, indeed protesting too much, that analysts such as himself have no access to patients suffering from *dementia paranoides*, after bemoaning the paranoiac's resistance to treatment, and then in a rather opaque fashion justifying his recourse to print, to a reading, an exposition and exposure of the Judge's book, we encounter the most remarkable statement in the entirety of the one-and-a-half-page introduction: 'It is possible that Dr Schreber is still alive today,' which is to say the summer of 1910. We can note again the stripping of the Judge of his juristic titles, a minor infraction here as his doctorate in law is elliptically acknowledged, but much more crucial is the fact that at that time, Schreber was not simply alive but according to the records of Leipzig-Dösen Asylum, to which he had been admitted in November 1907, he was experiencing relative peace and quiet, generally uninterrupted sleep and was scribbling away, although not in a manner intelligible to his attending doctor.[7]

What is staggering beyond comprehension is that Freud seemingly had virtually no interest in contacting the family, in finding out about the condition of the Judge, his subsequent history, cure or relapse. He showed no desire for engagement, no aspiration to meet the patient, his relatives, his fleeting-improvised wife, his daughter, neither the tested soul of Professor Flechsig, nor the director of the asylum whose reports Freud so relies upon, nor the attendants or lawyers who had experienced the Judge's various and variable manifestations.[8] This extraordinary lack of inquisitiveness, the insensibility that precluded looking for and meeting Schreber, amounts to a fear of encountering the subject of his analysis in case the experience may be resistant to his analyses, or because that encounter may unsettle the prescriptions and weaken the façade of the new method. Either that, or he simply thought it unnecessary, the case already determined: come the hour, come the conclusion. The point is that Freud is seeking in his book to provide a diagnosis of Schreber, he intends an analysis of the patient, and he then proffers a theory of paranoia that is supposedly predicated upon and exemplified by this singular patient, but, and it is a significant butt, the pun no excuse, he is entirely unwilling to even lift his pen and directly send a letter of enquiry as to the whereabouts, health or availability of the very patient who was currently being examined exclusively on paper and diagnosed in the Freudian imaginary as an instance of the sublimation of the symbol of the father. One

---

[6] Roberto Calasso, 'A Report on Readers of Schreber', in Calasso, *The Forty-Nine Steps* (Minneapolis: University of Minnesota Press, 2001) at 125.

[7] The hospital charts are generously provided as an appendix to Lothane, *Defense* at 469, 482.

[8] He makes one discreet enquiry in correspondence, an unpublished letter to Ferenczi, on 10 October 1907, but to my knowledge nothing more. See Lothane, *Defense* at 106.

interpretation of the analyst's resistance to the analysand, Freud's counter-transference, appears in a much-cited passage at the end of the case study of the written reports where Freud opines: 'It remains for the future to decide whether there is more delusion in my theory than I should like to admit, or whether there is more truth in Schreber's delusion than other people are as yet prepared to believe.'[9]

The remark should be put in its proper context. The paragraph that it concludes begins with Freud saying, 'I neither fear the criticism of others nor shrink from criticizing myself.' At the risk of a bad pun, the shrink protests that he does not shrink. The joke, however, carries a certain truth, which emerges just before Freud's tentative admission of his own possible delusion, his identification with his imagined subject. It is a very tentative and brief hint, almost a slip, and one that reveals the insecurity that has led Freud to his thoroughly dogmatic, deeply defensive and, in his own formulation, his some-what monotonous account of the text that he is purporting to use as a mode of treatment of the patient *in absentia*. He thus calls upon a 'friend and fellow-specialist' as witness to the fact that 'I had developed my theory of paranoia before I became acquainted with the contents of Schreber's book'. It is not in the end Schreber who is the subject of the project but simply its excipient, the vehicle of Freud's prior desire. He is but 'a fragment of a larger whole', namely 'the libido theory of the neuroses and psychoses'.[10] Freud, in the spirit of his embattled and turbulent disciplinary times, is much more concerned with manipulating Schreber to corroborate his theories and shore up his enterprise than he is with any analysis of the patient, diagnosis or cure of the subject, through attention to their speech and here their text. The glimpse provided by the comparative statement of the two delusions, those of the Judge and those of the analyst, manifests a degree of competition and more importantly of counter-transference, the projection of the analyst on to the discourse of the analysand, and is likely to transpire to be highly significant. There is, in Freud's account, a strong element of the Napoleonic, and in Foucault's' terms, of playing King and asserting his power against the institution of psychiatry, to be sure, but also against the truth of the other, over the discourse of the Judge. To borrow from Canetti's analysis of Schreber, Freud is seeking power and '[i]t is difficult to resist the suspicion that behind paranoia, as behind all power, lies the same profound urge: the desire to get other men out of the way so as to be the only one; or, in the milder, and indeed often admitted, form, to get others to help him *become* the only one'.[11]

[9] Freud, 'Psychoanalytic Notes' at 79.
[10] Ibid.
[11] Canetti, *Crowds and Power* at 435; emphasis in the original.

There are two principal reasons for Freud's waiving of the Judge's discourse and preclusion of the desires expressed in the text. The first, competitive, homosocial, relates, as adumbrated, to the precarious status of psychoanalysis, and Freud's own concern to be recognised as the author and principal protagonist of the method. His paternity of the discipline has been contested, disciples have abandoned him and Freud is himself in some significant measure subject to the crisis of authority that accosts his age: the father is dead, the *dispositif* or familial apparatus of heteronormativity, Prince Phallus himself, are all in a state of detumescence and disarray. Freud is bent on saving the father, curing the son's hatred of the imagined oligarch and so also keeping the son's sexuality within the confines of familial reproduction and the law of the father.[12] He is supposed to take up his pre-defined generative and gendered place, and for Freud is ill of not doing so.

There is a transitional passage at the end of Freud's introduction to his Case History, in which, so as to authenticate his analysis, he states: 'I am providing verbatim citations of all sections of the *Memoirs* [*Denkwürdigkeiten*] that support my interpretation.'[13] He then asks his readers themselves to read the book at least once before approaching his own text. This transitional passage stands as a mark of legitimacy, a sign of apparent truth to the discourse being interpreted, even though, as I have adverted often and already, Freud is not in fact interested in enquiring into Schreber's actual history, trajectory or current condition and circumstances, nor in paying attention to any aspect or depth of the text itself that does not support his monistic theory of the paternal principle of explanation. Freud needs his place as father, his monotony of interpretation, to shore up a historical past and symbolic security that is under threat, and an immediate history of his own disciplinary child, that is also in a fractured state. His goal is not to track the Judge's dysphoria, nor to enquire as to his status as hermaphrodite, cis-gendered, bisexual or as transitional, as a member of the 'third sex', which is to say his escape from the law of genre, but rather and only to cite verbatim those passages that support 'my interpretation', and thus that shore up Herr Dr Freud's method and movement. As if to prove his point and perhaps also to lure the lector into a sense of security, the first sentence of the *Case History* cites Schreber, rather conclusively, stating that he has twice suffered from nervous illness. That statement is already incorrect, if trivially so, insofar as enquiry would have led Freud to learn that Schreber is in fact suffering, at the time of writing, a third and final nervous indisposition. That aside, Freud then cites the

---

[12] This is, of course, in significant measure the thesis of Michel Tort, *Le Fin du dogme paternal* (Paris: Aubier, 2005)

[13] Freud, *The Schreber Case* at 5.

Judge referencing the juridical context and cause of both of the illnesses. That context, however, like the person of the Judge, is not of interest to Freud. He moves to the illness, to Schreber's breaking of the law of the father, his mad resistance to the familial and specifically paternalistic apparatus of sexuality without so much as a word remarking the juristic context and provenance, the legal aetiology of the case, precisely as a case, both analytic and juristic.

More surprising yet and in stark contradiction of the implications of his transitional reference to verbatim citation to Schreber, the second paragraph abandons the Judge, his person, his text, his thought, completely and moves immediately to extracting the history of the first 'illness' from a 'Pro Forma Assessment' provided by the Judge's first doctor, Professor Flechsig.[14] Only eight lines into his *Case History*, predicated as it supposedly is upon the Judge's book, although equally upon Freud's desire to prove his own pre-established theory, of which he is keen to claim sole authorship and title to, he has shifted almost immediately from the text to psychiatric reports of a formal kind provided by Schreber's doctors and captors, the discourse of the wardens. Escape from the text, from the voice of the subject, to the scripture of the institution, the books of the law, the psychiatric reporting that, paradoxically, Freud is secretly seeking to contest, has seldom been swifter. The stage is set by the discourse of the institution, by the psychiatric reports that are the not so secret subject of Freud's principal attentions and that form the family from whom Freud seeks recognition and reward. The pattern is repeated in the subsequent descriptions.

After citation to Professor Flechsig's pro forma report there is a brief interlude, a play between the illnesses, and citation to the leading dream, the dogmatic key to the good Dr Freud's interpretation, the hypnopompic reverie of the pleasure that 'submitting to' or 'undergoing' intercourse as a woman must occasion. Still proceeding as if simply describing the content of the book and the course of the condition, Freud moves then, two paragraphs after citing Flechsig's report, to a lengthy exposition of the second illness that is drawn initially almost exclusively from the assessments filed by Dr Weber, the director of the Sonnenstein Asylum, whose reports and testimony to the courts consistently and persistently sought to keep Schreber incarcerated. The director of the asylum's hostile diagnoses are the basis for Freud's approach to his subject, as if the psychiatric terminology and judgement will support and justify the psychoanalytic interpretation that follows. The father of psychoanalysis wants the paternal imprimatur and blessing of the medical establishment. He makes no secret of it. Freud thus staggers and carefully

---

[14] Ibid.

orders his use of the formal records to best support the thesis that he will be later propounding upon the conventional and now, of course, controverted presupposition, drawn from the dream, that homosexuality, if not recognised and successfully overcome, as Freud had overcome his homosexual libido, is the trigger of paranoia and thence of mental illness. As Calasso observes, the ghost of Fleiss hovers over the analysis of Judge Schreber and it is this unresolved investment, Freud's brush with homosexual affect, or in his own terms, his developmental 'weak spot', his latent paranoia, that could well be taken to explain the emphasis on the negative or abnormal character this as yet unspeakable affection.[15] It is this perceived sexual abnormality, the propositional shift from loving to hating the father, that projection of his thwarted love on to other figures, that is the fissure, the crack, the wound that Freud seeks to cure. Somewhat ironically, Schreber is in effect deemed to take his sexuality too seriously. He embeds himself in an erotic and erogenous self that does not conform to Freud's schema of development and does not treat homosexuality or better transitional desire, as a stage to be abandoned, passed through and left behind as not conforming to the law of familial reproduction.

Initially, it is the descriptive and diagnostic language of madness that silences Schreber's discourse. Hypochondria and hyperaesthesia (sensitivity to light) are rapidly superseded by 'notions of persecution', 'auditory delusions', 'pathological ideation', 'hallucinatory stupor', suicidal ideation and then 'more acute psychosis', 'hallucinatory insanity', a 'clinical picture of paranoia' and further delusions that definitively inscribe the Judge among the mad, a would be King in Bedlam. The promise of verbatim transcription of the Judge's discourse is already rendered irrelevant precisely because the institutional assessments have marked that discourse as insane and their author as a lunatic, whose sexual dysphoria and transitional desire are simply manifestations of incapacity and as such are threats to the symbolic order. The psychiatric discourse has projected the categories of psychosis and paranoia, pathology and delusion upon the Judge's text before it is even properly opened. And Freud has followed suit, both because he wishes to legitimate his method and because he is not interested in Schreber but only in the expostulation, exemplification and dissemination of the libido theory. There is then an air of inevitability and a tenor of déjà vu when Freud comes, soon after he has finished quoting Dr Weber's aggressive labelling of Schreber, to the substance of the Judge's system: 'For a comprehensive depiction of the delusion in its fully developed form we can turn to the Assessment supplied by Dr

---

[15] Calasso, *Forty-Nine Steps* at 128

Weber in 1899.'[16] No word from the Judge, it is Weber's system, the institutional apparatus, and not Schreber's declarations, descriptions and depictions that will set the stage and drive the analysis, one that is completely, adamantly, juridically and literally *in absentia*. The description that follows, which is taken, as adumbrated, from the reports of Schreber's attending physician, warden and captor, who was also his antagonist in all three stages of his court battle for release, details the culmination of the patient's 'delusional system' as perceived by the institution in which he was at the time involuntarily incarcerated. As Louis Sass has successfully argued, it is hardly an account of his philosophy, and I will add that it is in no sense a depiction of his jurisprudence, let alone a balanced overview of his discourse and advocacy of his transition and his sanity.[17] Equally, it ignores his puns, his style and his sense of the ludic, his *Luder*, hir humour. What is provided by the psychiatrist, and relayed as truth by Freud, because it suits his extrinsic purposes, is that Schreber has been called to bring salvation to the world, that his mission comes directly from God and that a prerequisite of salvation is his '*transformation into a woman*'. Armed with this overview, Freud intends to go beyond the psychiatric interest, which is simply in the day-to-day behavioural consequences of 'the patient's delusion' to an understanding of the 'peculiar trains of thought, so remote from habitual human thinking' that will explain 'the motives of, and the paths taken by, this transformation'.[18] And yet, even at this moment of declaration of the psychoanalytic project, this nailing of independence of thought to the banner of the new method, the next line reverts to the institutional descriptors and the reports of the director of the asylum: 'The two main points stressed by the medical assessor are the *role of the Redeemer* and the *transformation into a woman*.' The latter point has, of course, already been signalled ahead by Freud's discussion of Schreber's hypnopompic dream, but the broader dependency upon the psychiatric designators and descriptors remains stark and unforgiving. Freud the king, the champion, the innovator who opposes the established forms is here entirely subservient to the facts as set out in the institutional reports of the very discipline that he wishes to challenge or at the very least to supplement. If Freud seeks the protection of the psychiatric categories, the terminology drawn from the reports of the warders, director and doctors of the appropriately and

---

[16] Freud, *The Schreber Case* at 9.

[17] Louis Sass, *The Paradoxes of Delusion* at 25–33.

[18] Freud, *The Schreber Case* at 10. It is worth noting here that even then this train of thought was not without precedent or contemporary exemplars, as is well depicted in Laure Murat, *La Loi du genre: Une histoire culturelle du 'troisième sexe'* (Paris: Fayard, 2006), to which theme I will return later.

irreally named Sonnenstein Asylum, it is because there is another and greater portent that lurks in the Judge's discourse and that has to be suppressed. This is the threat, posed at the level of the institution and also on the plane of truth, of the discourse of the law. The question is as basic as that of whether Schreber has a right to his discourse, whether he is entitled to explain his behaviour, and vindicate his subjectivity so as to gain release from the asylum. Underlying this conflict of discourses is the centrality of law to Freud's discourse, the importance of judgement and specifically of a verdict, and his need in consequence to keep the analytic prescription of causes and cures free from juristic over-determination. It is trial, *in absentia*, by analysis and the process is one that may pay lip service to the analysand, but in fact does peculiarly little listening. Law, specifically the Judge and the Analyst, exist, for Freud, in different realms, separated by distinct methods and opposed projects and projections. This is apparent in an earlier essay that Freud published in 1906 and that has peculiar implications for the analysis of the role of the Father, the 'familiar ground of the father-complex', the 'monotonous solution' and the place of law in his attempts at interpretation.[19] When invited to contribute to a law class on the possible use of psychoanalysis in the courtroom as a means of eliciting evidence, Freud came to the unequivocal conclusion that these two worlds and epistemologies were ineluctably separate.[20] This non-relation between the theatre of trial and the drama of the couch is in one sense fairly obvious. Freud points out that while both court process and analysis are directed at discovery of the truth, the context and method of enquiry are antithetical. In the courtroom the accused, as also the witness or litigant, are subject to time pressure, hostile examination and an interrogation with potentially coercive results. There are rules of evidence, criteria and sanctions for perjury, further procedural protocols and hierarchical constraints upon what is said and how it is said in giving testimony in legal settings. The method of analysis, free association, by contrast depends upon unlimited time and the willing cooperation of the analysand in the shared project of discovering the truth. The only obstacle to be overcome in analysis is the repression barrier while in the trial the accused will likely be resistant to the truth and so deflective of the inquisitorial process of

---

[19] Freud, 'Psychoanalytic Notes' at 55; emphasis in the original.

[20] Sigmund Freud, 'Psychoanalysis and the Ascertaining of Truth in Courts of Law', in *Collected Papers*, vol. II (London: Hogarth Press, 1946 [1906]) at 13. This theory is developed somewhat further, in structural form, in Pierre Legendre, *Les Enfants du texte: Etudes sur la fonction parentale des Etats* (Paris: Fayard, 1992), translated as 'The Judge amongst the interpreters', in Goodrich (ed.), *Law and the Unconscious: A Legendre Reader* (London: Macmillan, 1997) at 164.

examination, which carries with it the threat of punishment or fine. Freud's conclusion is that the 'distinguished jurists' must go their own way while analysis carves out a dominion and truth of its own. It is a short interpretative step to saying that the Judge, as a member of this professional resistance, this coercive and combative métier of institutional incitation to falsehood, should not simply go his own way – that is very far from what Freud prescribes – but rather go away, get sent down in his turn. The essay on courtroom practice preceded the 'Psychoanalytic Notes' on *dementia paranoides* by five years, but Freud's interest in law, his lecture, his study of Judge Schreber's litigation, and then only two years after the publication of his book on the Judge, the appearance of *Totem and Taboo*, signalled of course in the postscript of 1912, all suggest a continuing, indeed a repeated investment, in the question of legality.[21] The persistent theme, what makes the psychoanalytic case and the law case *confrères*, is that they share the question of guilt. Fictive though it may be, the Oedipal guilt of the sons who have killed their totemic father is closely aligned to the guilt that the court seeks in the secular liturgy of trial. The distinctive feature of the trial is simply that the party on the stand – accused, litigant, witness – is more institutionally and immediately invested in denying their guilt than the analytic patient whose resistance to the truth is often primarily unconscious. What this means for Freud in the present context of his reading of Schreber is twofold.

First, the law of the father, the continuous and intransigent jurisdiction of the immortalised figure of the totemic paternal metaphor, the legend of the phallus, exists from the beginning. The founding myth establishes a norm of sexuality and the place of the father that the son can either take up in the mode of mastering the feminine and playing the paternal role, or descend into madness. Identify or dissolve are the choices on offer to the son, the Judge, the subject as such. This, as Michel Tort rather rambunctiously and feministically puts it, is the relaying of the Old Testament figure of the father as Führer and it merits recognition and cognition that 'this schema of the originary father is a fantasm which imposes itself in an obsessive fashion on Freud, without a scintilla of possible justification derived from anthropological studies'.[22] The roots of such a fantasm are in Freud's unconscious; he wishes to save the figure of the father, he wants to be an institutional father, the sovereign of his disciplinary, and so borrows from a religiously transmitted myth a 'pseudo determinism of origin,' which dictates the erotic submission of the mother to the father, of the feminine to the masculine

---

[21] Sigmund Freud, *Totem and Taboo* (Harmondsworth: Hogarth Press, 2001 [1913]).

[22] Tort, *Fin du dogme* at 105.

and thus institutes Schreber's sexual dilemma. Borrowing momentarily from Freud's disciple: 'If a man who thinks he is king is mad, a king who thinks he is king is no less so.'[23]

Second, and equally flamboyantly, the expulsion of the jurists is from the domain of truth. Their 'distinguished path' is by direct implication one of violence, circumscription and denial, in which the legal profession is viewed as practicing a lesser or lower law, a mendacious and coerced institutional pragmatics that hovers far below the psychoanalysts' access to a higher law and truth. Once designated a lawyer and a litigant to boot, the Judge is placed in the psychoanalytic position of resistance, evasion, deflection and, not to put too fine a point on it, he is by occupational designation a liar. Schreber does not and cannot tell the truth, for Freud, first because he is a lawyer and, second, because he has no access to psychoanalysis. Freud has to speak for the Judge, he has to peer behind the repression barrier and tell his truth. That truth, monotonously for Freud and later for Lacan, is that Schreber had failed symbolically to kill his father and so experienced the hallucinated ghosts of the paternal figure, the projection of what was excluded from the symbolic, as the principal symptom of his illness. By way of variant, and this is Santner's insight, the Judge's investiture crisis, his inability to take up the position and role of Senatspräsident, reflects his identification with the social and epistemic crisis of authority that came with the late nineteenth-centurt declaration of the death of God, which here expresses the social form of the Oedipus complex. Stick, however, for the moment, with the question of the lawyer, rather than that of the abstraction law. Freud places Schreber in the position, and profession, of someone who is not to be believed. The Judge's discourse is to be understood primarily as symptomatic of his resistances to his own truth, and being a lawyer precludes him from both the motive, and the ability, to attend to his symptoms and seek their cause. Freud recognises that the Judge does attempt to work through his dysfunction, we would say dysphoria, by means of the (paranoid) mechanism of projection: 'what we take to be the production of the illness, the formation of delusion, is in reality the attempt at a cure, the reconstruction'.[24] These delusional projections, as Freud terms them, are in effect lies that mask the truth, which in its turn arrives in the mode of law with 'the introduction of the father into the Schreber delusion'.[25] Fear of the father is, of course, the theory and theme that persists into *Totem and Taboo*. It is a facet of Freud's system and of the 'Postscript' of

---

[23] Lacan, 'Presentation on Psychical Causality', in Jacques Lacan, *Écrits: The First Complete Edition in English*, trans. Bruce Fink (New York: Norton, 2006) at 139.

[24] Freud, *The Schreber Case* at 60.

[25] Ibid. at 39.

1912, when Freud was at work on the later book, which signals this thesis in clarion terms. The mythological dimensions of the *Memorabilia* captivate Freud and produce a strong link between the Judge's delusions and 'the totemic thinking of primitive peoples', wherein the totem, from which the tribe traces its origin, comes to be worshiped 'as the father of their tribe'.[26] Signor Phallus arises in the mist of prehistory, before time, as the mythical apparatus of familial role and disposition. We can note again, with renewed justification, that Schreber's discourse is now, for Freud, a distant image in the rear-view mirror of psychoanalytic theory. The Judge's records and recollections are those of a lawyer, and so are structurally resistant to the truth, a series of deflections, lies and masks that paper over the wound, the 'severe psychosis' of Schreber's 'feminine fantasy' and its 'paranoid manifestations' in his fear of sexual abuse. The key for Freud lies, of course, in the hypnopompic dream in which the Judge thinks it would be rather beautiful to be a woman engaging in sexual intercourse, because this feminine identification signals his failure to take up the masculine paternal place, his avoidance of the paternal law, the guilt and transference that such occasions. In Freud's words, which should be read slowly, lucubrated, weighed and balanced: 'A surge of homosexual libido was, then, the cause of this illness.' Slightly later we read: 'We should not, I think, object any further to the supposition that the cause of the illness was the emergence of a feminine (passively homosexual) wishful fantasy.'[27] Its transferred object was first 'the doctor', Flechsig, and then God and the sun, but behind these, because Freud is commendably atheist, lies the father, the totem and the law. The question of the totemic role of the father, love of authority turned to hatred and paranoia, will be taken up further in the context of Lacan's Roman Catholicism, and *il Papa* emergent in the concept of the *nom du père*. For Freud, as Sanders forcefully and lucidly explicates, homosexuality is more the excipient or mode of transmission than the direct object of the aetiology and explanation of the presumed psychosis. There is a propositional structure to the theory that construes love of the father as mutating through paranoia into hate. The homosexual ideation is in itself normal, a moment, that the healthy subject, Freud, for instance, cathects and so resolves by directing the energy elsewhere. The psychotic, however, fails to repair the conflict, the love turns to hate, via substitute figures – Flechsig, God, Ariman – who are experienced as persecuting the paranoiac: 'Another way of saying this is that he or she is, in effect, before the law. But the paranoiac does not know this, since the contradiction cannot come to

---

[26] Ibid. at 69.
[27] Ibid. at 37.

consciousness in the requisite form; "guilt" is structural, but, for the para-noiac, not subjectively felt.'[28] It is thus that Freud can claim, in a letter to Ferenczi, on his own case, that 'a part of homosexual cathexis has been withdrawn and made use of to enlarge my own ego'.[29] That is apparently the 'healthy' response, the successful disposition, because it integrates the subject into the heterosexual norm of the family and into the paternal role as master of the feminine. As Freud puts it elsewhere, 'it is a question of detaching the homosexual component of the libido', of 'overcoming' the desire.[30] The prop-ositional structure, the paranoiac syllogism that Forrester inventively devises in his structural linguistic account of the talking cure, remains stuck in its minor premise, which is that 'he persecutes me'.[31] To this we can counter Sanders' acute observation that the subject is before the law, having trouble with the scales, hard of judging precisely because of this blocked desire, the wish to explore rather than escape the prohibition, the law of interdiction that back then assigned to the man who loves a man, and, excuse the jurid-ism, *a fortiori* the trans, the masculine that seeks the feminine, the man who wants to be a woman, the place of madness. It is this socio-political conflict, the law against desire, the institutional restraints and dogmatic pillars, the conventions of sexual place and the institutional codes of erotic desire, that Freud elaborates and emphasises in the subsequent interpretations. It is intriguing to note that when Freud first introduces this thesis, he pauses dramatically, 'in the face of a flood of remonstration and objection. Anybody acquainted with the psychiatry of today has to be ready for the worst.'[32] Then he goes on to pinpoint the cause of such a reaction: 'Is it not an irresponsible slight, an indiscretion, and an act of calumny to accuse an ethically so elevated man as the retired Presiding Judge Schreber of homosexuality?' There is, as others have pointed out, a degree of ambivalence and a certain identification that Freud appears to feel towards the judge's imputed, or better projected, sexual preference. We are all bisexual. The established order and genealogy of sexual places was already unstable, the third sex had emerged, the repressed had returned and Freud was busy shoring up the breached concept of paternity. That said, the surface of Freud's text hints rather loudly at a

---

[28] Sanders, 'Mourning' at 136.
[29] Cited in Lothane, *Defense* at 338.
[30] Brabant, Eva et al. (eds), *The Correspondence of Sigmund Freud and Sandor Ferenczi, Volume 1* (Cambridge, MA: Harvard University Press, 1994) at 5 and 243. For discussion, see John Forrester, *Dispatches from the Freud Wars: Psychoanalysis and its Passions* (Cambridge, MA: Harvard University Press, 1998) at 46–55 ('Casualities of Truth").
[31] John Forrester, *Language and the Origins of Psychoanalysis* at 154, and cited by Sanders, 'Mourning' at 123.
[32] Freud, *The Schreber Case* at 33.

conventional view, that homosexuality is an ethical flaw, to be overcome, and
if it mutates into the desire to be a woman it is an indication, a symptom of
madness, which, it should be noted, it remained in the medical diagnostic
manuals until the late twentieth century. Both these assumptions thus sit
squarely within the psychiatric and social *mores* of his day but in seeking
novelty and justification, in proselytising his method and promoting his
movement, Freud paradoxically intimates both acceptance of the norm and a
less than open desire to subvert it, a thwarted cathexis of his own, the displacement of homosexuality into homosociality as Freud the King leads the
movement, *his* children, the army of analysts.

Two lines of power seem to drive Freud's interpretation. The first, as
noted, is his struggle for recognition, his own claim to paternity of the psychoanalytic movement, which Santner details well, and that here has the
paradoxical expression of starting from and relying upon the psychiatric
reports on Schreber while at the same time claiming the novelty and independence of his psychoanalytic interpretation. If theory is a mode of seeing,
not just a grammar, then depending so slavishly upon the perceptions of the
Wardens, the carceral discourses of the asylum, should alert us to a limitation if not a certain flaw in the hermeneutic being manipulated. The second
theme is that of the theory of the law of the father, which precedes and
drowns out Schreber's text yet again, because he actually has relatively little
to say of his father, who he explicitly says he reveres, and then moves on. He
seems at this level in the main simply to share the common illusion of an
extant God, an omnipresent divinity, single and several as the Trinity postulates. The Judge, the untrustworthy lawyer, 'the primitive', whose psychic
life, and myth, is comparable to that of a 'savage', mentions his own father,
and also the kindly divine father, his father in law, and his birth father at
various points in the work. The one substantive mention of his father, the
doctor and author, of whom he seems proud, is a reference to 'my father's
Medical Indoor Gymnastics (23rd Edition, p 102)', and observes that his
father, like other physicians, does not seem to be informed about the woman's position in playing the female part in sexual intercourse.[33] The Judge
had very sweetly searched his father's popular book for advice. It had come
up lacking, as the father so often does, but there is little evidence of misplaced Oedipal drive in the reference as opposed to a certain recognition and
respect. Schreber not only seems to have a significant, although distant,
pride in his family history and his father's career, but the book that is mentioned, in its twenty-third edition, was a massive best seller. When the

---

[33] Schreber, *Memoirs* at 167.

publishing house responsible for the work went into liquidation, Schreber negotiated a new contract for publication and this furtherance of his father's fame, together with his juristic acumen in negotiating the contract and managing the legal documents, were cited as factors that influenced the Royal Court of Appeals, and persuaded his brother judges that he was legally competent and that he should be released from the asylum. It has, of course, been a popular and continuing theme of Schreber studies that his father tortured him with his strange orthopaedic machines and devices designed to promote upright posture. Niederland in particular, in an article in 1959, promulgated this thesis to dramatic effect, and in 1973 Schatzman popularised the thesis for a general audience.[34] As Lothane has shown in great detail, however, there is little evidence of any torture, misuse or sexual abuse by the father, Moritz, of the son, Daniel Paul.[35] Certainly Freud, who had no source other than the *Memorabilia*, would have had no grounds for attributing any tyrannical behaviour to the father. The speculative conclusions precede the cause because the case study is an attempt to prove the theory. In legal terminology, Schreber is guilty until proven innocent, and in medical nosology he is diagnosed mad before his book is trawled for evidence of the various tinctures and other occasions of his insanity. In Freud's words, the *ipsissima verba* always being of importance to jurists, 'I cannot be held responsible for the monotony of the solutions provided by psychoanalysis . . . In the case of Schreber, then, we once more find ourselves on the distinctly familiar ground of the father complex.'[36] Freud has found what he is looking for, a certain comfort in the restoration of the challenged father, a return of the repressed, the emergence of a higher law, an originary legality in the mode of psychoanalytic truth. What this reveals, however, is less an account of the Judge's *lapsus* than a representation of Freud's desires and specifically his wish to reinstitute, in torrid times, an unassailable authority,

---

[34] W. G. Niederland. 'Schreber: Father and Son', 28 *Psychoanalytic Quart.* 151 (1959); reprised in Niederland, *The Schreber Case: Psychoanalytic Profile of a Paranoid Personality* (New York: Quadrangle, 1974). M. Schatzman, *Soul Murder: Persecution in the Family* (New York: Signet, 1973). We find this theory repeated in Colin MacCabe's 'Introduction' to the more recent translation of Freud. MacCabe cites to Lothane but the misspelling of Lothane (as Lothan) is perhaps rather too indicative of his not having read that work. Certainly, *incredibile scriptu*, there is no indication in his text that he got as far as reading Chapter 4.

[35] Lothane, *In Defense of Schreber* at 147–98 provides a comprehensive reading of Moritz's work and an account of his educational philosophy and actual inventions that conclusively disproves the 'exaggerated descriptions' concocted by Niederland and the 'even greater distortions' of Schatzman.

[36] Freud, *The Schreber Case* at 42–3.

a sense of origin, a familiarity of law. The father, the masculine, reappears in Freud as the secular displacements of religious concepts. As there is nothing remotely monotonous about Schreber's *Memorabilia*, and little that is familiar, let alone familial, in his account of the juridical theology of the Order of the World (*Weltordnung*), it is time to signal a move from Freud to his inheritor, the extremist Jacques Lacan. Freud's theory of the father complex and of Schreber's homosexual desire projected on to his doctor, Professor Flechsig and then sublimated into the mythical figures of God and the sun is precisely a theory, a way of seeing the case, and in this instance, or so we are told, a monotonously familiar point of view for the analyst, not least because the lens through which he has viewed them is initially that of the reports provided by the psychiatric police, the warders of the clinics where Schreber was incarcerated. The element of repetition, of precedent cases, is a reference, of course, to Freud's self-legitimating method in the face of imagined reactions, and thus is likely somewhat exaggerated so as to defend his theory from the remonstrations and uproar of the psychiatric profession. The theory is certainly not based upon any actual knowledge of family, father, patient or childhood circumstances and thus must remain morphologically amorphous. For my purposes, I want simply to point out that the theory that Freud presents is a reflection in significant part of his own motives, drives, anxieties and projections. It is a manifestation in large measure of counter-transference. It is a matter of how Schreber can help Freud's cause or drop from view. It is the fact that Freud leaves so much out of the analysis, that he moves so rapidly to the reports of Schreber's wardens, that he offers such a highly selective traversal of the Judge's text, and provides an imagined aetiology of the illness in the family, in the Judge's childhood, in his relation to his father, all of which case histories are external to the book being examined. It is the omissions, the gaps and other clues in the interpretative tradition that stems from Freud that deserve attention. It is the jurist that is missing, the law that is present only in the form of a repeated, and so symptomatic, absence, reduced to *wider* or conflict in an unstable psyche that has to be interpreted so as to shore up the founding place of Freud upon the founding myth of the father. Freud, as Gherovici rather forcefully puts it, needs a sex change. If my reading of Freud is one that focuses upon his totems and taboos, rather than upon his express message, and views him in a historical fashion as a symptom of a sexual apparatus and institutional intransigence with which we no longer identify, Lacan represents something of a New Testament, a resurrection of the Freudian interpretation of Schreber in the hands of his children. Once again there is a curious parallelism between Schreber's brilliant madness and Lacan's mad brilliance.[37] This can be tracked in the paradoxical oscillation in Lacan's texts between attraction and repulsion, love and hate, play and judgement as if the disciple is somehow caught in the very propositional structure of paranoia in which, for Freud, the fundamental transformation is that of the verb turning into its opposite.[38] I would hazard, because hazard it is, that Lacan the scientist of the obscure is constantly lured into his other persona, that of the erotomaniac, law morphs into love and while the analyst glimpses and hints at this possession, the fact that he is internal to the dance, or mutation of opposites, means that it is desire that speaks him and the myth of the father that repeats in the fictions of the son. Lacanium, to coin a phrase, starts Schreebing.[39] It is Lacan, in all events, and in good Roman Catholic style, who most explicitly makes the link between the place and function of the father and the role of law, of the *nom du père*, in the aetiology of Freud's theory of Schreber's 'illness'. First, however, a few preliminary remarks. Some further notes on method and the dangers of imbibing too much Lacanium. Let's just say that Lacan does not start with the Judge and his text but rather with the psychoses, the topic of his seminar, and, these, 'there is no reason to deny oneself the luxury of this word – correspond to what has always been called and legitimately continues to be called madness'.[40] The setup, the theory that here precedes the encounter with Schreber's text, not only delights and plays, as one would expect of Lacan the linguist, with the ambiguities and the verbal luxuriance of lunacy, but also sets up a tone of judgement: 'Like all perverts, it sometimes happens that the paranoiac goes beyond the limits and falls into that frightful madness, the unbounded exaggeration of his unfortunate character'.[41] As Schreber is the only subject analysed in the book, it is a fair assumption that the pervert whose unfortunate character and frightful madness emerge in unbounded exaggeration is that of the Judge. And that perversion and madness, let it not be forgotten, is his transitional desire, his 'abnormal' sexuality, his refusal of the law of genre as

---

[37] I have to confess that I am here revising an elegant expression from Cornelius Castiadoris, *Crossroads in the Labyrinth* (Brighton: Harvester, 1984) at 129: 'Nevertheless, we cannot reflect too deeply on the fact that language only exists in the form of particular languages, and that a universal language exists only for Leibniz and President Schreiber [*sic*], or for a number of lesser pen pushers possessed of neither the mad brilliance of the one nor the brilliant madness of the other."

[38] Forrester, *Language* at 154.

[39] By way of unnecessary explication, the reference to the campus drugs Lacanium and Derridium, is to the fine and entertaining François Cusset, *French Theory: How Foucault, Derrida, Deleuze & co. transformed the Intellectual Life of the United States* (Minneapolis: University of Minnesota Press, 2008).

[40] Lacan, *Psychoses* at 4.

[41] Lacan, *Psychoses* at 5.

it comes to be thwarted by medical indictment and positive law, by psychiatrists and warders, court clerks and personnel, and now finally it comes to be
foreclosed by Lacanian theory. By the time that Lacan is writing, he is in a
sense correct to observe that 'the lunatic's printed discourse is all that we
have', but of course, Lacan is also returning to Freud and expanding his text
on Schreber, as supplemented by the linguistics of Ferdinand de Saussure.
Following on from Freud, it cannot be ignored that the frightful and per-
verse characteristics of the particular paranoiac under *postmortem* analysis are
those that the founding father of the movement had pointed out. Schreber's
latent homosexuality, his passive feminine desire, his relationship with the
divinity transferred into his belief that his doctor had tried to kill his soul or,
more plausibly, was guilty of medical malpractice, are the principal manifestations of his character deformation, although the presumption that they are
insane perversions and frightful paranoia seems extreme and open to alternative interpretations. There is also a certain metaphysical trajectory that
attracts analytic correction. Schreber thought that God should be kept out
of human affairs, that the proper Order of the World was one that was free
of the interference of the dead, of the chatter of automata and of souls 'tied-
to-celestial-bodies', and it is again quite possible to agree with such opinions
as being no more eccentric, as the Royal Court of Appeals helpfully pointed
out, than any of the many other species of theism, including, one can now
add, Lacan's own dream of the big Other. Divinities were to be excluded
from law and the legal evaluation of Schreber's case because the law transpired to be remarkably sympathetic to the ex-Judge's forensic rhetorical
ploy, which was that of insisting that all spiritualist interferences, be it God,
psychiatry or the priesthood, should remain excluded from the tellurian and
pragmatic, thoroughly impure because of the mundane routines of positive
law. For Lacan, the key to the interpretation of the *Memorabilia* lies in the
concept of foreclosure – *Verwerfung*. Continuing the patter, established by
Freud, and rather too common in the study of Schreber, Lacan's introduction of this concept comes before any substantive encounter with the text
and discourse of the *Memorabilia*. It is not, I hasten to add, that Lacan does
not spend considerable time in performing what is in essence a poetics of
psychosis, an ironic or perhaps conflicted celebration of the visceral qualities
of the Judge's language, hir *Grundsprache*, and reading extensive portions of
the text to his students, but rather the preclusion of aspects of that discourse
by virtue of the prior designations that nominate the Judge as perverse,
unfortunate, lunatic, paranoiac, an advanced case of madness and now foreclosed before and prior to attending in any detail to the text on its own,
which is to say on the Judge's terms. The concept of *Verwerfung* literally
operates as an analytic foreclosure, a preclusion and reorientation of the text

to come. The patient, because here again we are dealing with a text that we have been told in no uncertain terms, in advance, is a manifestation of insanity, has failed to enter the symbolic.

Lacan, on page thirteen of the translation of *Seminar on the Psychoses*, explains that 'what is refused in the symbolic order, in the sense of *Verwerfung*, reappears in the real'. Following on from Freud's briefly sketched theory of the paranoiac's hallucinations being attempts to heal the wound of interior, symbolic aphasia or akinesis, the patient's hallucinations are thus, for Lacan, to be treated as the reappearance in the real, as objects, of what was earlier negated in the symbolic order. The failure to take up the place of the father results in a Lacanian lacuna that displaces the speech of the subject into exteriority. The agonistic activities of the Judge are equally amenable, however, to an interpretation that takes his forensic adventure as precisely that, advocacy of his case. As I will argue later at length, the Judge sought, first page, line one, to win release from the asylum 'in order to live once again among civilized (*gesitteten*) people and at home with my wife'.[42] He wanted to recover his legal capacity, to return to competence, to prove in an indirect yet powerful manner that transitional desire was not an illegal or mad infraction of law, but rather, if anything, an attempt to change the priority of the law over desire.

The categorisation of litigiousness as a symptom of paranoia immediately forecloses discussion of the legal merit and jurisprudential significance of the Judge's advocacy and argument. It is dismissive, presumptive, and in no small measure condescending. Schreber's struggle in the symbolic order, his prolonged fight to gain acceptance and publication of his work, as well as his release from the asylum, his discourse as a lawyer, is thus foreclosed in the psychoanalytic reading by the very concept of the imaginary, of fantasy, desire and *jouissance*, that is supposed to explain them. These, to borrow from a more recent study in the same vein, are the delusional's devices for persuading doctors that they are not psychotic but have been born into the wrong body.[43] The psychotic, on this theory, litigates their pleasure and certainly for Lacan, in replacing the symbolic with the imaginary, with fantasy, Schreber sets up a dynamic that most often will take an adversarial, legal and conflictual form: 'the prevalence of litigiousness is stressed . . . because the subject cannot come to terms with a certain loss or injury and because his entire life appears to be centered around compensation for the injury suffered and the claim it entails'.[44] Which, one may riposte, is fairly unsurprising if one has been incarcerated without one's knowledge, and against one's will, for desir-

[42] Schreber, *Memoirs* at 1.
[43] Morel, *Sexual Ambiguities* at 192.
[44] Lacan, *Psychoses* at 22.

ing what lawyers term, *plus ultra*, something more, namely affect, body and
volition, in the space or on the vacated throne of the judge. Elsewhere, Lacan
notes that law is the pivot but in Schreber's case, the sagacious psychoanalyst
opines, rather surprisingly and certainly counter-factually, that such juridical
ambition lies entirely in the imaginary dimension.[45] I will address or better
give space to Schreber's transitional self and sexuality, his transformation into
a woman, in later chapters, and for the moment simply reverse the psychoanalytic projection that sees the Judge's successful attempts to advocate his
sanity and litigate his release as no more than proof of his psychosis. It is pass-
ingly ironic that it is the psychoanalysts who rush to treat Schreber's advocacy
of his desire, his drive to transition, and specifically his confrontation of a
masculine law with a feminine sensibility as evidence of madness rather than
as a complex expression of trans performance. *Verweiblichung*, feminisation,
the *jouissance* of the psychic feminine and interior body, the fantasy in the
place of the phantasy of the phallus, is given neither credence nor words by
the very discipline that invented the erotic drive as the structural principle of
human action. More than that, no attempt is made to address, let alone to
understand, the roots of the Judge's dispute, and cause of action, precisely
in the mistreatment and misdiagnosis that he had received from the medical
and legal professions. The discourse of the Judge and his critique of law are
alike foreclosed by the analyst's appeal to the higher and imaginary law of the
father. They project their own fantasy of desire unbound, the *nom de leur père*,
one may say, on to the patient and in that curiously counter-transferential
sleight, end up accusing the Judge of their own sin.[46]

Pause and consider what Schreber had experienced at the hands of the
medical profession and then by virtue of the covert actions and ineffective
representations of lawyers. He received an initial treatment from Professor
Flechsig in the Leipzig University clinic and then returned, seemingly cured,
to work as a judge for a further eight years. When he suffers his relapse, he
returns to the clinic and receives a rather peremptory chemical treatment, a
very strong (and potentially lethal) sleeping draught, which does not work.
After the failure of the prescribed medication, Flechsig offers little further
treatment and seemingly loses interest in the patient. As Lothane elaborates
it, Flechsig's research interests and reputation lay elsewhere, in the surgical
treatment of madness, and Schreber offered no prospect of furthering that

[45] Ibid. at 69–70.
[46] A point made at a general level, with especial reference to the multiple significations of
Lacan's 'Disourse of Rome', and with great elegance in Michel Tort, *Le Fin du dogme*; and
see also Michel Sylvestre, *Demain la psychanalyse* (Paris: Albin, 2003).

work.[47] So Flechsig effectively kicks the Judge out of the clinic and into the asylum. Once admitted to the asylum, Schreber has lost his judicial career, as the ordinances of the Ministry of Justice exclude a Judge who has been admitted to such an institution from ever returning to their office. More than that, while in the asylum, Schreber's wife, unbeknown to the Judge, who believes he is a voluntary patient, obtains a temporary court order incarcerating him as insane and relieving him of control of his financial affairs. The rest of the story, the prolonged litigation and eventual release are well known, but it does seem somewhat far-fetched to regard Schreber's investment in his lawsuit as a 'litigious delusion', without more.[48] You don't have to be Franz Kafka to recognise that we are all before the law and that in this instance that was quite immediately and literally the case. The Judge had every reason for his attention to the litigation and considerable justification for his view that he had been harmed and misrepresented by those who were paid to care for him. In the vernacular, his legal concerns were perfectly real. They are not obviously merely the hallucinations that the analyst too readily takes them to be. The Judge, the lawyer, had legal concerns. He set out a philosophy and a practice of law with considerable originality, detail and success. Lacan, at points, comes close to recognising this. Freud had early on admitted both his profound interest in the uniqueness of Schreber's book and a certain degree of identification with the putative delusions that it relayed. He, too, admitted to homosexual feelings, but he was 'healthy' enough to be able to sublimate them into his work. Lacan goes somewhat further, arguing that the Judge 'is as coherent as many of the philosophical systems of our time ... I do not see how Schreber's system is of any less value than philosophers whose general theme I have profiled', referring in the main to Kant and to Kojève. Indeed, in a moment of extraordinary clarity, Lacan remarks: 'wasn't it because they didn't go far enough in listening to the insane that the first classifications were impoverished and problematic ... weren't you struck ... by how much more alive what one obtains is if ... one simply listens to the subject?'[49] There is an undoubted truth in that perception and point of method, but it is not one to which the analyst remains particularly constant. Two points are key.

---

[47] When Alexander van Haven, in the course of working on his PhD visited the University of Leipzig Clinic, where Flechsig had worked, and asked if they had Schreber's brain in their collection, the response was puzzlement and a clarion no.

[48] Lacan, *Psychoses* at 18.

[49] Ibid. at 206. The same point is made much earlier, in 1845, by Dr Jacques-Joseph Moreau de Tours: 'Although the patients sometimes spoke, we did not take sufficient account of what they said", cited in Murat, *The Man Who Thought He Was Napoleon* at 228.

First, the listening actually performed is highly selective. Indeed, I have argued that it was foreclosed by the analytic apparatus projected on to the discourse prior to its elaboration, by Freud, Lacan's father, and then in the seminars, by the maestro himself. Lacan believed the psychotic, and our Judge in particular, were amusing, rich in insight and original, and that the contribution of psychoanalysis was to make the language of psychosis understandable and meaningful, but this is always according to the terms that the analyst brings to the reading. It is meaning within the system of analytic interpretation that is the Desideratum, the Lacanium. That said, madness made meaningful is still madness. The problem of expression remains. Thus, it is a mad meaning, the lunatic's laughter, the insane insight of the perceptions that appeal to Lacan because it is the subjective criterion of Lacan's own truth, his pursuit of his fantasy, his desire, his psychosis, which in an even more pronounced form than with Freud, leads to the displacement of Schreber's treatise and argument, his syntagm, into a rigorously if paradoxically foreclosed space of displacement in which the brilliance of the madness is an entertaining and often illuminating accessory to the monotony of interpretation. Lacan may laugh with the Judge, he may recognise the madman within, but he distances himself in the mode and trajectory of interpretation. The *Memorabilia* thus suffer the dual status of mythic objects: they are texts pregnant with covert meaning, signs and supports of the analysts' theory, and they are mere fantasy and imagination. The second point is that Lacan is focused entirely upon the linguistics of psychotic utterance, upon the symbolic at the expense of the imaginary. That is, of course, the Lacanian theory and the embellishment that Lacan offers to the propositional structure of paranoia that Freud had devised. The unconscious is structured like a language, and Legendre adds that the unconscious is like a jurist, but intriguing though this may sound from the perspective of analyzing the discourse of the Judge, it restricts analysis to a perspective located exclusively in the chop logic of syntax, with at best a veneer of rhetorical complement. The focus on language, upon linguistic phenomena such as phonetic homonymy, repetition and morphology, neither recognises nor moves beyond the linguistic to the image, the 'picturing pleasures' and other visions that so motivated and moved Schreber throughout the involuntary course of his residence in Sonnenstein. These, for Freud and for Lacan alike, are hallucinations, visual delusions that are no more than the form that the symptoms of psychosis take, rather than expressions of intent, metaphors of desire or modes of thought. Perhaps, as adverted earlier, it was the proximity of the birth of cinema that led Freud to treat hallucinations as the projection of an unreal, entirely fictive and discountable set of imagistic delusions. The train on the screen, racing towards the audience, as Vertov famously showed, will not actually harm anyone in any directly physical sense because it will not leave the screen. For Freud, that seemed to be the end of the matter.

The cinematic character of projection removes the hallucinated image from the domain of analysis – it is the equivalent of the hallucinated qualities of the filmic image, a self-conscious fiction, an evanescent and vanishing spectre upon the template of the imaginary, and one that is instantly dissipated when the technology of projection is understood. The image for Freud is suspended, suppressed within and after a process of distortion is registered as an external phenomenon.[50] It then returns from without, and thus is projected back as a fantasy that will cover over the fissure in the self that has caused the paranoia[51] – which is all, in its way, very pretty, and satisfyingly circular. That said, however, the image is reduced by Freud to being only a sign of illness, the projection is nothing but a hallucination, a visual delusion that comes back to haunt the subject as a hieroglyph, an opaque clue as to the cause of their condition. The hallucination has no value in itself, and the image is deemed illusory in the sense of being without object, a pure chimera, and thence not subject to the rigour of interpretation or multiplicity of possible meanings and erotic excursions that redound to the hermeneutic benefit of the dream narrative. The apparatus of the image is displaced into the linguistic and propositional structure of paranoia. The same ambiguous status of the image is found in Lacan. He starts from the observation that Freud has the 'genius of the linguist'.[52] When it comes to images, the point of departure is still language, the decipherment of the hieroglyphs of dreams, to which Lacan cannily adds that the notion that dreams are expressed in images is altered when one realises that the hieroglyphic depiction is an image that occurs in writing.[53] After which, Lacan works tirelessly to reduce the image to the word, and specifically to the primacy of the signifier. The image exists only as a marker of the psychotic fantasy that places the subject outside of the signifier and so beyond the symbolic: 'The classical theory of the image and the imagination is obviously surprisingly inadequate. This is ultimately an unfathomable domain.'[54] Hence the concentration on other things, on the linguistic sign and on the meanings that Lacan, who is in his turn exterior to Schreber's signifiers, chooses to impose. It is the absence – the abeyance – of the father that forms the core of Lacan's profoundly Freudian interpretation, and thus in his terms a question of the unsaid, an absent signifier, the Lacanian

[50] Freud, *The Schreber Case* at 56.
[51] Ibid. at 60.
[52] Lacan, *Psychoses* at 10.
[53] Ibid. at 247.
[54] Ibid. at 165.

lacuna. It is, however, a problematic unsaid. First, empirically, Schreber does, as mentioned earlier name his father and not simply in the reference to Moritz's book and the renegotiation of the contract for its publication. Schreber also, and indicatively, mentions his father at several points as one of the souls that spoke to him, inhabited him and on occasion advised him.[55] The propositional transformation, from love to a displaced or transferred hate, has not taken place, nor has the impossibility of speaking the name of the father, as Lacan invents, in fact occurred. Early in the *Memorabilia*, Schreber explains his theory of the nerves that make up the human soul. He opines that the nerves contain the recollections, the 'memory impressions' of lineage and progenitors: 'This new entity – the child to be – thus recreates anew the father and the mother, perhaps more the former or the latter', and whichever predominates, there is no question but that the child incorporates a paternal nerve and memory.[56] This theory is later enacted in the references to his father's, and in one instance his brother's soul as voices that were in contact with him during that period of his nervous breakdown when he believed the world had ended. At a later juncture, to make sure of the point, to give the full textual support for what follows, Schreber references his father's soul as a source of medical advice, by virtue of its 'scientific experi-ence during its life'.[57] Finally, in discussing tested (impure) souls and the role of divine rays in interfering with his plans, Schreber again mentions his father's soul as one of those manipulated by the rays in the course of their elaborate efforts to confuse him and impede his purposes.[58] These references to his father, who was indeed dead, are respectful, considerate and appropri-ate. It has also to be remembered that Schreber's mother was alive and thus merited different and more direct treatment, which included the poem that the Judge composed for her ninetieth birthday. The enigma of the father in the analytic interpretation, however, remains. The fact of the references to the father in the text do not, of course, disprove Lacan's theory of the case. His argument is that the interrupted sentences keep abruptly halting before naming the father. The 'interrupted sentences stop at precisely that moment at which a signifier which remains problematic is on the point of emerging, charged with a definite meaning', and that signifier, for Lacan, that ultimate and unsayable, foreclosed word is the name of his father. Thus, he goes on: 'I shall give you an indication and, to reassure you by showing you that we are in our own domain, I shall tell you that in Schreber's entire work his father is

---

[55] Schreber, *Memoirs* at 51, 96, 116.
[56] Ibid. at 7.
[57] Ibid. at 96.
[58] Ibid. at 116.

cited only once.'[59] There is, of course, the enigma of the citation, of the half-said (*mi-dire*), which Lacan discusses elsewhere, but the distinction between citation of the deceased father's book, and failure to note the references to his soul, to paternal experience and advice, and to his incorporation in the son's nerves, is tenuous in the extreme.[60] The exclusion of these other references, the refusal to attend to the discourse of the Judge, the failure to listen to the text, to address the detail outside of its 'entertainment' value or its utility in the projection of his own theory of the foreclosure of the son's discourse by virtue of the absence of the signifier, the unsaid father, has another significance. The excluded references, the foreclosure of the text and specifically of its citations to the father, is an expression of Lacan's belief that these other instances are merely hallucinations. They are psychotic fantasies, paranoid delusions, part of the apparatus of the imaginary whose operations are expressly 'unfathomable'. The notion that the hallucination is without object or reality, if Lacan had cared to listen, as opposed to telling others to listen, is lengthily contested by Schreber. The Judge is quite clear that certain of his visual perceptions, his visions, are idiosyncratic to him and would not be shared by others.[61] He spends considerable energy and ingenuity in discussing and contesting Kraeplin's theory of hallucinations, concluding: 'I trust that I have proved that I am not only not "controlled by fixed and previously formed ideas", but that I also possess in full measure the "capacity to evaluate critically the content of consciousness with the help of judgment and deduction".'[62] Aware of the idiosyncrasy and at times singularity of his visions, Schreber nonetheless proffers the view that it would be entirely incorrect to discount them as merely subjective and spends much energy on detailing the vividness, persistence and underlying reasons for his visions of rays, nerves, fleeting-improvised-beings, as well as his own physical changes during the internally contested process of unmanning. There are reasons, objective circumstances that explain many of these perceptions and, as Schreber rather jocastically puts it, throwing the 'slogan' or 'catchword' hallucination at them, does little to explain, interpret or even address them. In part, the Judge seeks simple recognition, acknowledgement, which the psychoanalysts should

---

[59] Lacan, *Psychoses* at 283.

[60] Jacques Lacan, *The Other Side of Psychoanalysis* (New York: Norton, 2007) at 36–7.

[61] As, for example, Schreber, *Memoirs* at 74: 'I would, however, concede the possibility that what I had seen outside my door could have been a hallucination'; or again, at 274: 'It is of course far from my purpose to wish to convince other people of the truth of my so-called "delusions" and "hallucinations". I am fully aware that at the present moment that would be possible only to a very limited extent.'

[62] Schreber, *Memoirs* at 78. The reference to Kraepelin is to his *Psychiatrie. Ein Lehrbuch für Studirende und Aerzte*, 5th edn (Leipzig: A. Barth, 1896).

be the first to provide, that his visual perceptions have meaning. Thus: 'In my opinion science would go very wrong to designate as "hallucinations" *all* such phenomena that lack objective reality, and throw them into the lumber room of things that do not exist'.[63] In a later footnote, Schreber goes further and rather touchingly declares, 'I would count it a great triumph for my dialectical dexterity if through the present essay, I should achieve only *one* result, to make the physicians shake their heads in doubt as to whether after all there was some truth in my so-called delusions and hallucinations.'[64] It is a plea that to date has fallen pretty much on deaf ears. Certainly, Freud and Lacan avoid any substantive recognition of truth or value in the dismissively labelled hallucinations, and so again we have to take our queue from Schreber. The footnote on Kraepelin's theory makes a prescient connection between the 'visual hallucinations' and real visions 'which I also have experienced, that is dream-images'.[65] Lothane confirms this connection in his paper on hallucinations and argues that their clinical definition as 'a sensory perception without external stimulation of the relevant sensory organ' is a prima facie contradiction in terms, ignoring that 'as an awareness in absence, the hallucination properly belongs with other such forms of awareness in absence as the dream and the image'.[66] Schreber is very specific in his theory of his images. They are generated by picturing or they are sent by the rays and need to be sorted and differentiated to allow for their different roles. The image is both a salve and an idea, a projection in the more dispositive sense of rectifying the real, of planning change, of dreaming – both reverie and project – the goals of his own struggle. For Laure Murat, too, the connection between the oneiric image and the hallucination is politically and hermeneutically central: 'madness has perhaps as much to teach us as dreams, to which it is secretly related'.[67] That relation is nowhere more evident than in the visual connections that Schreber draws between body and desire, the proper order-of-the-world and the miracles that intervene and threaten to interrupt his politico-juridical project. As Murat puts it in relation to the revolutionary madness that swept France at the turn of the nineteenth century, it is incumbent on the historian to examine the archives and to listen to the plurality of

---

[63] Schreber, *Memoirs* at 79; emphasis in the original.

[64] Ibid. at 135; emphasis in the original.

[65] Ibid. at 78.

[66] Zvi Lothane, 'The Psychopatholgy of Hallucinations – A Methodological Analysis', 55 *British Journal of Medical Psychology* 335 (1982). For André Green, *The Work of the Negative* (London: Free Association Books, 1999), Freud's failure to address hallucination in any detail is a significant lapse and ignores the importance of what he terms the work of the negative: 'Freud's brilliant analysis says almost nothing of Schreber's hallucinations' (164).

[67] Laure Murat, *The Man Who Thought* at 2.

voices and visions to be found in the records, the books of the law. 'Is it possible to detect, in the joint murmur of patient and doctor, or rather beneath the official discourse of psychiatrists – those scribes of insanity – the potential political discourse of the mad? We know that psychiatry is a political field, but what does madness have to say about politics?'[68] The answer is that madness is in many respects an extreme expression of political desire, a discourse of rebellion and defeat, a utopian blueprint or a rage at abuse. That there is meaning in madness, that its discourses merit attention on their own terms, as discursive projects as well as visual projections, leads back to Schreber and his own highly unique extra-judicial disquisition. Freud and Lacan both discount the visual perceptions, the hallucinations that are depicted in the *Memorabilia*. As discussed, they are treated dismissively, they are merely filmic, without object, regressive or external and purely paranoid. What this dismissal achieves, I have argued, is a foreclosure of Schreber's discourse that mirrors the theory that his work is the expression of foreclosure. Lacan's argument, following and expanding upon Freud's, is that it was Schreber's father who precluded the Judge's entry into the symbolic, who foreclosed his capacity to reason. In ignoring and excluding the 'fantasies', depictions, *prosopopoeia* and other images in the Judge's book, Lacan effects a further and perhaps even more fundamental foreclosure. Lacan comes to play the role of the father, takes on the habit of the imaginary Moritz, and imposes his own theoretical machinery and corrective devices, his Trinitarian system and rigid argot upon the text that he is supposedly listening to attentively. He becomes, to borrow from his disillusioned daughter Sybille, *Un Père*, a distant and dominating figure of control, whose apparatus of surveillance closely mirrors that which Schreber himself depicts as that of God in the forecourts of heaven.[69] Schreber was a jurist and a judge. His nervous breakdown was legally generated, and his subsequent visions were populated by numerous lawyers, counselors, court attendants and clerks, as well as by figures of sovereignty, justice and governance. His text is replete with copious legal maxims, along with rights, duties, obligations, trespasses and other wrongs. If we turn to his visual depictions of the supernatural, we again find an intriguing juridism in his description of the automatic writing system, in the rays, in the tied-to-celestial-bodies that inscribe everything said, as well as in his quest for justice and a return to the proper order of the world. His was *morbus juridicus*, a legal ailment, and one that gained an expansive and highly articulate expression in the metaphysical system that he portrayed. It offers, I will argue,

---

[68] Ibid. at 9.
[69] Sibylle Lacan, *Un Père* (Paris: Gallimard, 1997).

a lengthy and complicated critique of law and a novel jurisprudence. This is in many regards unsurprising. He spent much of his life uncomfortable with and at times attempting to escape from his legal persona, or more dramatically from the apparatus of sexual difference and the religious figures of paternity and law that Freud and Lacan continue in displaced form to relay. He devoted a large portion of his work to juridical critique, in this instance the depiction of the inadequacy of law. It is that aspect of the *Memorabilia*, more than any other, that has been foreclosed, ignored and dismissed. It deserves recollection and rescue.

3

Morbus Juridicus: Crisis and Critique of Law

There must be an equalizing justice and it can never be that a morally unblemished human being with feet firmly planted in the Order of the World should have to perish as the innocent victim of other people's sins in a struggle carried on against him by hostile powers.

In the wake of a translation that deletes the bulk of the title of the work and removes the juristic credentials of the author, and of psychoanalytic interpretations that denude the Judge of his discourse and hir visions – 'the growing disaster of the imaginary'[1] – it is time to rectify and rescue the jurist from her doctors. There is no question but that Freud and Lacan were somewhat in love with Miss Schreber, identified with his delirium and admired, were informed and entertained by hir discourse. It is indeed that identification and amusement, their sense that they too were ill in part of the same delirium, that leads to the projection of their own interpretation, their foreclosure of the Judge's text, by rather too quickly inserting the figure of the absent father into the space that could equally well be occupied by the plurality and complexity of images and figures of paternity and law that Schreber himself proposes. This constitutes a certain conflict of laws, that of the interpreter as against that of the jurist, and two rival conceptions of the paternal metaphor. For the analytic schema, the figure of the father is that of an absence, the lack of the signifier engendering the fantasy of the patient, as against the Judge's perception of a struggle to institute a novel governance and *oikonomia* in the place of a failed sovereignty and a useless deity. The psychoanalytic critique of the subject forecloses the critique of the law. It is not only a question of clearing the ground, of finding a position from which to listen to the subject's discourse, but also of taking account of the tradition and theoretical framework that the Judge inhabited and, however variably, expressed. As Laplanche puts it, in a study of Hölderlin that is not far removed from the case of Schreber, when the study of law comes into the equation it has a very

---

[1] Lacan, *Écrits* at 481.

particular significance: 'there is no doubt that it involves a search for the father, but under the very specific aspect of a search for the law or, if you will, for a certain figure of the father as connected to a law'.[2] The father is historically the principle of genealogical legitimacy and hence also of authority and nomination. The search for paternity, literal and metaphorical, is a quest for the variable figure of deity, sovereign, monarch, legislator, president and precedent, which terms are etymologically the same, that will fulfil the problematic function of source of legality for the subject, both social and subjective. The figure of the father is inextricably tied up with the question of law and it is always an all too human question, a slightly mad intonation, because the father is inevitably absent, in that the source of law can never be seen. There is only ever the mask of the sovereign, the apparel of monarchy, the paint of popery, the *imago* of the familial and social father that Lacan interprets as a hole in the subjectivity of the subject triggered by this absence: 'But how can the Name-of-the-Father be summoned by the subject to the only place from which it could have come into being for him and in which it has never been? By nothing other than a real father, not at all necessarily by the subject's own father, but by One-father.'[3] Hence, and the jurist Legendre makes great play upon this, the legal desire for paternal figures and the monotheistic trajectory of Western law that sets out from the figure of the Holy Roman Emperor Justinian as the author of a single and comprehensive body of laws, contained in one all-inclusive series of texts, the *Pandects*, the signifier that establishes the scripture and territory of the social, the singular space that the subject will inhabit.[4] A single Code, the *Corpus Iuris Civilis*, governs in a spectacular fashion and establishes the social sites of subjectivity, administration and family, governance and disposition or *oikonomia*. It is fair to say that Schreber struggles with both, but it is an unjust foreclosure to suppose that because he is subjectively troubled, because of the familial disruption that he experiences, he cannot have a perspective or say on the social distribution of power and thus has to be deprived of his theory of law. First, a preliminary observation. The point has been made many times that Schreber's text lacks

---

[2] Jean Laplanche, *Hölderlin and the Question of the Father* (Victoria, BC: ELS Editions, 2007) at 34.

[3] Lacan, *Écrits* at 481. I will note here that this thesis remains popular among Lacanians and that Maria Aristodemou, *Law, Psychoanalysis, Society. Taking the Unconscious Seriously* (London: Routledge, 2015) devotes the bulk of her book to a highly engaging exposition of the hole at the heart of the legal subject and social law.

[4] Most notably, Pierre Legendre, *Le Désir politique de Dieu* (Paris: Fayard, 1996). In translation, see P. Goodrich (ed.), *Law and the Unconscious: A Legendre Reader* (London: Macmillan, 1996). Pierre Legendre, *Dieu au mirroir* (Paris: Fayard, 1995) is forthcoming in translation from Routledge in their Discourses of Law Series.

'anything that resembles a metaphor'. *Ipse dixit* Lacan, and MacCabe follows suit, to name but two.[5] Take MacCabe, who mimics Lacan on this point: 'Schreber's text is strikingly free of metaphor, the fundamental trope where we find ourselves transformed in language, just as it is almost completely free of femininity.'[6] Such a remark raises the question of whether MacCabe has even read the *Memorabilia*, because it is an opus that begins, page 2, with the Judge stating: 'To make myself at least somewhat comprehensible I shall have to speak much in images and similes, which may at times perhaps be only *approximately* correct.' It would be fine for MacCabe to distrust the Judge and challenge his use of images, but there is only the assertion, as if he has simply read Freud and Lacan on Schreber or maybe he has read and forgotten, as Bayard notes can frequently and justifiably occur.[7] In either event, it is hard to credit the view that there is no femininity in a text that bellows in pain at the process of becoming a woman, that sets its greatest store for alleviation of the pain of sex change in dressing as a woman, and that recognises constantly the changing shape of breasts, buttocks and genitalia as part of the process of transformation. Or is it perhaps that MacCabe believes that it is unfeminine to write on theology and law, that women should somehow be kept away from such discourse? As if that were not sufficiently opaque, the argument that there is no metaphoricity in the nerves and rays, in the miracles, in the skeletal changes and episodic visions, in the manifestations and conversations, let alone the sexual intercourse with the divinity is as much lack of attention to detail as it is projection on to the text.

Schreber is frequently explicit on imagery and non-literal senses: 'The Christian teaching that Jesus Christ was the Son of God can be meant only in a mystical sense which but approximates the human sense of these words, because nobody would maintain that God, as a Being endowed with human sexual organs had intercourse with the woman from whose womb Jesus Christ came forth.'[8] The other dogmas of the Church, which Schreber contests, revises, rejects and refigures are equally subjects that unfold in a continuing allegory of the Judge's new world order. Take another very explicit and obvious instance of metaphor: 'A person who wishes to pave a way for a

---

[5] Lacan, *Psychoses* at 281: 'Something struck me – even when the sentences may have a meaning, one never encounters anything that resembles a metaphor.'

[6] MacCabe, 'Introduction' at xvi.

[7] Pierre Bayard, *How to Talk about Books that You Haven't Read* (London: Bloomsbury, 2009). It has always also struck me that Gilles Deleuze and Félix Guattari, *Anti-Oedipus: Capitalism and Schizophrenia* (London: Penguin, 2006) had also either not read, or had rather selectively remembered Schreber's text. *Memoirs* at 2; emphasis in the original.

[8] *Memoirs* at 3.

new conception of religion must be able if need be to use flaming speech (*Flammenworten sprechen*) such as Jesus Christ used towards the Pharisees or Luther towards the Pope and the mighty of the world.'[9] Moving on to expressly discuss his style, his rather graphic depictions and imagery, it again strains credulity and defies rhetorical acumen to claim that this incendiary style, a latter day speaking in tongues, is somehow not to be read as a consistent and extensive transfer of meaning and accentuation of feeling through allegorical expansion. Equally, borrowing from Euan Fernie's finely observant analysis of Schreber, when the Judge becomes aware that von W.'s soul has disappeared, 'I found myself moved to play the funeral march from Beethoven's "Eroica" on the piano in honour of its departing'.[10] The Judge exercises a Pythagorean law, dissipating animosity and resolving conflict, even as here a struggle unto death with soul murderers and raping spirits, through music, the lyre, the original and most structural *nomos*. How then does this dimension, this textual figuration and rhetorical play get foreclosed and ignored? It is almost as though the metaphor is so great, the allegory so expansive and ambitious, that those whose gaze rests constantly on the fiction of the life behind and beyond the text, the mirage of the author, entirely fail to apprehend the humour, the play, the figures, the rhetorical divagations and the symbolic permutations of the Judge's style.

Lacan expends considerable time on the point, discussing metaphor and metonymy as defined by Saussure and developed by Roman Jakobson and Maurice Halle, but scotomises the point, subjects it, that is, to his blind spot, which is the centrality of rhetoric to his own practice. It is as if the rhetorical has to be his and no-one else's. Start at the beginning. Metaphor is classically defined as a sensible figure, one of transport that changes the meaning of a word so as to affect the sense and thus also the mind of the auditor. From Aristotle on, the metaphor manipulates the meaning of the word, it dissimulates so as to persuade or at least to alter the intentions of the addressee. Extended use of metaphor is termed allegory and, borrowing from the English jurist Puttenham, we learn 'because inversion of sense in one single word is by the figure of *Metaphor*, of whom we spoke before, and this manner of inversion extending to whole and large speeches, it makes the figure *allegory* to be called long and perpetual Metaphor'.[11] Understood thus, and properly, as a central feature of the juristic art of persuasion, as the fabrication and dissimu-

---

[9] Ibid. at 443.

[10] Ibid. at 193, discussed in Fernie, *The Demonic* at 268–9.

[11] George Puttenham, *The Arte of English Poesie* (London: Richard Field, 1589) at 156 (spelling modernised); emphasis in the original. One could equally turn to Tom Sloane (ed.), *The Oxford Encyclopedia of Rhetoric* (Oxford: Oxford University Press, 2001) s.v. metaphor.

lation of forensic rhetoric, it is likely that Lacan and his epigones have been deceived, that they have not seen what they did not want to look for, rather than that Schreber made no use of metaphor and allegory. Lacan's use of metaphor borrows from Saussure in that he distinguishes the figure as one of substitution, a paradigmatic shift of meaning, as opposed to being a question of metonymic contiguity. 'Meaning is the dominant datum and . . . it deflects, commands, the use of the signifier to such an extent that the entire species of pre-established, I should say lexical, connections comes undone.'[12] Here Lacan struggles to move from the lexical conception of metaphor as 'improper', which is to say inventive, use of the word, to the extended use and implication of metaphor for the signifying chain, which is precisely what Puttenham indicates in the concept of allegory. The shift in meaning expands into the signifying chain, indeed it becomes metonymic, it starts a narrative, and in Schreber's case, it becomes epic. To recognise this *allegoresis*, to understand and read the *Memorabilia* as legal discourse, means straight off that it is necessary to be aware of the rhetorical character of the text, to attend to such metaphors as fleeting-improvised-men, rays tied-to-celestial-bodies, play-with-human beings, miracles, visions, and visitations, sightings of sovereigns through keyholes, the various interferences with the Order of the World, the feminine expressions, all of which are inventions of Schreber's designed to capture his altered sense of his own transitional materiality and his changing view of social disposition, the governance of the human as such. He insists that he is not mad. He is aware of the questionable reality of his perceptions – they are simply real to him – and acknowledges that some are imagined, wholly subjective, and some he believes can be proved to be objective. Take the example of Schreber's unmanning, his transition to becoming a woman. This is something that he most often understands literally as the objective process of his body, his nerves and skeletal structure transforming into those of a female corporeality and sensibility, but he is also aware that others may not always see it as such, and that this physical transformation waxes and wanes in different contexts. This is not simile, it is not 'like' he is becoming a woman, but rather the ambivalent and visceral sense that even though others may not apprehend this, he is a woman, that this is a material state of transformation, an incarnadine metaphor in which the subject becomes other. Refusal to recognise this corporeal and immanently real dimension to the narrative is simply to force it into categories that pre-exist and dismiss it. To this we can add that the becoming feminine of the body is also replete with numerous metaphorical and allegorical significations of which the Judge is fully aware, not the least

[12] Lacan, *Psychoses* at 218.

of which is that she can now, when travelling under the banner of the feminine, no longer play the virile role of a lawyer. Ironically, of course, she had to play the lawyer again to litigate his release but his choice, his sensibility had in between times tranced and trans'ed, the *metaphoros*, the *morphosis*, had happened as far as he was concerned, the metaphor was live and real, *allegoresis* manifested. The text can thus be read as metaphor upon metaphor, an allegory of transition to woman and to critique of the law, from supine constraint to creativity, from rules to freedom, letters to images. To borrow from the master of juristic allegory, Ernst Kantorowicz, 'the judge, Law's son becomes Law's father', and to this we can add, that law's father is also, and classically, a nursing mother.[13] There is rebellion, anger and critique, as also there are visions and bellowings, philosophies and theologies at play throughout the *Memorabilia* and it is only the rush to diagnosis, the pathologisation of the patient, the rather unimaginative exclusion of his doctrine, that precludes attention, let alone appreciation of his play of metaphor and allegory, and the crucial attendant role of *allegoresis*. The reason that *Lacan et Cie* refuse the allegorical character of Schreber's text is interesting. It is a structural impossibility for the psychotic, whose entry into the symbolic has been foreclosed, to speak metaphorically because the figure requires the priority of the signifier over the signified – the transfer of meaning is occasioned by the overvaluation of the signifier, to which the psychotic does not have access. By way of contrast, Schreber, in Lacan's account, misrecognises an imaginary signified as the signifier of the real. This interpretation, however, ignores Schreber's awareness of the eccentricity of his depictions, as adumbrated above, and equally misses the key point, which is the inversion of the symbolic order that the Judge seeks to effectuate. Viewed from the perspective of his theory of the social and judicial body, their transformation, as also the vanishing of the real, there is no substantial basis for discounting the theoretical value – the mode of perception – that the *Memorabilia* elaborates. It is Lacan, to coin a phrase, who acts as a shrunken-headed scientist terrified of a desire that emanates from outside his own system and its Trinitarian epistemology. Psychoanalysis here confronts and excludes fantasy, just as positive law banishes literature as a mode of knowing. If Schreber's text, however, is to have an equivalent value, if justice is to be done to what he writes, then the transfer of meaning from the symbolic to the imaginary that constitutes one concept of metaphor can be mirrored in

---

13 Ernst Kantorowicz, *The King's Two Bodies: A Study in Medieval Political Theology* (Princeton: Princeton University Press, 1958) at 151. The king as nursing mother is from the Psalms, although we find it as well in early modern constitutional texts, such as Roger Coke, *Justice Vindicated from the False Fucus put upon it, by Thomas White Gent., Mr Thomas Hobbes, and Hugo Grotius* (London: Tho. Newcomb, 1660) at 21, 98.

the transfer of meaning back. The signifiers of authority and law, writing and judgement, of body and person, doctor and wife, birds and bees to name but some, are hollowed out by Schreber and transferred into his novel system. What has too much meaning, the signifier dominated by meaning, in Lacan's theory, becomes in the *Memorabilia* an immediately contested meaning, a hollowed-out signifier that is characterised by the stuttering of interrupted thoughts, the pointlessness of automatic writing down, the interference of voices, the intrusion of medical opinions and the apparition of improvised, indubitably sketchy beings. Positive law haunts these spaces and, for the Judge, most often adopts these vain, immaterial and tested figures. Moving to the juridical tenor, the legal themes and language of the *Memorabilia*, metaphor plays an immediate and highly significant role. The transition between consciousness and dream, the real and theoretical presupposition, the prosaic and what may be termed a transitional style, meaning a highly charged and alternately dysphoric and ecstatic modality, an affective style in flux, but also a mode of *fictio iuris* or legal fiction, which occurs early in the course of the nervous indisposition. Shortly before the advent of the second illness, in the course of discussing the feeling of being overworked in a context where his colleagues were older and better informed as to court procedure than he is, Schreber admits to having trouble presiding over the Court. He is a newcomer and overtaxed, which results in sleeping badly. He describes being woken several nights by 'a recurrent crackling noise in the wall of our bedroom. Naturally we thought of a mouse.'[14] Subsequent experience explains otherwise: 'I have come to recognize them as undoubted divine miracles – they are called "interferences" by the voices talking to me.' It is the footnote explaining this reference that deserves the closest scrutiny. The voices are those of departed souls, and they are improperly attempting to return and to disturb Schreber. The dead, which is to say tradition, precedent, the *nomos* of custom and use, of prior determination is rustling and disturbing the Judge. Something is amiss in the tradition, wrong with law and with his place, and needs to come to consciousness. What is crucial is that it is, for Schreber, a juristic as well as subjective disturbance, of which he notes: 'I must not omit to add that it amounted to nothing more than a *dolus indeterminatus* – if a legal expression be permitted – carried to an extreme.'[15] In a psychoanalytic frame, the *dolus indeterminatus*, the 'general intent to do harm', has the symptomatic significance of being marginal. It is a legal reference secluded in a footnote, the apparent referent of which is insomnia, but whose general context is that of

---

[14] *Memoirs* at 37–8.
[15] Ibid. at 38, fn 22.

law induced anxiety – the Judge's fear of decision, engendered by elevation to the Presidency of one of the three chambers of the Royal Court of Appeals, and also a resistance to identification or stasis in a role that has come to seem improper, lacking in affect and so a constraining and constrained form. Start with the doctrinal signification of the juristic term, *dolus*, meaning evil intent, fraud and deceit, and *indeterminatus* meaning unlimited and undefined, a category that was developed initially by the German – indeed the Saxon – jurist Benedictus Carpzovius.[16] The intent to harm, in civilian systems of criminal law, to which the law of Saxony of course belongs, is usually direct. An individual intends, by means of an act, to harm a specified person. That is termed *dolus directus*, but it fails to cover a series of exceptional situations in which harm is occasioned by less direct means. The law frames a variety of possibilities, *error in objecto* and *aberratio ictus* being the most frequently debated, including *dolus indeterminatus*, where the intent to harm is indefinite, meaning that the actor plans to harm someone but has no particular person or victim in mind.[17] The object of the unlawful act is generalised and any of a class of foreseeable casualties of the act are grouped as intended objects of the harm for legal purposes. Schreber is here invoking a key legal concept of subjective intention, a very elaborate and expansive form of a liminal *mens rea*, in inveighing against the various perturbations and generic interferences, the harm done by nocturnal noises, the voices of the dead, tested souls as he calls them, who return from the forecourts of heaven to disrupt the proper Order of the World, who bring with them a false or at least improper law. The immediate point is that the sophisticated juridical conception of intent that the Judge uses evinces that it is not some private and personal vendetta that is at issue, nor is it here simply paranoia. The crackling noises, the rustling thoughts, represent tested, impure, souls, the emissaries of return, illegal spectral presences that threaten the *ius commune*, the custom and use that constitutes the moral order, the patterns of time that have hitherto generated the juristic norms of the secular polity as tellurian expressions of mundane practice. That the disturbances are occasioned by the visitations of impure spirits expelled from the firmament does not excuse their interventions and interfer-

---

16 Benedictus Carpzovius, *Practica Novae Imperialis Saxonica Rerum Criminalium* (Wittenberg: n.p., 1652).

17 For the sake of definition, *error in objecto* concerns an error in the object of the prohibited act – A, thinking C is B, and planning to harm B, harms C. *Aberratio ictus* concerns the situation where A directs a blow at B, but it is deflected, and C is injured. *Dolus eventualis*, finally, covers the scene where a possible consequence of the act is harm to another and the actor is held to have constructively intended to harm someone whose well-being they recklessly impacted.

ences, their miracles and soundings, precisely because the indefinite intent of the divinity, God's failure to control and retain these souls, need not be definite to be wrongful. It is not Schreber who is directly affronted, but rather it is the law that assigns blame to such vague yet heedless intent. The crucial point, juristically, is that the Judge is not addressing his own illness as the principal cause of concern, but rather viewing it aetiologically in terms of a breakdown in the legal system, a derangement of the juridical order, and a crack in the social hierarchy of law. For Schreber, the *dolus indeterminatus* of extimate intrusions is not simply a representation of imaginary dark forces aimed at his demise, but rather is an attempt to explicate in an uncannily appropriate form that there is something rotten in the state of the law. It is after all his own elevation in the judicial hierarchy, his high-altitude appearance, and his unease in relation to this procrustean plateau, as also discomfort with his colleagues that triggers the sleeplessness. The most immediate interpretation of such malaise and unsettled affect is that the situation reminds him, so to speak, of that earlier trauma, namely his failure to get elected to the Reichstag that led to his initial nervous breakdown. He is repeating the originary wound, the blocked desire to escape law, the failed attempt to become a legislator, which is the trauma that arguably lies at the very origin of his critical indisposition. For a second time, Schreber succumbs to sickness at law and, as Sanders and Santner both suggest, the crucial issue juristically relates to the question who is to judge and how they are to judge. The recourse to *dolus indeterminatus* is not just to a legalistic expression, but it signals a sense of general and, as yet, indeterminate wrong, an as yet unspecified disorder, generative here, as we know, of the Judge's anxiety, reminding Schreber of work undone, of corrections, legislations, edicts that he has yet to inscribe and pronounce. Anxiety, nervousness, *chaleur*, are motives for action, spurs to critique and reform. It is not so surprising, after all, to elicit from auditory disturbances, hypnopompic interruptions, a preconscious inquietude and a sense of something wrong that attaches to the existential and the official, to *oikonomia* and office. It is from these auricular intrusions that the Judge jumps to a sense of injustice. The connection of hearing to law, and of listening to the other side as the indicator of justice being done, also suggest the metaphorical significance of the noises and press towards the conclusion that the polity is in a parlous state, that it needs to change, that reform, mutation, transition are necessary, and new identities have to be built. Pressing on with the aetiology of *morbus juridicus*, the next moment and metaphor is again one that connotes failures of judgement and justice, and in this instance the symbol of the scales is the figure that is foregrounded. It is Mark Sanders who brilliantly elicits the symptomatic significance of Schreber's early and seemingly minor complaint about his treatment at the hands of Professor Flechsig. The eminent Professor, if you recall, had failed to instruct the Judge on how to use the scales in the clinic to weigh himself. Had he been able to operate the machine, he felt he may have recovered sooner. The complaint is not mentioned again, but Sanders points out the crucial judicial implication of this reference:

> Let us therefore strip Schreber's sentence of its negative form: 'auf die ich kein großes Gewicht lege' (on which I lay no great weight) becomes 'on which I lay great weight'. Why should Schreber lay any great weight on what is, as his book is organized, the second of Flechsig's mistakes – and which, in any case, relates to his first illness, from which he recovered? I think we can guess why, if we allow that the scales that he chooses to mention are, in addition to being an instrument for monitoring the weight of patients, also a symbol of justice, a reminder – even if he was not conscious of it – of Schreber's métier as a judge.[18]

Initially, Schreber simply appears to want to be able to use the scales, to understand how to judge, how to do justice, to his condition, but the implications rapidly expand as the Judge becomes increasingly aware of the extent to which justice is awry and things are wrong in the Order of the World. For Sanders the implications are expansive: 'Schreber can no longer judge well. He sees himself as having become emaciated – *Abmagerung* is starker than "loss of weight," closer to emaciation – because, he tells us, he does not understand how the scales work, and is not given leave to operate them himself. The scales may work perfectly, but his faculty of judgement does not.'[19] The rustling in the walls can be linked here to the dysfunction of the scales, the loss of balance indicating disorientation, an inkling of something wrong with the institution, with the doctor as well as with *nomos* and law. The ever-expanding *dolus indeterminatus* requires a response to scale, an appropriate reprise and reordering that will wrest back the seat of judgement or as Schreber puts it in his forensic essay, *sedes materiae* – the seat of the matter, namely jurisdiction – in deciding what is law and what is proper for the Order of the World.[20] Bearing this in mind, the expansion of the scales, the increased range of reference of this metaphor for justice becomes more vivid and pertinent to the trajectory of the Judge's transition. His critical project becomes that of wresting back the scales and seizing justice for himself. For Schreber the scales return with a crescendo of juridico-theological implications late in the work: 'the scales of victory are coming down on my

---

[18] Sanders, 'Psychoanalysis, Mourning, and the Law' at 131.
[19] Ibid. at 132.
[20] The juristic term *sedes materiae*, is used, again correctly, which is here to say metaphorically, in *Memoirs* at 366.

side more and more, the struggle against me continues to lose its previous hostile character, the growing soul-voluptuousness makes my physical condition and my other outward circumstances more bearable.'[21] The harmony of the Order of the World is, for Schreber, being restored and it is this that feeds his soul voluptuousness, his sense of erotic and aesthetic ease, his coming to terms with transition, with a feminine soul, even if his body is frequently resistant, slower and inconstant in its change. Schreber seeks to cast off or at least to repel an inauthentic authority and unbalanced order, in favour of a living law, a creative and feminine body and self that will take up the place of an abandoned and so self-determining ethical and sexual social schema. The scales that come down on Schreber's side, the palms of victory, feminine sensibility and the emergent woman, come as the conclusion of a lengthy struggle to right the wrongs of imbalance. Schreber's critique is waged against the alternative seat of judgement and the interferences of the divinity in the human world: God deals only with corpses and so does not understand the living, and hence for the Judge the need for leadership, for a new theory of law, precisely because 'incredibile scriptu, God cannot judge'.[22] What is wrong with the polity, and awry specifically with law, is the absence of a proper site of judgement, the ironic displacement, the abdication of the scales of justice to the divinity, which is defined by Schreber precisely as that that cannot judge. The struggle, the equalising justice, is aimed at wrenching back the scales of justice, the right to legislate, to invent law appropriate to a secular humanity by human means. It is Eric Santner who makes the point that it was in form and content an investiture crisis that Schreber suffered and this is powerful and correct so long as we first understand that crisis historically and literally.[23] The referent of the investiture crisis is primarily to the struggle between Church and State and specifically to the so-called *dictatus papae*, the Papal edicts of Gregory VII, promulgated so as to reassert the primacy of the Pontifical jurisdiction over all secular sovereign rule. The medieval tables of the law were emitted precisely so as to reassert that the Roman Church was founded by God alone and that the temporal Emperor could thus be appointed and deposed by the Pope, acting as the Vicar of Christ. It was thus within the remit and power of the Church to make and break the impermanent and merely temporal dominion of secular rulers. The investiture crisis is a reference in consequence to an earlier and exemplary struggle for power, the fight for the scales of judgement, between the spirituality and the temporality, in a form that predicts the later anti-crusade conducted by Schreber. The

---

[21] Ibid. at 293.

[22] *Memoirs* at 245.

[23] Santner, *My Own Private Germany* at 11–12.

dictatus papae that emerge from this first conflict are aimed at investing the Pope with sole and universal authority. Edict one, *primus canonicus*, is that God alone founded the Roman Church. Edict two states that the Roman pontiff alone can rightly be called universal. Edict five proposes that the Pope alone may depose the absent, and by Edict seven, 'That for him alone is it lawful to enact new laws according to the needs of the time.' Later Edicts spell out that he alone can use the imperial insignia, and 'that the pope is the only one whose feet are to be kissed by all princes'. Edict twelve is that the Papacy 'may be permitted . . . to depose emperors'.[24] In sum, the Roman pontiff was supreme, *vicarius Christi*, *lex loquens* or mouthpiece of the higher law, and in direct and immediate line to divine decree. Schreber's apparent investiture crisis is close to being a direct mirroring and complete inversion of the earlier assertion of papal supremacy. Schreber's dictates aim to undo all that the previous pontifical edicts had sought to institute and maintain in that first revolution of interpreters, in the birth of the Western legal profession in the textual corpus of a universal law.[25] Where Santner interprets the investiture crisis as a failure on Schreber's part, a crisis engendered by somehow refusing investiture in the role of Senatspräsident, in the office of judge, the *Memorabilia* in fact expand and reorient this narrative in a radical way. For Santner, in the wake of Nietzsche's declaration of the death of God and the attendant crisis of faith, Schreber refuses his fate, his nomination and conse-cration as judge.[26] His breakdown is an expression of the collapse of social authority and legal legitimacy. That much is both insightful and accurate but somewhat vague, a touch generic. The Judge's refusal and his corporealisation of his resistance to the office of judge as then defined is less a failure than a rebellion against a prior definition and jurisdiction. The office of judging

[24] The *dictatus papae* are reproduced in S. Z. Ehler and J. B. Morall (eds), *Church and State through the Centuries: A Collection of Historical Documents* (London: Newman Press, 1954) at 43–4. Pierre Legendre, *L'Amour du censeur* (Paris: Seuil, 1976) at 68 also reproduces and discusses the dictates.

[25] The concept of Papal revolution is taken from Eugen Rosenstock-Huessy, *Out of Revolution: An Autobiography of Western Man* (Norwich, VT: Argo, 1969 [1938]); and is developed in juristic terms by Harold Berman, *Law and Revolution: The Formation of the Western Legal Tradition* (Cambridge, MA: Harvard University Press, 1983); as also synoptically, in Berman, 'The Origins of Wester Legal Science', 90 *Harvard Law Rev.* 894–943 (1977); and by Legendre, *Désir politique de Dieu* at 156–64, and Pierre Legendre, 'Hermes and Institutional Structures', in Peter Goodrich (ed.), *Law and the Unconscious: A Legendre Reader* (London: Macmillan, 1995) at 148–55.

[26] Santner, *My Own Private Germany* at 12: 'The (repetitive) demand to live in conformity with the social essence with which one has been invested, and thus to stay on the proper side of a socially consecrated boundary, is one that is addressed not only or even primarily to the mind or intellect, but to the body.'

appears empty to Schreber; it needs to be revolutionised, taken back, the scales realigned and reordered, wrested from exterior and spiritual precedents and placed back in human hands. The investiture crisis is thus a challenge to a particular jurisprudence and conception of law. It is, I will argue, a burgeoning critique of law and of its abstract geometric schemata, the pure theory of a hierarchy of norms operative solely and fictively through logical subsumption, in favour of what lawyers rather appropriately term *lesbia regula*, a flexible, and Schreber may add feminine, rule. There is a sense, of course, in which critique of religion is also and paradoxically a recognition and validation of the importance of the sacred and theistic. Borrowing the concept of revolution from Berman and latterly Legendre, this crisis of faith in authority that began in the late eleventh-century papal reformation that contributed significantly to the institution of the legal profession, the relay of the antique scriptural norms of the social Text of law, the faith of the exegetes, gains a second elaboration at the turn of the nineteenth century. The extremity of legal modernism, particularly in Germany, is challenged by Nietzsche, by Marx and by Freud. The second revolution of the interpreters is indeed that of a belligerently atheistic critique that culminates with Freud who undoes the prior certainties and liberates both the unconscious and desire as motive forces, drives, sovereigns who potentially legislate the manifestations of self and sociality. Thus, in Legendre's terms, Freud opened up the second revolution of the interpreter, an extra-territorial and indefinable discourse on limits that have been fundamentally misunderstood. The formulation of this error is worth scrutiny, 'Freud took the place not of the interpreter, but of the figure of the sovereign, of the icon or Reference; his work, the Text that devalues all other Texts, now awaits its own devaluation.'[27] In sum, the second revolution of the interpreter placed reproduction of religious and political structures in the hands of the analysts, and it is this investiture crisis, ever present and conflicted in Freud, that Schreber inhabits in the mode of uncertainty and the questioning of limits, conceptual and corporeal. Schreber explicitly conceives his struggle, his demand for investiture as a woman, as a crusade and indeed adopts the motto, *in hoc signo vinces*, from the earlier fight to reclaim Jerusalem.[28] But his goal is a very different reclamation, a reiteration

---

[27] Legendre, 'The Judge Amongst the Interpreters', in Goodrich (ed.), *Law and the Unconscious*, 164–210.

[28] *Memoirs* at 78, referring to the Emperor Constantine's well-known vision *in hoc signo vinces* 'which was decisive for Christianity's victory'. It is interesting that this motto is later taken up in truncated form – *in hoc signo* – as the mark of battle won, and thus, eventually, of *PAX*. See Diego de Saavedra Fajardo, *Idee de un principe politico Cristiano* (Monaco: n.p., 1640) at 174–6.

perhaps of his desire for election, in that his crisis is neither simply with
investiture in Santner's sense, nor with the misinterpretation of Freud as
sovereign, but with investing and investment as such: he wishes to establish a
new scales of justice, to appoint new judges, and in sum to refigure the Order
of the World and promulgate new law, free of the theistic structures and
imperial inheritance of the theologico-juridical tradition and its interpretative institutions. The Judge wants revolution, a third revolution of the interpreters, one that frees the body from the law of genre, and liberates the mind
from faith in the sovereignty of the hierarchy. It is not that his new post is too
much for Schreber; it is rather too sparse, too limited, desiccated, ossified and
much too constraining. The Judge wants to express his desire, to be a woman,
to create, to write laws and none of this fits within the timid plan and institutional constraint of his appointment to the position even of one so elevated
in the juridical hierarchy as a Senatspräsident. He has large plans, but then
name a critic of law who does not wish to invert and realign the legal order,
its procedures and personnel. Marx, Proudhon, Nietzsche?[29] The New Left
Criminologists, the postmodern jurisprudes, the critical legal scholars, the
abolitionists, *Critique du Droit*? The free law movement? Foucault, Deleuze
and Guattari, Luce Irigaray, Jacques Derrida, Giorgio Agamben, Antonio
Negri, Patricia Williams, Roberto Unger, Kimberlé Crenshaw, Duncan
Kennedy, Thanos Zartaloudis? The list could go on but this particular madness, this possession by the visceral desire for critique is not a madness in
which Schreber is alone. He is, of course, specific, and as he readily admits,
he is extreme. For him the rule of Pope Gregory VII is over, the dogmas of
the Christian Church are to be rewritten, and the investiture crisis means
primarily that the edicts of the divinity are to be kept in the distant realm of
the divine, away from the human and from the legislation, the spiritual order
and novel forms that Schreber will introduce. As stated in Edict 5, if the
absent are to be deposed, then it is God that should definitively be removed
from the scene of politics and law, and this is the very task to which the Judge
devotes substantial portions of his drive and text. It is that impetus to a new
order, to rectification, equalisation and cure of the divine *dolus indeterminatus*, as also the corresponding trespasses, wrongs and abandoned duties of
lawyers in the temporal sphere, that coalesce in his crisis and its drive to critique of law. It is the Order of the World that forms the starting point of
Schreber's legal doctrine and so also of his eventual critique of law. It is this
threatened state, this fractured and invaded tellurian harmony, that the Judge

---

[29] On the earlier history of critique of common law, see Peter Goodrich, 'Critical Legal
Studies in England', 12 *Oxford J. Legal Studies* 432 (1992).

intends to defend. The Order of the World is in essence the law of human nature, the spirit of the tellurian, *justissima tellus* as will emerge more thoroughly in the discussion of Schreberian jurisprudence in the next chapter. For the moment, it is enough to note that the Order of the World is that of Being in its totality, which force and presence is characterised as omnipotence, such that 'nothing can maintain itself permanently which contradicts it', or that is 'unlawfully (*Auflehnung*) achieved'.[30] It is characteristically, symptomatically enough, in a footnote that the definition of the lawful and moral order of things gains expression: 'I believe I can remember having read somewhere sometime in one of the sources of our religion the sentence: "The Lord – *scilicet* when the work of His creation was finished – went away"; this sentence seems to be a figurative expression of what I wanted to convey.'[31] The recognition of the figuration of the passage again indicates, if such is necessary, an awareness of metaphor, and equally importantly introduces the Latin juridical term *scilicet*, which translates in legal argot as 'to wit', the term that triggers legal fictions, the juridical invention of counter-factual statements that will allow either jurisdiction or remedy in specific cases. The fiction is a device that allows the court, here the Judge, to do justice, the relevant maxim being *in fictione iuris semper est aequitas*, meaning fictions of law must always be used to equitable ends. If necessary, a woman will be treated as a man, so as to allow a cause of action – legal standing – in cases of need, and for Schreber, clearly, a man must by fiction of law, become a woman if morality and the Order of the World so require. We will see later that for Schreber, they do so dictate. As Rita Felski nicely elaborates it, a century and more after the *Memorabilia*, but then the Judge, like Nietzsche, never expected to be understood soon, there is more to life than critique, more to interpretation than simple suspicion, and so affect, mood, pleasure and person, the body, mingle with the objects of hermeneutic elaboration.[32] Schreber wants to escape the catechisms of the theologically inspired juridical, he wants not to be governed, he seeks to escape the Text so as to transform himself, so as express and inscribe a novel text, a body that he can claim as hir own. The Order of the World, in its juridical sense, as *justissima tellus*, is predicated upon the separation of the divine and the human. After God's ultimate goal of the creation of the human was achieved, God left the world and humanity to itself: 'He Himself retired to an enormous distance.'[33] God's *actio in distans*

[30] *Memoirs* at 193.
[31] Ibid. at 252 n. 101.
[32] Rita Felski, *The Limits of Critique* (Chicago: University of Chicago Press, 2015) at 172–84 on post-critical reading as an affective engagement with being.
[33] *Memoirs* at 252.

is definitive of both morality (*Sittlichkeit*) and law (*Recht*). Thus, in various famous passages, Schreber elaborates how God only deals with corpses in the forecourts of heaven, how the rays and miracles are immoral (*Unsittlichkeit*) intrusions, and intriguingly that God cannot comprehend the distinction between dreams and waking thoughts, images and rules. Also important is the fact that when Schreber does reference God's understanding, he amusingly remarks that being extant at a great distance from the world, the divinity gains knowledge of human affairs through the nerves of generations of departed human beings. This is a slow and incomplete process and most of the information that accrues is of little interest, as, for example, the fact that there can be no doubt that 'God is acquainted with the idea of railways'. According to conditions consonant with the Order of the World, God 'gains only the external impression of a travelling train, as of all other events on earth' and while He could always gain more knowledge of their purpose and function, 'it is hard to imagine why he should want to'.[34] Both law and administration, symbolised appositely here by the proper running and scheduling of trains, are matters beyond the jurisdiction of the divinity, precisely because they are human affairs, administrative functions, modes of disposition that operate or unravel according to an interior logic, a living presence and judgement, dreams and waking reasons of which God is ignorant. That God withdraw from tellurian affairs and temporal governance is the project and goal of Schreber's jurisprudence. If we turn to the process and mechanisms of divine interference, the attractors, the lures and the misunderstandings that draw God down, most often uncomprehendingly, into the human and secular it is in the domain of the juridical, and in infraction of the Order of the World, and of the rule of law – *sub lege et non sub Deo* – that this confusion and clash of jurisdictions most often occurs. The primary symptom of Schreber's *morbus juridicus* is precisely his ire at the malpractice of lawyers, the wresting of freedom of thought and balanced judgement, the confinement and arrogation of reason from the human practitioner to the representatives of the ever-present divinity in His multiple modes of manifestation in rays, nerves, plants, bees, birds and further miracles, as well as other fleeting improvisations in the mode of voices, visions and spectral apparitions of both living and departed human figures. Catechism, Collect, comprehensive Codes, are all attempts to subjugate the Judge's new-found sense of freedom of body and thought. God's efforts, transmitted through the variegated assemblages of legal figures and functionaries, are aimed at annulling both the *dictatus Schreberiae* and the erotic transformation of his body into that of a

---

[34] Ibid. at 300.

state of voluptuousness and openness of soul. Start with the human figures that appear, usually metaphorically, in the text. There are a number of sovereigns and petty sovereigns, Christ is invoked at one point as also the figure of the crusades in the previously adverted motto *in hoc signo vinces*, and so too Napoleon, Prince Frederick, Luther, the Pope, and the cloud of Pharisees. There is Dr Weber and his assistants Dr Täuscher and Dr Quentin, and Dr Pearson, figures of authority who treat Schreber, who appear at times as spectres and who in all contexts try to manipulate the law so as to continue the Judge's incarceration in the asylum. Then also there is Professor Flechsig whom Schreber deems to have abused and abandoned him, in infraction of professional ethics and legal norms. The 'God Flechsig', the 'Prince of Hell', constantly interferes both with the divine nerves and with Schreber's. What is significant is that Flechsig transgresses the Order of the World, while at the same time abandoning his treatment of the Judge: 'Thus began the policy of *vacillation* in which attempts to cure my nervous illness alternated with efforts to annihilate me as a human being.'[35] Schreber wanted out of the walls of mental health, and vilified those that had locked the doors. Flechsig, now partly absorbed into the domain of the divine and the nerves of God, is resident in the transient space of tested souls, of impure corpses and of incomprehension of the human. It is as an annihilator that Flechsig devised 'a plot laid against me . . . the purpose of which was to hand me over to another human being after my nervous illness had been recognized as, or assumed to be, incurable, in such a way that my soul was handed to him, but my body – transformed into a female body and, misconstruing the above described tendency of the Order of the World – was then left to that human being for sexual misuse and simply "forsaken", in other words left to rot.'[36] Flechsig is a figure of misadventure, one that seeks to subjugate the transitional patient, through confinement, through definition, through labels, and finally by means of abandonment, the noisy silence of bedlam. The Judge goes on to say that however spectral, homicidal and extreme this attack upon him may seem, 'I have not the slightest doubt that this plot really existed, with the proviso always that I do not dare maintain that Professor Flechsig took part in it in his capacity as a human being.'[37] Which sentiment we should, I think, take literally, which is to say metaphorically, as descriptive of how Schreber felt about his infantilization and incarceration at the whimsical hands of dubious professionals. There is then the matter of Flechsig's abandonment of any treatment for Schreber, and his ejection of him from his Leipzig clinic.

[35] Ibid. at 56; italics in the original.
[36] Ibid. at 56.
[37] Ibid. at 56-7.

Flechsig, the relevant initial representative of the psychiatric institution, improperly, contrary to the Order of the World, arrogates the right to play God and judge the Judge. Such hubris immediately raises the question of authority and justification for a course of non-treatment or mistreatment that falls squarely in the juridical domain. For Lothane, it is a question of medical negligence, a failure to respect the paramount interest of the patient and it is but a short step from that attribution of professional failure to the Judge's own lawsuit, as well as to his vivid perception of the failure of the legal profession, the pseudo legists, *leguleos*, to use Valla's term, to assert and protect his rights in their proper form. What is most immediately out of joint, indeed rotten, in the state of Saxony, is the law as most proximately represented by all the legal personnel and court officials who have obstructed Schreber's release, who signally fail to argue his case coherently, and from the bench succeed only in misapprehending his cause and misinterpreting the law. These are the characters that the Judge initially attacks, in the metaphoric mode of seeing them as dead, as fleeting-improvised-men, which is to say as ghosts, impure *revenants*, and consistently as hostile and abusive figures. Thus, the County Court Clerk appears in the company of an asylum attendant, both as fleeting-improvised beings, and gradually disappearing human shapes. Even more significantly, the Court Attendant 'had the habit of occasionally dressing in my clothes'.[38] To drive the point of this unholy and illegal alliance home, Schreber next comments upon the apparition of someone who was supposed to be the medical director of the asylum whose 'conversation was confined to a few empty words'. The Judge seeks to escape these dissimulating spectres by going into the garden, but he immediately encounters, among other figures, the most noticeable, 'the Councillor of the County Court K, of Dresden, with an ungainly enlarged head'[39] – a head full of improper decrees, inflated edicts, misapprehensions of the freedom that the Judge is trying to assert and attain. After this interface the parade of legal spectres, all negatively depicted and impugned, continues as a description of transmigrated souls and manifestations of the illness, the madness of those seeking to constrain and judge the Judge.[40] The lawyers are patrolling the asylum, they are conspiring with the psychiatric guards, they are in cahoots with the doctors and their empty enunciations, and are busy imposing limits,

[38] Ibid. at 103.
[39] Ibid.
[40] For the sake of completeness, mention is also made of County Court Councillor W, Prosecutor B, 'who remained immobile in a bent, devout, almost praying posture', and 'President of the Senate of a Court Dr. F., the Country Councillor Dr M., the lawyer W. from Leipzig'. *Memoirs* at 106.

instituting illegitimate genres and purveying false truths by umbrageous means and thoroughly nebulous arguments. A fleetingly improvised jurist puts on Schreber's clothes, another patrols the grounds of the asylum, a prosecutor starts praying, while one further key legal figure has an unattractively enlarged head. The critique of the political theology of law could hardly be more directly and vividly conveyed. Swollen heads, bended knees, supine torsos and stolen costumes are all signifiers of the unattractive and disfigured character of this masculine profession, this derivative and subordinate, in effect plagiarised art. Lawyers are thus depicted quite unequivocally as being complicit in the corruption and malfeasance of the doctors. They appear as fools, as illicit and vanishing images and even as linguistic figures of the mechanisms of divine interference with the temporality and with humanity. More than that, the spectral forms of illicit and unjust legal personnel attempt to perform the religious task of the early legal tradition, they try to bind the Judge, to arrest and punish his person, to abuse and confine him in a body without desire. The attacks on Schreber's nerves at one point take the form of mechanical fastening, in which tested souls are tied to celestial rays emanating from the divinity: 'the souls hung on a kind of bundle of rods (like the fasces of the Roman Lictors)'.[41] These *emblemata*, indeed stigmata, exemplify the empty role of the jurist that the Judge has so persistently and painfully sought to avoid. The jurisprudential implications of this 'tying-to-celestial-bodies' is then spelled out as introducing and facilitating not simply a rupture in the Order of the World, through the interference of the spiritual in the temporal, but much more specifically 'it continues to the present day and led to further consequences, particularly the "writing-down-system".'[42] The adumbrated link between 'tying-to-celestial-bodies', Roman law and the 'writing-down-system' requires careful and detailed elucidation. In his forensic essay, Schreber argues cogently, and as it transpires convincingly, that spiritualism, belief in, or as here war with God, are metaphysical questions that are to be kept strictly separate from questions of law. The passages and inclinations of the soul are not matters of law, nor is spiritual belief a ground for incarceration, a point that the Judge makes in his *Memorabilia*, in the most apposite of ways, citing the German Civil Code: 'Although I have a nervous illness (*Nervenkrank*), I do not suffer from any mental illness (*Geisteskrankheit*) which would make me incapable of looking after my own affairs (¶6 B.G.B. for Germany) or which would allow my detention in an institution against my will on the grounds of administrative law.'[43] In thoroughly prosaic,

---

[41] Ibid. at 125.
[42] Ibid. at 126.
[43] Ibid. at 268. Quite disarmingly, Schreber observes in a footnote: 'I wrote an essay at the

coherent and lucid logic, Schreber thus argues successfully before the Royal
Court of Appeals that it is a juristic error to confuse belief with law, truth
with judgement. The Order of the World ordains a separation of powers that
assigns different roles and rules to the two jurisdictions. A non-relation
between God and the world, between the theological hierarchy and mundane
administration, is what the revolutionary Schreber is advocating. So far, so
good. What has been almost universally missed in the myriad interpretations
of Schreber is the critique of law that is lodged in his description, his allegory
of the illicit invasion of the polity, the temporal body and law, by the rays and
the nerves of the celestial realm. It is the moribund and unthinking practices
of lawyers that have through weakness of thought and arid dogma conspired
to allow the spirituality to interfere, to mix jurisdictions, and to confuse the
Order of the World. The lawyers that appear in the *Memorabilia*, the officials,
clerks, prosecutors, judges, are all 'fleeting-improvised-men', miraculous
apparitions, sketchy and tenuous beings, ghosts returning as 'tested souls' tied
to rays, nerves and other celestial bodies as they enact the dictates of the
higher power. They are neither subjects nor free but rather images, occasionally devils, possessed by the dissonant divine law and jurisdiction. They are
conduits not persons, means and not ends, unthinking functionaries, the
inhabitants of the dust and smoke of texts. It is by virtue of 'compulsive
thinking', the 'writing-down system', the 'automatic-remembering-thought',
the 'head-compressing-machine'[44] that spectral lawyers, the ultimate dogma-
tists, zombie jurists seek unthinkingly to relay an abstract, immaterial and
externally given law. It is against this ethereal, unwritten *lex divinae*, this pure
tradition, that Schreber revolts. It is his investiture as a lawyer and his elevation to the high office of senior judge in particular that, as has been diversely
pointed out by the critics, leads to Schreber's disillusion and rebellion: law is
not enough, it does too little, it is the semi-existence of the sleepwalker fulfill-
ing the functions of an office that is bereft of both thought and creativity. It
is an empty-headed, unlovely, imprisoned existence, offered in figurative
depiction in the mode of jailers, automata, bound and manacled beings
operative not according to thought but simply at the dictate of imaginary
higher orders, and celestial bodies. The lawyer, within the German tradition,
that of *mos italicus*, that of the continuing and uninterrupted validity of the

beginning of this year entitled "Under what circumstances can mental patients be held in
public institutions against their will?", and tried to get it accepted for publication in a law
journal. Unfortunately the editors of the journal refused it on the ground of lack of space.'
[44] Ibid. at 159: 'The "little devils" . . . compressed my head as though in a vice by turning a
kind of screw, causing my head temporarily to assume an elongated almost pear-shaped
form.'

classical Roman law codification, treats the inherited text, the *Corpus iuris civilis*, as the sum and total all law. The BGB, the German Civil Code that was soon to be promulgated in the newly unified Germany, and upon which Scheber had worked as a young jurist, was modelled on the same exemplum of a complete and exhaustive code of all relevant law, as *pan-decta* – the receptacle of universality.[45] Law pre-exists all events and the letter of the Code will be applied directly to resolve all disputes. The text, or as Legendre prefers, the Text, precedes all sociality and subjectivity and the lawyer is simply the exemplary inhabitant of that Text.[46] The trauma of law, in this model, is that of the demand of investiture that the subject abandon all subjectivity and simply become the obedient servant, the pure medium of the prior text of written law. The subject is to be erased so that the speech of the law, the application of the text, can be unequivocal, certain and without variation. The lawyer, supine and subservient, is merely the mouthpiece, he who speaks in the name of the law, or, in the Lacanian idiom, in the name of the father. In the civilian tradition law is written reason – *ratio scripta* – an enclosed and unerring textual system in relation to which the jurist is at best an exegete and exemplum, an ambulant script, a cipher, a parchment nose. If we turn to Schreber and his critique of the numerous fleeting-improvised-lawyers that appear in his writing, we find that at each turn it is the abdication of responsibility, the denial of authorship, the refusal of judgement, avoidance of the body and hence an overwhelming passivity, what Fernie elaborates upon as demonic possession, that causes Schreber such visceral contortions and pain. The Judge almost dies of the struggle to rid himself of these awful spectres, these ghouls of the law. It is thus law that rips the Judge apart, that flays his nerves, that masks his vision and tries in innumerable ways to penetrate, interfere and control him. It is lawyers who try to take over his mind in the manner that law always will, through text, through automata, through compelled and so compulsive thinking and writing down. In Schreber's schema the lawyers are sent by the divinity acting out so as to stop the Judge from thinking. So as to take him over. So as to suspend his sentences. The ultimate goal of the divine project is to annex humanity and for this to be possible

---

[45] The *Bürgerliches Gestzbuch* of 1900. For an introduction to the history of Roman law in the West, see Peter Stein, *Roman Law in European History* (Cambridge: Cambridge University Press, 1999); Alan Watson, *The Making of the Civil Law* (Cambridge, MA: Harvard University Press, 1981); Berman, *Law and Revolution*.

[46] On law and text, see Pierre Legendre, *L'Autre Bible de l'Occident. Le Monument romano-canonique* (Paris: Fayard, 2009). An introduction to such themes can be found in Legendre, *De la societé comme Texte* (Paris: Fayard, 2001). In English see Goodrich, *Law and the Unconscious*; Legendre, *God at the Mirror: Study of the Institution of Images*, trans. Peter Young (London: Routledge, forthcoming).

Schreber has to be unmanned. In its hostile mode this unmanning aims to deprive the Judge of social personality and all capacity to act in the public sphere both metaphorically and literally. First, he is to be subjected, made into a *dispositif* of law, an assemblage of ministerial functions activated from a distance, abstractly, by rules, so as to become a juridical marionette. And then literally, he is to be locked up, both in the sense of being deprived of reason and thought and also incarcerated so as to ensure that he does not even appear in the social. Hence the bellowing, the voice that escapes the prison walls. The crucial mediating concept is the legal one of representing and is to be found explicated, appropriately enough, in a footnote: 'The notion of "representing", that is to say of giving to a thing or a person a semblance different from its real nature (expressed in human terms "of falsifying") played and still plays a great role generally in the idea of souls.'[47] In this negative form, the souls represent Schreber as 'given to voluptuous excess', as an emasculated, castrated, inoperative and abject subject and thus as incompetent, and demented. In proceeding through representation, which is to say legally, these spectres of the juridical, these impure souls enact the Judge's trembling incompetence upon the social stage while internally they work to silence the Judge in exactly the manner in which they, too, are silenced. They are the very metaphor of an absolute sovereign decree. The interferences are gauged to unbalancing Schreber, to stopping him thinking by filling his mind with an unrelenting noise. Compulsive thinking is at base non-stop meaningless thought, relentless chatter, a steady stream 'of unconnected phrases' and interrupted sentences.[48] The goal of this incessant thought was both to represent the Judge as insane, to unhinge him and keep him thereby within the asylum, and to evidence to him that his thinking, like that of the spectral lawyers, lacked all originality, that he could never be different from them, that conformity, rote and machinic repetition were all that the Judge could ever be. The incessant interference of these tested souls, of the nerves, the voices, the fleetingly and dishonestly improvised, constitutes an enormous 'infringement of the freedom of human thinking' because it occupies the entirety of mental space and energy, precluding the right to think nothing, the 'not-thinking-anything-thoughts' that alone allow the space for creativity, for art and, in Schreber's case, for poetry, music and the invention of a new scales of justice and law.

Among the mechanisms that the spirits use to preoccupy and derail the Judge's thoughts is that of the writing-down-system, that of enslaved scribes

---

[47] *Memoirs* at 129 n. 62.
[48] Ibid. at 223 n. 96.

scribbling superior decrees as amanuenses of other powers. The lawyer is here
reduced to a filing clerk and inhabitant of the scriptoria where everything is
written down: the plea rolls, the tables, the fines, the endless procession of
instruments, indentures, deeds, records, judgments and more. The practice of
law, from a critical perspective, is that of the amanuensis whose technique of
intervention into Schreber's thinking is based on the belief that his 'thoughts
could be exhausted by being written-down, so that eventually the time would
come when new ideas could no longer appear in me'.[49] In good juristic fashion, whenever Schreber had a thought the scribes would respond with the
phrase 'we have already got this', '*scilicet* written down' or 'it has been
recorded'. It is law that seeks to perpetrate the wrong (*unrecht*), the trespass
of shutting the Judge up by dampening and deranging his thoughts, by
engendering delirium and dementia through the combination of interrup-
tion, incompletion and unremitting inscription: '*Books or other notes* are kept
in which for years have been written-down all my thoughts, all my phrases,
all my necessaries, all the articles in my possession or around me, all persons
with whom I have come into contact, etc.'[50] The writing-down is done 'in the
manner of the fleeting-improvised-men, but lacking all intelligence; their
hands are led automatically, as it were, by the passing rays for the purpose of
making them write down'.[51] It is through the possessed, through legal
servants, the amanuenses of the divine, that the attempt at possessing Schreber
proceeds by way of the scriptorium of law. In old legal terminology the
automatic writing systems that the *Memorabilia* describe are those of the logographer inscribing the speech of the client so as to speak as and for the litigant, as a mouthpiece of the other in a manner that will be mirrored in
the formalisation of a judicial hierarchy in which the divinity speaks through
a delegate – *delegatus maiestatis* – who hands on and passes down the messages
of the ultimate sovereign, the absent source of law, Lacan's big Other,
Shakespeare's nothing, Kelsen's *Grundnorm*. Jurists may have represented
this as speech but it is dictated, written, they would say, upon the heart,
inscribed by nature and in nature and there for the faithful to see, obey and
relay.[52] The thoughtless transmissions of fleeting-improvised-lawyers, of automatic inscription, of compulsive thinking, with its interruptions and incom-
pletions, as also the miracles and other apparitions and visions that are sent to

[49] Ibid. at 131.
[50] Ibid. at 125; emphasis in the original.
[51] Ibid. at 125–7.
[52] On this juristic account of *ius non scriptum* as a secret writing, an *acheiropoietic* form, see
Peter Goodrich, *Legal Emblems and the Art of Law* (New York: Cambridge University Press,
2014) at 181–90.

disturb the Judge's composure and ratiocination constitute a system of attempted possession. It is against this all too prolonged and painful inhabitation of his soul by law and lawyers, against the deadening effects of endless recording and compulsive relay, the turning of the Judge into a typewriter, that Schreber bellows, so as to speak, so as to think, so as to be heard beyond the walls of the asylum.[53] The legal figures, the blind exegetes, adopt an unrelentingly negative strategy of unmanning the Judge, with the goal of turning him into a corpse, an object of vivisection. The intermediate stage is that of legally representing him as feminine, frightened, fickle and a fool, as diminished, incompetent and infantilised, all terms that lawyers of the period associate with femininity and the uncorroborated witness, the teller of tales. This is why femininity is the site of struggle and the point of resistance. Schreber finally comes to claim his femininity as a strategy of reversal and reclamation. His transitional impetus is to the feminine voice, to giving birth to something new, to writing and creating, text and poem, a new law against an imposed law. It is against this automatic writing that the *pousse à la femme* reacts, and rewrites in a different voice. The unmanning, the delegitimisation, gets reversed and put to positive use and effect. The Judge's struggle is to quiet the voices, to make space to think, create and legislate a novel philosophy of law. This means returning to the roots of the tradition, following as he puts it at one point the etymologies of words and by extension the roots of juristic tradition prior to the interferences of the divinity and the near collapse of the Order of the World in his own unsettled and revolutionary times. Seeking the grounds of *nomos*, Schreber wants to establish a criterion of measure, a scale of judgement, that is both just and human. It is music that restores harmony and calms the Judge's mind: 'Playing the piano in particular was of immense value to me; I must confess that I find it difficult to imagine how I could have borne the compulsive thinking and all that goes with it during these five years had I not been able to play the piano.'[54] Music recollects a longer tradition of jurisprudence, a positive and uncensored mode of apprehension, thought and feeling, in the Judge's view, that is 'deeply ingrained' as can be seen from 'very characteristic instances when in poems rhymes (refrains) recur, or when in musical compositions a certain sequence of notes expressing the embodiment of beauty occurs not only once but is

---

[53] On this theme of inscription, see the excellent discussion in Friedrich Kittler, *Discourse Networks 1800/1900* (Palo Alto: Stanford University Press, 1990) at 291–304.

[54] *Memoirs* at 169. He goes on to say that 'musical-not-thinking-anything-thought' was a refuge that the falsehood of 'representing' could not intrude upon or dissipate because of the 'real feeling one can put into piano playing'.

repeated again and again'.[55] There is the foundation of custom and use, *ius commune*, the practices of time that became law as a musical *nomos*, a harmony of actions, before the interventions of virile anthropomorphisms, male divinities, and then popes, emperors, sovereigns, trumps and lawyers. It is against the latter interferences and novelties that Schreber bellows, adopts feminine attributes and accoutrements, plays chess and plays the piano in the hope of re-inscribing and relaying a norm that precedes law, a harmony that exceeds legalism and promises an exorcism of the barren and ghostly law that possesses the juristic figures that police the Asylum, inaccurately record what Schreber does and misinterpret its implications. It is not necessary to claim that Schreber is mad only of and only with the juridical. Law is a structure whose manifestations are variably linked to the legal in the political, administrative, governmental and *oikonomic* or dispositive and less visible domains of social life. What is rather at issue is the fulcral role of law in Schreber's nervous breakdown and in his subsequent visceral and painful indisposition as he struggled existentially with all the ways in which legality as a framework of closure possessed and constrained him. It was lawyers who incarcerated him and the lower courts that kept him in the Asylum and, thus, in the most immediate of senses it would seem evident and obvious that his struggle to rectify his position and claim his right to freedom, expression and legal personality would entail a significant critical animus towards his erstwhile profession, the strictures of its scriptural tradition and second-hand practices that had so shrunk their capacity for thought and invention. Crisis is ever the fount and pulse of critique and nowhere more so than in Schreber's little recognised juristic work. The invocation of the art of law, *otium cum dignitate*, and its reference to a broader conception of doctrinal and professional practice returns analysis to a more humanistic definition of knowledge of law. For the early modern tradition, *ars iuris* was a multifaceted invention of legal offices, scrivening practices, rhetorical elocutions and ethical duties that explicitly incorporated the authority of the poetic and the literary and, in a more antique version still, of the rhyme, rhythm and musical harmony that formed the original meaning of *nomos* as the measure and method that precedes and subtends law.[56] Schreber's attempt to exorcise the possessed and

---

[55] Ibid. at 165.

[56] The relevant maxim, in full, is *auctoritates sanctorum et dicta doctorum, philosophorum et poetarum*, comprehending a full panoply of disciplines and knowledges divine and human. The maxim has a lengthy philology and roots, although for an expansive discussion of the themes on a relatively equal footing, see the doctoral thesis of Wilhelm Cornelius Ackersdyke, *Disputatio philologico-juridica. De utilitate et auctoritate poeseos et poetarum in jurisprudentia, nec non de utilitate jurisprudentiæ in legendis et explicandis poetis* (Paddenburg,

possessive, to eviscerate in its turn the demented rigour and blinkered reason of late nineteenth-century law and lawyers thus renews in an admittedly idiosyncratic but by no means unprecedented depiction a critique of the vacuity of law and of the emotional and spiritual emptiness of its interpretative practices. In honest Pauline fashion and with a certain carcerally cenobitic tone, the Judge wishes to fulfil the law and that, as is well known, means abandoning the blackletter and dead practices of textualist implosion in favour of the spirit of the rule, the breath or *pneuma* of justice. The automatic writing system of the blind exegetes, the *flatus vocis* or empty noise of their fleeting-improvised-thoughts and paltry representations all constitute a hollowing out of legality, an apparatus of mental torture and a death-bound subjectivity. The fulfilment of the law, the devising of a method appropriate to rendering justice and giving effect to a spirit of legality that ultimately dispenses with blackletter legalism and its interpretative restraints is no small endeavour. It takes the jurist not simply into the enigmatic, because forgotten, disciplines of music and poetry, philosophy and theology, but also leads into the mysteries of governance, the *arcana imperii*, whose esoteric and dark contours have historically been hidden from social purview. It is the crisis-driven candor of critique, the willingness to confront the opaquely hierophantic beliefs of the veiled authors of law, the theology of origin and the abasement of the legal profession that founds the significance and lasting value of the thoroughly sceptical juridical theology that is packed into the varied and divagating trajectory of the *Memorabilia*.

1779), helpfully – if unimaginatively – collecting and collating all the pertinent Greek and Latin legal and poetic texts.

4

The Impure Theory of Law: The Metaphysics of Play-With-Human-Beings

'What will come of this cursed affair?' and 'What will become of me? Should he' (*scilicet* say or think) – such are the questions that have for years been spoken into my head by the rays in endless repetition; even if they rest on falsifications and do not render my own thoughts, yet they give a hint that even God is aware of a thoroughly mismanaged affair.[1]

The *morbus juridicus* from which Schreber suffered was not simply a sickness with law but equally an ailment of a deeper kind, a dissatisfaction with the grounds of *lex,* with the absent authority and lack of justice in the jurisprudential trajectory of his epoch. Not only is his constant reference to juristic figures, professional terminologies and jurisprudential categories, both Roman and German, a mark of his struggle to obtain release despite his inept legal team, it is also symptomatic of a metaphysical concern with a system that he in turn diagnoses as 'out of joint' and smelling rotten. The narrative and trajectory of the *Memorabilia* is directed constantly towards the theological and theoretical bases of legal structures. His critique is of abstract impositions, external interferences, an inhuman law operated by automata, machines, rather than a material and embodied law. If we return momentarily to the figure of the scales, and the Judge's dissatisfaction with his initial treatment, his complaint that he was never taught to use the machinery for weighing himself at the Leipzig clinic by the over-busy, and latterly professionally negligent, Professor playing God, Flechsig, we can open the question of justice that is the most immediate referent of the symbolism of the scales and, indeed, in the French, of *La Dame de Balance* whom Schreber was striving, often against himself, to invoke and to become. Schreber couldn't weigh himself; he was unable to measure and so contribute to and speed up his cure. We can note first that the symptom is a manifestation of bodily unease, malaise of a corporeal kind that requires attention, care. The primary meaning of the inability to weigh is at this stage, as Sanders notes, that of a

[1] *Memoirs* at 287.

deficit of judgement and jurisdiction. He cannot play the part of judge, but we should also note that this early, marginal complaint relates to the body and to weight, as also to body image, all of which signal clearly the transition to come. Becoming woman means physical change, reorientation of bodily nerves and ligaments, diminution of size, enlargement of breasts and such like. Justice also will need to be done to the body, but, initially, it is as judge, as office holder and in his official capacity that Schrebrer feels that he suffers a certain *aphasia* of judgement. The machine, the scales of justice, temporarily eluded and escaped him. So much so that the rest of his work is comprehensible as being in significant part a description of the epic struggle, the intellectual and corporeal quest to grasp the scales and to rectify the imbalance that he had earlier both embodied and symbolised. The scales had to be wrested back from an inequality generated by the divinity and disruptive of both body and law.

The Manichean struggle, *Deus contra Deum*, may seem excessive in its figures and incorporations, but put in its historical and jurisprudential context it is neither as outré nor as delirious as the history of commentary and the much larger body of work that ignores this dimension of the *Memorabilia* has tended to portray. At one level, Schreber offers a system of natural law, of *justissima tellus*, of a most just earth that can contribute to the diversity of radical jurisprudential systems. One can borrow from Foucault's concept of archaeological analysis and see the *Memorabilia* as offering a break in the continuous chronology of reason 'invariably traced back to some inaccessible origin', in place of which the Judge presents a more discontinuous and agonistic plurality of scales 'sometimes very brief, distinct from one another, irreducible to a single law, scales that bear a type of history peculiar to each one, and which cannot be reduced to the general mode of consciousness that acquires, progresses and remembers'.[2] Schreber's fight is to devise his own scales, a novel equilibrium in the sphere of juridical theology and of the *ius naturae* that inhabits a specific space within his conception of the institution and various scales of practice, procedure, doctrine, advocacy and theory of law. The Judge may want in the end to judge himself as a woman, to weigh another body, as will be elaborated in the next chapter, but before this question of transition to the feminine can be addressed, it is necessary to work through the jurisprudence of the legal subject, the persona and gender of law as a discipline and profession from which the Judge has become increasingly estranged. It can also be observed, by way of introduction to his jurisprudence, as a corrective to the foreclosure of his discourse in the psy-disciplines, that

---

[2] Michel Foucault, *The Archaeology of Knowledge* (New York: Pantheon Books, 1972) at 8.

this legal metaphysics is not so uncommon a genre for his period, and that the Judge is far from alone in his visceral yet speculative insights into the sources and purposes of law. Specifically, with respect to his contemporaries, and drawing first upon a text within the 'auld alliance', Germany and Scotland, the example of *The Reign of Law*, a popular work of juridical theology by the Duke of Argyll. Appearing in 1871 in its fifth edition, and reprinted several times after that, the work occupies a theoretical domain surprisingly similar in level and theme, if not in orientation, to that which Schreber traverses and contests in a contrary and thoroughly vivid manner. For Argyll, the purpose of his philosophy of the dominion of law was to reassert the proper Order of the Mind, and specifically to contest the materialistic and atheistic philosophies that had sprung from Darwinism. The enemy is science, insofar as it denies the Supernatural and, by extension, the Supramaterial. In brief, because the proofs are very lengthy, Argyll asserts in natural law fashion the 'universal Reign of Law' as the immutable Will of the Divinity, fixed and invariant, but unknowable to humanity: 'there is no secret Presence where its bonds are broken', and at another point, the Will 'knows no parallax' and thus is immune to alteration.[3] Belief in the Supernatural, Argyll affirms at length, is 'essential to all Religion' in that 'Belief in the existence of a Living Will – of a Personal God – is indeed a requisite condition'.[4] To this he adds that 'the Mind is as much subject to the Law as the Body is. The Reign of Law is over all.'[5] The operation of the Divine Mind in all the workings of nature, body and thought is proven best through miracles, the Supernatural manifestations of Divine power for Divine purposes. Argyll's theory of miracles differs not at all in epistemological level or ontological manifestation to that of the Judge. The two jurists may hold contrary views of the value and interpretation of miracles; they are manifestations of a higher law for the Duke, and they are improper interferences in the human realm for the Judge but the object of their theories and descriptions of the miraculous are the same. These expressions of God's Will, whether positive or negative, explain phenomena, such as, in an intriguing example used by Argyll, the 'preservation of the Jews as a distinct People during so many centuries of their dispersion . . . It is at variance with all other experience of the laws which govern the amalgamation with each other of different families of the human race.'[6] The mystic hand of a Higher Will has, in Argyll's account, hewn their fate and their survival is accountable only through such theistic presupposition. Ironic in many

---

[3] Duke of Argyll, *The Reign of Law*, 5th edn (New York: Alden Press, 1884) 30.
[4] Ibid. at 32.
[5] Ibid. at 38.
[6] Ibid. at 30.

respects though the example may be, it resonates with Schreber's 'extraordinary identification with an exemplary Jew', 'perhaps the relatively most
moral' of beings, 'the one single human being to be spared'.[7] The identification is based, as Fernie brilliantly elaborates, upon the exemplary Jew sharing
in Schreber's fate, in being unmanned, transformed into a woman so as to
be able to bear children, so as to save the world. In immediate terms, it is the
resonance of the metaphor, expressly the 'legend' of foundation, the miracle
of transformation and the institutions that support it that fairly expressly and
self-consciously transcend the natural and temporal and prefigure the Judge's
own trajectory towards confronting and contesting the divine interferences
both with himself and with humanity. If anything, Schreber is more aware
of the symbolic dimension of such miraculous metaphoricity than is Argyll
who contends only that beyond nature lies the unilateral legislative power of
an unknowable will and its absolute decree. It is precisely that supine view of
knowing and its accession to blind faith that Schreber will impugn at length.

The island of human knowledge, for Argyll, has tenuous borders and it
is the fact that we do not know those borders that makes it hard to recognise
the boundary across which the Supernatural begins. Time and again the good
Duke of Argyll, in a surprisingly popular work of jurisprudence, endeavours
to prove the eternal apparatus, as the expression of His Will in nature and
in mind.[8] The Law, in its proper sense, its fifth meaning in Argyll's account,
is a 'purely Abstract Idea, which carries up to a higher point our conception
of what phenomena are and of what they do'.[9] And to this end, just so as to
conclude this brief glimpse of a popular work of metaphysical jurisprudence,
an expansive defence of the supernatural, Argyll intones in horror that 'there
are men who would stare into the very Burning Bush without a thought
that the ground on which they stand must be Holy Ground'.[10] It requires
a radical series of leaps of faith to understand this example, drawn from an
Old Testament *parabola* or parable. We are supposed somehow to prove the
supernatural by projecting ourselves into scriptural apparitions and standing
before elliptical manifestations of the divine as witnessed in the spontaneous
combustion of bushes in an extremely arid climate. In that Argyll is offering an epistemology of divine law, it is necessary to acknowledge the break
that occurs, the shift to miracle and fiction as devices of metaphorical and

---

[7] *Memoirs* at 53. I owe this point to Fernie, *The Demonic*, 279–80 who provides an inspiring
reframing of these passages in Schreber.

[8] The fifth edition of the work is expressly a popular edition, produced cheaply so as to make
it easily 'available to the working class'.

[9] Argyll, *Reign of Law* at 108.

[10] Ibid. at 113.

metaphysical description and to acknowledge the homonymy of this schema with the method of the *Memorabilia*. If one can paraphrase one of Lacan's finer observations, we can hazard that *'if a man who thinks he is a Duke is mad, a Duke who thinks he is a Duke is no less so'*. The Duke, too, has a finger in psychosis, but no-one to my knowledge has yet dismissed his work as the raving symptoms of a spiritualist who wanted to become a man.[11] Even in its positive assertions, Schreber's theory of law, of the Order of the World, of miraculous manifestations, of his struggle with God, is very close to Argyll's subject matter and doctrine. They are different in detail and in tone, but they initially share a comparable epistemological domain of knowing pushed beyond 'the island of knowledge', of faith or intuition as the heuristic that explains experience and generates both purpose and meaning for the subject who wishes to extract solace and strength from the unknown. After the exemplary instances of what I will term the trigger devices of *scilicet,* to wit, and *als ob*, 'as if', the argument shifts suddenly to narrative depiction, to the imaging of a domain beyond, an unknown, an unconscious. It also embarks upon a quest for what Rabelais termed the great 'perhaps', although for both Argyll and Schreber doubt is far removed from their purview, save in its projection upon others, the Darwinians in one case, the lawyers and the doctors in the other. Turning to the latter, the Judge, and granted his initial atheism, his status as the last figure of the Enlightenment, his epistemology is if anything more rational and muted than Argyll's. Schreber makes frequent use of the Latin term *scilicet*, so much so indeed that Lacan borrows the word as the title for his journal, thereby aligning, yet again, and yet again somewhat covertly with the 'lunatic's printed discourse' and imputed state of mind. The composite Latin word *scilicet* combines *scrire*, to know, and *liceto*, meaning lawful, that it is permitted, and, thus, combined, indicates to know lawfully. As Lacan perhaps intuited, the term, being permissive and opening, suggests a trigger, a point of entry into thought, a trajectory, a mental space of invention and fabrication. Thus, when the interrupted thoughts end and Schreber adds the parenthetical *'scilicet,* say or think' he is implicitly cutting off the voices and projecting his own thoughts into the lawful space of imagination that the severance has permitted and facilitated. What follow are technically licit thoughts, and in his case extra-judicially approved elaborations. Translated into English, although the Latin has the same connotation, *scilicet* is properly 'to wit', and to wit is that starting point of metaphor that in law becomes the *fictio iuris*, the legal fiction of jurisdiction. *Scilicet* is, to wit, the assertion

---

[11] See the discussion in Maggie Nelson, *The Argonauts* (Minneapolis: Graywolf Press, 2015) at 14–15.

of juristic power in the form of a fiction, most usually of place, personality, temporality or identity. Dating back to the Twelve Tables, the *fictio iuris* is a feature of all of the more or less distant forms of Western law, including the common law systems, and allows for the expansion or retraction of rules, and the intervention of equity to provide a just resolution for, as the maxim goes, *in fictione iuris semper est aequitas*. Two features of this equitable invention, of the reshaping of the symbolic by the imaginary, are of interest in relation to Schreber. First, the uses of *scilicet* in the *Memorabilia* are always in relation to the (miraculous) voices that the Judge experiences and they relate most directly to interrupted thoughts, signalling, 'to wit think', about the cursed affair in the epigraph to this chapter, about the Order of the World, about his defence against the power of the rays, about his wife's feelings, and lastly about his conception of the soul.[12] In each instance, even where the voices are negative in content, the liminal device of *scilicet* marks a break and triggers a passage to possibility, to options neither yet stated nor previously available. They instance thought in its most generative and transgressive moment, and in Schreber's case at that very point where 'the father's no' is challenged and His law overcome.

An easy example can be taken from a common law borrowing from the Roman tradition in the form of developing the concept of 'estoppel', a law French term for inventing a ground in equity for enforcing gratuitous promises.[13] The civilian basis of the concept is from Justinian: no-one can change their mind to the harm of another – *nemo potest mutare consilium suum in injuriam alterius*. In the case of someone who has made a gratuitous promise, law refuses to enforce the promise, but equity triggers the fiction of preclusion, treating the second party, the promisor, 'as if she has given something, *scilicet* a *quid pro quo*, a detriment, in return, and so meets the legal requirement for intervention, namely that there be a contract. In formal terms, the promisor is estopped from denying the truth of their original statement. The preclusion prevents the promisor, legally 'the master of the offer', the father of the contract, from speaking further or, as an early judgment puts it: 'It seems to us that the true reason is the preclusion of the defendant, under the doctrine of estoppel, to deny the consideration.'[14] The fiction, the *scilicet*,

---

[12] *Memoirs* at 49, 186, 245, 252, 312.

[13] Now termed reliance detriment in US common law, where this device is much better and more fully developed than in the UK. For its early roots in the doctrine of moral obligation, see, for example, *Caul v Gibson* 3 Pa. 416 (1846): 'A moral obligation has ever been held a sufficient consideration to support an express promise, but not an implied one'; and *Ryerss v Trustees of Presbyterian Congregation* 33 Pa. 114 (1859).

[14] *Ricketts v Scothorn* 57 Neb. 51 (1898) 53.

thus, stops the prior speech and propels the discourse of fiction, an imaginary elaboration so as to achieve the desired equitable end. The preclusion as it is technically termed is quite simply a foreclosure of law, the arrest of *certum ius* or strict law and the silencing of the juristic patristic or simply abstract regimen in favour of a redistribution according to imaginary forms. The father is silenced by equity in a fashion not dissimilar to that in which Schreber seeks quite explicitly to foreclose the divine father who is consistently engaged – as theology, as tradition, pattern and law – in trying to silence him, in trying to thwart his desires. In Schreber's usage, the *scilicet* performs the function of establishing his jurisdiction, his right to discourse, and, in the process, as the marker of his entry, it forecloses the voices, it interrupts the interrupted speech and contrary to the Lacanian analysis it precludes the father, the metaphor of prior speech, so as to allow the Judge his discourse upon the crimes and torments imposed both spiritually and physically upon him, and upon his perception of the proper Order of the World. Where the Duke of Argyll appears, at least to rationalist perceptions, to be wholly unaware of the delusional, although conventional, nature of his theories and images of the Supernatural, of the Divine Will, and moving hand of the miraculous as the context and ground of limitation of science, Schreber inaugurates his theorems and advocacy with the notification that these are legal fictions, variations upon the (tenuous) reality of the symbolic for the purposes of providing insight and imagining justice. They are what a philosopher contemporary with Schreber termed heuristic fictions, part of the *ars inveniendi*, the rhetorical and forensic craft of invention of arguments, whose most usual linguistic form in German is *als ob*, as if, from which very phrase Vaihinger took the title of his substantial treatise.[15] It is a phrase that Schreber uses numerous times, which as adverted earlier is usually ignored by the translators, but that bears, I will argue, a very heavy weight in the apprehension of the juristic theory that the Judge propounds. Vaihinger's theory of the 'as if' was influential upon the neo-Kantians of his day, and specifically upon the Marburg School of legal philosophy that today is remembered most for the work of the Austrian jurist and theorist of the juridical 'as if', Hans Kelsen. Fiction, the 'as if' of error and play, is intrinsic to all thought, all concept building and elaboration of theories. In a formulation that would appeal to Schreber, Vaihinger proposes that it is really only insincerity that leads most philosophical systems to hide their fictive basis, 'their irrational side', because 'the consciously false plays an enormous part in science, philosophy and life'.[16]

---

[15] Hans Vaihinger, *The Philosophy of 'As If'. A System of the Theoretical, Practical and Religious Fictions of Mankind*, trans. C. K. Ogden (London: Kegan Paul, 1924).

[16] Vaihinger, *Philosophy of 'As If'*, xli.

Fiction, from the Latin *fingere*, to mould, to give shape to, has a common root with the terms 'figure' and 'figuration'.[17] The fiction is an allegory, or to borrow from Vaihinger, metaphysics is metaphoric, and on each occasion that Schreber manipulates an 'as if', not as a trope but as a concept, as the mode of discursive thought, he embarks upon the work of *fictio rationis* by means of which the symbolic fiction operates: 'A new intuition is apperceived by an ideational construct of concepts' as analogical fictions. 'All knowledge is analogical because thought operates through categories and these are only analogical apperceptions.'[18] Dogmas, in theology and law, are thus classified by Vaihinger as fictions, rather than hypotheses that claim a causal relation to the real: 'the most sublime fiction of a practical kind is the idea of the moral world order'.[19] One can hear the echo of these very words in Schreber, in the Order of the World and its moral dictates, systemic equilibrium and legal intimations. Jurisprudence is the domain of the 'as if', of inferences drawn from fictions, of the *praesumptio iuris*, as opposed to the specific and practical domain of the *fictiones iuris*, which operate by altering facts and treating something that has not happened as if it had. The 'as if' expands upon the consciously false claim of fact in the legal fiction and builds its case, its 'general picture', as Bentham also opined, through contest and debate, the *pro et contra* of disputation, allowing Vaihinger the observation that fictions are aids to thought, and most particularly responses to contradiction and opposition: 'man owes his mental development more to his enemies than to his friends.'[20] The worst error, meaning the least productive fiction, is that which forgets that the fictive is a conscious falsehood. It is an error from which theorists such as Argyll and analysts such as Lacan have sometimes suffered, and so it seems appropriate to move to consider Schreber's own manipulation of the 'as if' in his text, and to trace its import for his jurisprudence, his juridical theology. It transpires that '*als ob*', the 'as if', precedes many of the Judge's key conceptual inventions. Stick with the highlights. The first use of 'as if' occurs

---

[17] On the etymology, morphology and concept of figure, see Erich Auerbach, 'Figura', now available in Porter (ed.), *Time, History and Literature: Selected Essays of Erich Auerbach* (Princeton: Princeton University Press, 2016) at 65. See also James Porter, 'Disfigurations: Erich Auerbach's Theory of *Figura*', 44 *Critical Inquiry* 80 (2017).

[18] Vaihinger, *The Philosophy of 'As If'* at 27.

[19] Ibid. at 46.

[20] Ibid. at 12. The early nineteenth-century work of Jeremy Bentham, *Theory of Fictions* (London: Kegan Paul, 1932) is an important forerunner, and his concept of fiction, 'the syphilis that runs through the veins of the juridical body', gets taken up in a more positive vein in Lacan. See Paul Audi, *Lacan ironiste* (Paris: Mimésis, 2015) at 18–22: for Lacan, rejecting the *non fingo*, 'the fictional is not that which deceives, but, properly speaking, it is what we call the symbolic'.

early in the text, symptomatically enough for any close reader of the marginal, and here the footnotes, in relation to the fleeting-improvised-men, who appear to be figures in a dream and 'as if' they were incapable of engaging in a sensible conversation.[21] That the spectres lack sense and sensation, that the oneiric is not the rational, seems apposite and well directed, especially as the next 'as if' relates precisely to the basic language (*Grundsprache*), the vulgar German that is the medium of divine speech, the diction of the nerves and voices that intrude upon Schreber's nights and interrupt his days.[22] The unconscious, the 'as if' of the dreamer, has its own symbols, its own relatively crude language and images, which the Judge is far from believing to be straightforwardly rational, let alone factually accurate. The fiction, the virtuality, marks and triggers entry into the domain of theory as incarnadine cerebration, Leibnitz's compossible worlds, which exist as expedient and in the best instances fruitful inventions: 'In fictions thought makes deliberate errors, in order to understand the nature of Becoming.'[23] Following Vaihinger's postulate that fiction addresses possibility and becoming, that it is, as Freud also noted, heuristically useful, it can be inferred that there is a certain gradation and accretion to Schreber's use of the 'as if'. The progress of the ideational fictions elaborated moves broadly from the conditions of possibility of the spiritual world, the description of its language, its mixing of rational and irrational, to the details and then the implications, the struggle, that this imagined and properly compossible world presents. Thus, after the discussion of the basic language, the human and spectral inhabitants, the dead souls that return from the forecourts of heaven are addressed, 'as if' their goal was to help their living relatives to attain a state of Blessedness, but always allowing that 'the soul's own happiness was not clouded by learning of their relatives' unhappy state on earth'.[24] The souls that return, even when benign and instructive of purpose, are still those that have failed to achieve the purification necessary for entry into the state of soul voluptuousness, Blessedness, and also have not achieved separation from the living as ordained in the proper Order of the World. Whatever their intentions, they interfere, and none more so, in his metaphorical and metaphysical emanations, than Professor Flechsig, who somewhat later is referred to 'as if' his plan to cure the Judge was that of 'intensifying my nervous depression (*Nervendepression*) as far as possible' and thus to bring about a sudden change of mood. Only later

---

[21] Schreber, *Memoirs* at 5.
[22] Ibid. at 14.
[23] Vaihinger, *The Philosophy of 'As If'* at 109. As Vaihinger remarks slightly earlier in discussing Kant, 'what we call truth is merely the most expedient error' (106).
[24] Schreber, *Memoirs* at 17. Their detachment is the result of their limited memory.

is Flechsig turned into the plurality of features, genealogical, amorous, violating, malevolent, murderous and hypnotising that prompt Lyotard to remark that 'all these contrary properties simply form a polysemia around the name of Flechsig'.[25] There in the 'personificatory fiction' of Flechsig, Schreber begins to figure that which he most wishes to exclude from his life and from the living. As Kittler points out, it is the 'as if' of the God Flechsig, 'the insane neurophysiologist', who has tried to manipulate the nerves in Schreber's head and who, like the rays, attempts to impose an alien law in his brain.[26] After the introduction of the 'as if' of Flechsig, Schreber provides a triplet of direct expressions of the deliberately erroneous character of the fictions. He opines that it was 'as if' single nights lasted centuries; 'as if' building a wall around God's realm could protect him; 'as if' the clinic would become a fairy (*Feenpalast*) palace.[27] Each indicates an expansion and flexibility in Schreber's thought which allows the role of the nerves and the emergence of his own nervous condition, his feelings of dysphoria and the desire to become a woman. First, in a discussion of the desired unity of the soul in the proper Order of the World, according that is to *nomos* as the Judge understands it, Schreber reports a 'picture which I have in my mind is extremely difficult to express in words, it appeared that nerves – probably taken from my body – were strung over the whole heavenly vault'.[28] While it may seem peculiar – English for deranged – to attribute the abuse and splitting of the soul to the malicious machinations of the polymorphous tensor Flechsig, that personificatory dispositive theatrical device and more immediate mark of the psychiatric apparatus oppressing the patient is used primarily as a mechanism for explaining the splitting of the soul, the fraying of the nerves. At this stage of the book, the divine nerves are unified and working in harmony with Schreber and it is the doctor who is the figure of their perversion and division, their unlawful entry into the world. For the Judge, however, the principal 'as if', the distant mirage yet visceral hope of unifying his soul, of achieving the desired state of voluptuousness comes later and with the next invocation of the always telling 'as if'. The crucial chapter XI, on his physical transformation, opens with the declaration that from the beginning of his contact with God, right up to the present moment, 'my body has continuously been the object of divine miracles.'[29] These have been painful, sometimes paralyzing, but to the degree that they are contrary to the Order of the World they have

[25] Jean-François Lyotard, *Libidinal Economy* (London: Athlone Press, 1993) at 57.
[26] Kittler, *Discourse Networks* at 299.
[27] Schreber, *Memoirs* at 71, 74, 108.
[28] Ibid. at 111.
[29] Ibid. at 148.

failed to impede or incapacitate the Judge, but rather come to take on the appearance of play. What is 'most nearly in consonance with the Order of the World' are those miracles, which is to say those interventions 'which were somehow connected with a process of change being carried out on my body.' These included the removal of his beard and the vanishing of his flourishing moustache, as well as changes to his sex organ and diminution of body size, '*as if* my body had become smaller . . . that is to say approximating the size of the female body'.[30] Of all Schreber's symbolic, or in Vaihinger's coinage *tropic* fictions, that of a soul divided, torn between masculine and feminine is without doubt the most powerful and in many respects prescient. While the feminine initially stands for threat, unmanning, and the possibility of sexual abuse, as the scales are tipped in Schreber's favour, he is also able to acknowledge the virtues of the other gender, female pleasures, desires, adornments and most of all the creativity of engendering life, the phantasm of giving birth, the projected joy, for him, of being woman. Aside from certain further references to nerves and rays, the miraculous interventions, positive and negative, of a divided God, there is only one further 'as if' to be mentioned at this juncture and that is a later passage where Schreber discusses his supernatural insights in relation to the creation of worlds. After discussing the Kant–Laplace 'Nebular Hypothesis', the Judge moves on to state that it is '*as if* [*als ob*] one must make a fundamental distinction between the mode of creation of the plant world and of the animal world'.[31] This distinction as between modes of creation is not so much a technical fiction as a conjecture and this cognitive operation is depicted by Vaihinger as *praesumptio iuris* rather than as a fully fledged invention, an alteration of the real.[32] The Judge wants to treat the animate as ontologically distinct from bare matter and indeed bare life both in terms of the earth, whose *nomos* should be self-conscious and human, and in respect of the divine rays (nerves) whose manifestations and transformations should be subject to the Schreberian law of the unity of the human soul as separate from the divine and from the *humus* of the earth. It is not a coincidence then that when the Judge discusses his perception of the divine rays as they intervene and impact his body, he insists that they take a tellurian and secular form: 'Above all I want to mention that the rays . . . often appear in my head *in the image of a human shape*.'[33] It is that transformation, that morphosis, that opens up the theory of the mutability of

---

[30] Ibid. at 149.

[31] Ibid. at 253; emphasis added.

[32] Ibid. at 33.

[33] Ibid. at 254; italics in the original. On the next page, we also read that 'it was as if the nerves were trying to overcome an obstacle to their descent' (255).

personality, the fragility of subjectivity and the possibility of transition, of becoming a woman while remaining within a more expansive and imaginative lawscape. Alongside the drive to become a woman, to embrace the feminine principle of creativity, Schreber also asserts a humanitarian ethic, a legal right to his feelings and to their expressions, corporeal, sartorial, oral and written. It is on the strength of that particular assertion that he wins his lawsuit and is released from the Asylum and it is there, in the face off between positive law and the Judge's juridical theology, that the positive and impure character of his jurisprudence can be addressed. The lawsuit is interesting and deserves brief note. Schreber has to fire his lawyers, primarily because these automata, these writing-down machines both fail to understand his cause of action and lamentably lack in the rhetorical ability to persuade the court. As he notes, the only elements of the original court pleadings that were both relevant and correct were those that he had penned.[34] The Judge, for his part, when he takes on the role of advocate, most successfully plays the judges, just as they are thinking that they are playing him. Far from being foreclosed, Schreber expatiates upon the errors and misrepresentations of his lawyers before contesting the medical opinions upon which the lower courts had rested their judgments. As we have seen, he denies any mental illness, and contests the aspersion of 'pathological imaginings'. He can contain his feelings, hide his desires, even if, given free reign, he declares that in response to the medical diagnoses, he would cry out, '*Oh sancta simplicitas!*', meaning, 'Oh! What fools!'[35] After that, Schreber sticks to his themes, outlines his metaphysics and, in effect, as Trüstedt so well notes, proves his sanity by means of what are in conventional terms insane arguments. Thus, he knows God, that he deals with divine miracles, that his knowledge 'towers high above all human science'. He sees behind 'the dark veil which otherwise hides the beyond from the eyes of man', and has written a work that belongs 'to the most interesting ones ever written since the existence of the world'.[36] It continues in a similar fashion, of which Schreber is well aware others may view as vain or megalomaniacal but continues in vivid detail to depict the miracle of broken piano strings, the reality of his visions, the delusion of his doctors, and then announces, with brilliant rhetorical skill, that all of this is irrelevant, 'an arabesque around the real core of the question', which is that the judges of the Royal Court of Appeal have no choice: they are bound by what the great authority Georg Friedrich Puchta had earlier termed scientific juridical law – *wissenschaftliches Juristenrecht* – and so by the automatic writing system

---

[34] Ibid. at 405.
[35] Ibid. at 410.
[36] Ibid. at 410–11.

of law, the very system that Schreber has so viscerally and vividly sought to escape.[37] The irony or the brilliance of the Judge's presentation of his case is that he in effect flaunts his femininity, his affective pleasures, his transitional being before a Court that is trapped by his knowledge of their knowledge that they are within the jurisprudence of their day incapable of any other decision than that which the so-called 'mad' Schreber dictates to them. He will live with his miracles, his femininity, even his bellowing, and publish his book in fulfilment of the final prophesy of his pleading before the Court, citing Luther: 'If it is man's work it will perish; if it is the work of God it will last. I will quietly await whether unequivocal events will not compel other people to accept the truth of my delusions.'[38] The work lives on and ironically the judgement, too, but by virtue of the book and not the other way around. The Judgment itself begins in good juristic and psychotic fashion with the declaration that the Judgement is 'IN THE NAME OF THE KING', capitalised, as given.[39] It is not so much the fiction of the Court speaking literally in the mode of *nom du père*, but rather that under their own theory, mad as they maddeningly perceive the Judge as being, they are bound by positive law, by the total and pure system of legal science, by an *indifferent* law that cannot take account of the extraordinary arguments put by the plaintiff *pro se*, or for himself. It is Schreber's desire that ironically forces the Court to accede to his forensic argument, that the Code does not allow his incarceration: 'The way he personally took up the fight against the tutelage' persuades the Court. His passion was expressed in measured form, his affect in acuity, his feelings in 'logical and juristical operations', all of which imposed upon the Royal Appeals judges no choice but to 'arrive at the conviction that plaintiff is capable of dealing with the demands of life . . . the orderly regulation of which is the object of the Law'.[40] The patently disordered Judge, dressing as a woman, bellowing, conversing with God, witnessing miracles, fluent in inventive masturbatory techniques, dismissive of the medical profession and profoundly hostile to the lawyers who put him into the Asylum, cannot but be released, the judges themselves being caught in the machine of the dictates and dictation of a higher power. They may be ill themselves of law but Schreber, indeed Miss Schreber, is able to flirt and flaunt a theory of affective order and a transitional self in front of lawyers themselves imprisoned in the Weberian iron cage of law. The critique of law that I have associated in the preceding chapter with *morbus juridicus*, with the Judge's erstwhile virile

---

[37] Ibid. at 423.
[38] Ibid. at 433.
[39] Ibid. at 473.
[40] Ibid. at 515.

profession and previously calm objectivity, is characterised primarily by a machinery of thoughtless recording and mindless repetition, Kittler's blind exegesis. The automatic writing-down system, the endless invocation 'it has been recorded', the compulsive thinking and inscription all signal a servile and wholly vicarious mode of quasi-legal existence, worship of legal science leaving the decision maker bereft of any decision to make, so pure is the logical-mechanical application machine – the *Subsumtionsautomat* that Schreber had so vividly fought, in body and soul, to escape. It is the judges who are judging the Judge that are, to coin a phrase, *en quelque façon nulle.*[41] It is, for our transitional protagonist a destitute institution, a failed form and an inept array of formularies. It is a barren play of abstractions, a pure theory, but a lifeless one. All of Schreber's terms indicate his hostility towards a system without creativity, lacking a soul, lost in an atemporal and cadaverous automatism. The Judge, however, comes not to denounce the law but to fulfil it. He seeks to move from the letter to the spirit, from the dead text to the living body and it is this trajectory that the *Memorabilia* outline and track in their visceral and frequently all too corporeal form. Piecing together the roots, the oppositional and positive dimensions to the Judge's juristic think-ing can best begin by tracking the references in his text. To what discourse does his impure jurisprudence seek to oppose itself? The specific answer, proleptic as well as retrospective, comes in references to Luther, Pope Honorius, Kant–Laplace, Goethe, Luthardt, the Bible, and the German civil code of 1900, the BGB – the *Bürgerliches Gesetzbuch.* There are Kings, Dukes, Gods and Emperors aplenty to depose. There are figures such as Puchta, Savigny, Jhering, legal science incarnadine, the Princes of the academy, the purists, the Gothically blackletter law professors, schemers and dreamers of the great Code, of the vocation of our age for legislation, who have to be confronted in all their aura of certainty and righteousness. Starting by work-ing backwards, there is first the Code and the fact of its being sidelined by Schreber when it first appears in the text, with the perilunar marks of the incidental, betraying a psychic significance. It is not so much that Schreber had, as a young lawyer, worked on the BGB, although that is important, but rather that the Code represents the reassertion of the autonomy and so purity, the purported self-enclosure of the legal system as separate from the political and social domains. It is in Weber's terms the expression of formal legal rationality, or as Jhering puts it, it is a pure science that will emerge in the

---

[41] I am borrowing this bon mot from Regina Ogorek, 'Inconsistencies and Consistencies in 19th Century Legal Theory', in Christian Joerges and David Trubek (eds), *Critical Legal Thought: An American-German Debate* (Baden-Baden: Nomos Verlagsgesellschaft, 1989) at 37.

codification as 'a higher unity of science', a sovereign dogma in need of disciples.[42] If we look at the system in which Schreber was trained, it is the strict conception of legal science, and along with it the drive to codification, the enactment of an exhaustive, closed and complete textual body of law that most strongly characterises the German tradition, the *mos italicus iuris docendi* as it used to be called.[43] The roots of the Teutonic drive to positivisation of law and to codification lie in a mathematical conception of legal science that has expansive roots going back at least to the mathematician and jurist Gottfried Leibnitz, whose *Nova methodus* was published in 1667 and whose method lies hidden, in Berkowitz's authoritative interpretation, at the root of the ills of the positivistic tradition of legal philosophy.[44] Leibnitz's conception of legal science takes its subject matter from the unsurpassed works of Roman law and applies a mathematical method of treatment to the rules and solutions produced by the early jurisconsults. Legal science was to proceed *more geometrico*, and, for Leibnitz, much more than for his European and Anglophone contemporaries, this meant the establishment of a purely logical system derived from first principles and elaborated from consequence to consequence in a pure and untainted order. The method that he introduces is explicitly schematic, although hostile to Ramus' interpretations of Aristotle, which he terms the source of *paedogorum odia exercuerunt* in both *Germania* and in *Gallia*, and the immolation of Aristotle.[45] He offers in their stead a universal system of rational study, and a method, line one of Part One, through which the perfection of action can be attained. The task of the jurist is to take the conclusions of the jurisconsults, the *generalia iuris*, and weave them, by means of the art of combination (*de arte combinatoria*) into the *systema iuris*, an unbroken system of rules. As Leibniz puts it in another essay:

[42] Rudolf von Jhering, *Law as a Means to an End* (Boston: Boston Book Co., 1913) at 31.

[43] On the earlier history of legal science in Germany, and the path of the *mos italicus*, see Donald Kelley, *The Human Measure: Social Thought in the Western Legal Tradition* (Cambridge, MA: Harvard University Press, 1990); and for specifically on the *mores Germaniae*, see Harold Berman, *Law and Revolution II: The Impact of the Protestant Reformations on the Western Legal Tradition* (Cambridge, MA: Harvard University Press, 2006) at chapter 3 ('The Transformation of German Legal Science').

[44] Gottfried Leibnitz, *Nova methodus discendæ docendaque jurisprudentiæ, ex artis didacticæ principiis in parte generali præpræmissis, experientiæque luce* (Frankfurt: Zunneri, 1667). Roger Berkowitz, *The Gift of Science. Leibnitz and the Modern Legal Tradition* (Cambridge, MA: Harvard University Press, 2005). Goethe, in a not dissimilar vein, observes that Roman law was like a duck. Sometimes it is prominent, swimming on the surface of the water; at other times it is hidden from view, diving amid the depths. See Stein, *Roman Law* at 116.

[45] Leibniz, *Nova methodus*, *præfatio* (p. 23 in the digitised copy available at http://digital.slub-dresden.de/fileadmin/data/356830047/356830047_tif/jpegs/356830047.pdf).

'the doctrine of law (*doctrina iuris*) belongs to those sciences that depend on definitions and not on experience, on demonstrations of reason and not of sense, and are matters of law, one can say, and not of fact.'[46] It is this position, associated also with the mathematician and philosopher of law Christian Wolff, for whom law followed in the 'track of Euclid' through definitions and their logical arrangement, that is taken up in the nineteenth-century *usus modernus* and its *interpretatio logica* as the basis of scientific jurisprudence. The method is axiomatic and is thus to give rise to a universal jurisprudence and one that for Leibniz grounds all knowledge in the putative science of law, including, as the definition goes from Gaius onwards, knowledge of things divine, because 'theology is a species of general jurisprudence'.[47] The geometrical method of legal science, termed the *usus modernus*, was inherited by the nineteenth-century tradition that Schreber enters. For Savigny and Jhering, the principle pedagogues of the Judge's formative years as a jurist, there was a constant struggle to revivify jurisprudence, as history, as *Volksgeist*, the spirit of the people, and as *Volkslied*, as their basic language, but most strongly in the form of codification and thus as system and science of law.[48] Despite a certain hesitancy and his title as the leader of the Historical School of Jurisprudence, Savigny believed in and sought the perfection of law in the 'guiding principles' of *Recht*, the transcendental deductions from juridical definitions, *consilia* and rules: 'it is this that gives our work its scientific character'.[49] The result was *usus modernus pandectarum*, or *Pandektenrecht*, a science based on and abstracted from Roman method and texts understood according to the mathematical model: 'through Roman law, beyond Roman

---

[46] Leibniz, *Elementa juris naturalis* (1666–7), in *Philosphische Scrhiften Erster Band 1663–1672* (Berlin: Akademie Verlag, 1990) at 460. Discussed by Gordley in *Jurists* at 176.

[47] Leibniz, *Nova methodus* 37 (*quia Theologia species quædam est Jurisprudentiæ universim sumptæ*); and at 38: 'almost all of theology devolves in great part out of jurisprudence' (*Breviter tota fere Theologia magnum partem ex Jurisprudentia pendet*). The view ends up in Jhering's view, *Law as a Means* at 30, that science 'unites all its members into an invisible community. They all exert their powers for the purposes of science, and the total result of the co-operation of all its disciples consists in the preservation, extension, and increase of science.'

[48] Berkowitz, *Gift of Science* at 83–6, terms it 'the triumph of legality' and the 'reign of *Gesetz*', the latter term invoking again the unlikely spectre of the Duke of Argyll. It is worth noting that Langdell was announcing a new scientific method of law at Harvard in the mid-1880s and John Wigmore, 'Nova methodus discendæ docendaeque jurisprudentiae', 30 *Harvard L.R.* 812 (1916) borrows Leibniz's title to argue that Langdell's science represented an innovation in legal scholarship that over the past millennium has happened only once every 200 years.

[49] Savigny, cited in Berkowitz, *Gift of Science* at 117. See also Gordley, *Jurists* at 199–201.

law' to the universal, as Jhering, Savigny's successor succinctly formulates it.[50] Law was a self-completing and thus autonomous system, or taking from Jhering again: 'universal sovereignty comes to science of itself. How? By its own power and force of attraction.'[51] The most visible result of this drive to rigour, universality, sovereignty, was the German civil code of 1900, viewed by the English legal historian Maitland as 'the best code that the world has yet seen', a highly abstract, rigorously conceptual, set of rules, free of almost all detailed casuistry. The Code provides a radical degree of closure by dictating that where it is silent and contains no rule on a specific point 'in the absence of such rules the principles given in themselves from out of the spirit of the legal order are controlling'.[52] There are, in other words, no gaps, no *lacunae* in the Code, but rather it stands complete and self-completing with neither threat nor weakness in the face of facts for the simple reason that it never has to deal with them. It is the latter point, the architectonic of the system, the belief in closure that comes to define the era and gain its most consistent and lucid elaboration in the *Pure Theory of Law*.[53] Nascent in the drive to codification of Schreber's pedagogic and then practical experience, the theory of purity, of a method of legal cognition entirely divorced from empirical support and distinct from all other disciplines gains its most forceful expression in the lifework and *Rechtswissenschaft* of Hans Kelsen. Founded upon the fiction of a basic norm, the *Grundnorm* that is presupposed for the exclusively normative system of law to be possible, legal cognition is treated, in strict Kantian manner, as 'objectivist and universalistic. It aims at the totality of law in its objective validity and seeks to conceive each individual phenomenon in its systematic context with all others . . . The law is an order and all legal problems must be set and solved as order problems. In this way law becomes an exact structural analysis of positive law, free of all ethical-political value judgments.'[54] The science is axiomatic; it deals only with norms, ought statements that have no necessary relation to any empirical practice or factual basis. Validity, that the norm is generated by the system of norms, is the only criterion of analysis as the 'Pure Theory of Law is a theory of positive law, of positive law as such'; it is legal science, not history, policy, sociology or

---

[50] Most notably in the three volumes of Rudolf von Jhering, *Der Geist des römischen Rechts* (Leipzig: Breitkopf und Härtel, 1852).

[51] Jhering, *Law as a Means* at 31.

[52] BGB s.1.

[53] Hans Kelsen, *Reine Rehchtslehre* (1911) translated as *Introduction to the Problems of Legal Theory* (Oxford: Clarendon Press, 2002 [1911]), had its roots in the late nineteenth-century neo-Kantian movements in philosophy, the Marburg School in particular.

[54] Hans Kelsen, *The Pure Theory of Law* (Berkeley and Los Angeles: California University Press, 1960) at 191–2.

interpretation.[55] The analysis of Kelsen's system is sufficiently profuse, available and even revived to leave for others. There are two features to his theory, however, that merit some elaboration as the mirror and inverse of Schreber's *Jurisprudenz*. First, there is the structural character of the dogmatic science of law as conceived by Kelsen. It depends upon the hierarchical chain of validity of commands from the founding fiction, the *praesumptio iuris*, the *Grundnorm*, the basic conceptual legislation that grounds and closes the system. Once the basic norm is in place, assumed, then all other norms can flow from it. The system thus has its enigma, its vanishing point, its big Other, its moment of irrationality, the fruitful error that leads in the first instance to the construction of the system. The *Grundnorm* is in Vaihinger's schema a summational fiction, a General Idea, 'an assumption that makes thinking easier'.[56] As a general ideational construction, the summational fiction faces the risk of hypostatisation, meaning that what starts as a conscious fiction becomes a dogma and then a hypothesis that seeks a grounding in fact. The *causa ficta* presses to become a *causa vera*, meaning a *causa non fingo*, or not of the scientist's invention because its author either seeks to hide it or has forgotten. The summational fiction, the 'general picture', is the means of creation of the object of cognition and is the necessary predicate of the purity of the system, which Kant had earlier defined rather baldly in the following aphorism: 'Any knowledge is entitled pure, if it be not mixed with anything extraneous.'[57] This purity is the impelling force behind the new science; it is the primary image, the first line: 'As theory, the Pure Theory of Law aims solely at cognition of its subject-matter'; it is legal science and not policy, and it is free of the interference of other disciplines, and most especially of morality and fact.[58] For Jellinek, writing in 1905: 'Among the vices of the scientific enterprise of our day is the vice of methodological syncretism',[59] a position of exclusion of other disciplines, methods and fictions that has an almost military character in Kelsen's determination to 'secure' the purity of the theory against all 'threats' of intrusion, all menaces of violation.[60] The alien, the foreign, the tainted and adulterated are to be excluded and this means very specifically that the corporeal, the factual, the emotional and the psychological are all also excluded. The Pure Theory, because it is pure, has nothing to say about the

---

[55] Kelsen, *Problems of Legal Theory* at 7.
[56] Vaihinger, *Philosophy of 'As If'* at 38.
[57] Immanuel Kant, *Critique of Pure Reason* (London: Macmillan, 1929) at 11–12.
[58] Kelsen, *Problems of Legal Theory* at 7.
[59] Elvin Morton Jellinek, *System der subjektiven öffentlichen Rechte*, 2nd edn (Tübingen: J. C. B. Mohr, 1905, repr. Aalen: Scientia, 1979) at 17.
[60] Ibid. at 8.

tellurian, the actual interpretation and application of norms, the life of the law as governance, because these are matters of politics and policy, of ambiguity, discretion and fact, which are unamenable to systemic normative resolution. The position is sufficiently extreme to provoke the Russian jurist Pashukanis to comment caustically of Kelsen that, 'as a result of his undaunted consistency, he reduced neo-Kantian methodology with its two categories, to absurdity. For it turns out that the pure category of Ought, cleansed of all impurities from the Is, or the factual, and of all psychological and sociological "dross", neither has nor possibly can have any rational definition whatsoever.'[61] The jurisprudential environment in which Schreber fell ill of the law was one of extreme fiction dressed up as hypothesis and fact. The problem, as with all religion, was that of treating the imaginary as real. Kelsen's theological science of law, founded upon the almighty *Grundnorm*, is but the extension and perfection of the fictions that generated the *imperium* of science and the codification of law upon which the Judge worked and within which he practiced and rebelled. It was against the enclosed and rigidly hierarchical system of norms, the writing-down-system, the automatism, the application through the concretisation of higher norms, the obsession with validity – the only question the Pure Theory could ask and answer – that Schreber rebelled. As against purity and enclosure, the exclusively scriptural and the rigidly defined, the Judge argues for a thoroughly novel and equally extreme juridical theology, a *justissima tellus,* a most just earth, a *nomos* of dirt, inhabitation, the human and the bodily. His is an incarnadine and material, even visceral, juridical theology that is most obviously on a par with that of the Duke of Argyll, although obviously more vivid and sanguinated, more honest about its pain and its joy. It is equally commensurate with the Pure Theory, and even the capital letters betray a lot, although it is the very menace and threat, the very emotion and fact, exactly the impurity that it fears.

Schreber's juridical theology clearly passes through several stages, and most immediately his conception of divine and of supernatural forces moves from rejection to resistance to struggle to acceptance and indeed soul voluptuousness or *jouissance*, at its culmination. First, however, there is the theology of struggle, the spiritual fight to remove God from the realm of the living. The antinomy is lucidly depicted in the form of purity and impurity. The flesh is of the earth and the temporal. It is prone to putrefaction, to rotting, to smell and to pollutions. The human is impure. The divine, by contrast, is pure and thus is the antithesis of the human. The process of separation and of purification of souls occurs in the forecourt, the *propylaeum*, or in classical

---

[61] Eugeny Pashukanis, *Law and Marxism* (London: Pluto Press, 1978) at 52.

terminology and image theory the atrium (*Vorhof*) of heaven: 'Only pure human nerves were of use to God – or if one prefers in heaven – because it was their destiny to be attached to God himself to become in a sense a part of Him as forecourts of heaven.'[62] Pure souls – white, moral souls – become divine, 'pure rays', which recur constantly in the text as intrusions upon the domain of the living and the body of the Judge but that are eventually deemed benign, or indeed blessed when not in conflict with the human. Impurity is the state of the living and of the 'tested soul', a 'soul still endowed with human faults like all impure souls'.[63] Flechsig, for instance, in his telepathic and miraculous nerve interventions, and especially in his attempts at soul murder, is characterised as thoroughly impure, and profoundly 'tested'.

In that Schreber's legal theology is at least in part an exercise in a great 'as if', a theoretical fiction, its most immediate object is the exclusion of purity and of its rays and nerves. The exile of God to a colossal distance comes at a considerable cost, in terms of the pain and sleeplessness that such a struggle will cause the Judge, by virtue of the nerves and rays, and machinations of the lower God Ariman, by means of which the divine maintains its immoral links and 'tested' contacts with the world. Each voice is like a banging inside Schreber's head and this is because in the last instance purity within the world and within the body is a lie. Abstraction to the point of purity and colourless whiteness, in the Judge's theory, is a lie. There is a concealed theology in the theory of purity, in the Kantian architectonic and in Kelsen's concept of law as a purely normative system, with its absolute divide of form from content, and with it the separation of being from law. As Kelsen remarks at one point, in expatiating the necessity of absolutely distinguishing 'is' (*Sein*) from 'ought' (*Sollen*), their mutual opposition may not preclude 'a higher level that would comprehend these two concepts that exclude one another'. This is the allure of the sovereignty of science to which Jhering refers, the call of a self-completing system, the self-constitution of a community of superiors. To this trajectory, *cette implacable blancheur*, in a moment of extreme candour, Kelsen adds that if he has committed himself methodologically to renouncing any link between the two domains, then how the 'higher level' union is possible remains expressly a mystery: 'I have not, at bottom, found a sincere response other than this: I am not a monist.'[64] So no response. Just a negative. Denial perhaps, if one accedes to the monism of his science. Elsewhere, addressing the same point, that cognition creates its own object, Kelsen elaborates that cognition is subject to its own immanent laws: 'it is their conformity to laws

---

[62] Schreber, *Memoirs* at ix.
[63] Ibid. at ix.
[64] Hans Kelsen, *Hauptprobleme der Staatsrechtslehre* (Tübingen: J. C. B. Mohr, 1911) at vi.

which guarantees the objective validity of the process of cognition', resulting in the implicit conclusion that the binary division of cognitive objects leads to two distinct orders of legality.[65] These, as Agamben elaborates them, constitute separate duties – modes of conformity to law – and distinct ontologies. The result is that 'Kelsen's program of constructing a theory of law without any reference to being cannot be completely actualized. The two ontologies (being and having to be), while clearly distinct, cannot be entirely separated, and they refer to and presuppose one another.'[66] In becoming pure, law evacuates the world and so, for Schreber, it should remain separate, beyond, the imperative of the divine being properly over the celestial and not the tellurian. The latter requires its own laws, its impure forms, and particularly its bodies free from being tied to celestial nerves, interfered with by rays or played with by means of miraculous intrusions. And in Scheber's case, bodies that can transition, flesh that can become woman.

The laws immanent to the two realms are quite distinct, each properly internal to its own sphere and state of being. Only in prospect, in the dance of death, are the two potentially and even then only transitionally connected according to the image of the forecourt of heaven, the atrium that houses the mask of the father. Schreber's project is the radical one of a singular and human ontology and law, immanent to and embodied in the flesh, the nerves and tensors, the libidinal economy that striates the skin and renders the corpuscles and tendons, the feelings, erotic flesh, nomadic and transitional. Schreber's struggle is ultimately to claim the body in the radical dual demand that the human can speak or be silent in their own way, and that their embodiment of erotic desire and performance be according to their own determination. If femininity is their chosen banner, then so be it, with its costs and benefits, its pain and pleasure. Those are the immanent laws of the human, the expressions of the impure and earth bound, of self-commandment according to the proper modes of apprehension and public expression that humanity dictates.

The cause of the human, of the corporeal and tellurian, of *justissima tellus*, is subject principally to the threat of hidden powers and the various other modes of automatism that the celestial order keeps trying to impose

---

[65] Hans Kelsen, *General Theory of Law and State* (Cambridge, MA: Harvard University Press, 1946) at 434–5.

[66] Giorgio Agamben, Opus Dei: *An Archaeology of Duty* (Palo Alto: Stanford University Press, 2013) at 174. On the jurisprudential implications of this statement of dual ontology on Agamben's part, see the discussion in Laurent de Sutter, '*Contra Iurem*: On the Two Ontologies of Giorgio Agamben', in Peter Goodrich and Michel Rosenfeld (eds), *Economies of Interpretation* (New York: Fordham University Press, 2018).

unseen by all except Schreber's keen theoretical intuitions and depictions. Thus, it is constantly the threat or practice of 'being tied to' some alien form that causes Schreber's complaint, his wretchedness – *Ludertum* in Santner's reading – because of the bondage, the *iuris vinculum* or the being chained to the alien law that such mechanisms and media of bondage represent.[67] All of the wrongs committed by the divinity are trespasses upon the human domains of mind and body, speech and desire, and are to be consistently controverted by the immanent laws of tellurian and manifold self-expression. Schreber's *Luder*, his fiction, his game, his play is that of untying, of liberating, of embodying the all too human of the flesh. Thus, a law that depends upon purity is an irrelevant law, a commandment that emanates from non-being and from an atopia or elsewhere that is also nowhere, and manifests only in the servile and inhuman form of souls tied to celestial bodies, compulsive thought, automatic writing and all the other manifestations of improper and retarded transitional being that gain miraculous though damaging expression in voices and the fleeting improvised appearance of dead lawyers and conjured but unreal souls. They are unmasks not flesh, hallucinatory, which is to say fictive, dream-like forms that endeavour to express the impossible presence of non-being, of what has passed, and so, too, the fact of the self-contradictory inscription of the pure law.

It is against God, in competition with and then in embrace and internal exclusion of the divine that Schreber's juridical theology, what we can now term his jurisprudence, takes shape. *Justissima tellus*, the tellurian law of the earth, Schreber's 'as if', is grounded in the founding *praesumptio iuris* that a human law can be wrested from the divine *imperium* and freed from the bonds of servitude to an impossible purity. For this, the Judge devises his own unique method of theoretical invention, the ecstasy and effectivity of picturing. Pure law takes the form of *logos* and *graphos*, miraculous voices and non-volitional recording and writing down, in variable modes and manners of intervention. This is the *Grundsprache*, the basic language, which is the foundation of the symbolic order and its law, and that the Judge tirelessly contests and seeks to expel as the remnant of an antiquated monotheistic metaphysics. Against this, Schreber devises an imagistic medium with a tangible corporeal substrate as the ground of his method and as the basis of his overturning of the existing order of *logos* and law.

The hidden powers and duplicitous manifestations of the divine law can only be excluded and exiled if the Judge can invent a novel order and *modus*

---

[67] Eric Santner, *The Royal Remains: The People's Two Bodies and the Endgames of Sovereignty* (Chicago: University of Chicago Press, 2011) at 47.

vivendi. This he does by foreclosing *logos*, precluding and silencing the symbolic so as to begin again, imagine again in the domain of images. The image, picturing and its pleasures are Schreber's defence against the rays and the mode of his advancing towards independence of thought and so conception of his own *leges terrae*, the order of the earthly and embodied. The rays, we learn relatively early on, endeavour to close the Judge's eyes and so in depriving him of image and imagination, control him.[68] Picturing, the conjuring of images and the creative drive of the imagination are the ground of identity over time in that they are the mechanism of preservation of experience, the mnemonic of personality, of the trajectories and pluralities of a life as an embodied and hedonic experience: 'Picturing . . . may be called a reversed miracle', to which he adds that anyone 'who has not experienced what I have cannot form any idea in how many ways the ability to "picture" has become of value to me.'[69] It is as a defence against the monotony, the mental torture and 'nonsensical twaddle' of metaphysics that picturing plays its initial role. It is a 'great joy' to picture, to conjure thought as image, and it provides relief by reviving the spirit and awakening the senses: 'the entertainment I obtained in this way was an essential means to conquer the otherwise often unbearable boredom. I often accompany my piano playing with the relevant "picturing", particularly when I play piano arrangements.'[70] The connection to music is suggestive of the appeal to harmony, the alternative order and thought that images can provide as against the celestial modes of what we may nominate angelological intrusion.

There is another and deeper sense of *justissima tellus* that emerges in the theory of picturing, the 'as if' of the image, which is that the image attaches not to the ontology of purity, the vacancy of the excised 'ought', but rather to sense, matter and decay. It is experience that is revived, re-wrought and rejuvenated, turned to new uses, by the act of picturing: 'man retains all recollections on his nerves, *as pictures* in his head. Because my nervous system is illuminated by rays, these pictures can be voluntarily reproduced, this is in fact the nature of picturing.'[71] A vivid imagination, his words, allow the

---

[68] Schreber, *Memoirs* at 157: 'attempts were made early on and kept up throughout the years, to close my eyes against my will, so as to rob me of visual impressions and thus preserve the ray's destructive power.'

[69] Ibid. at 233.

[70] Ibid. at 234–5.

[71] Ibid. at 232–3. We can note here the commonality that Schreber's theory here shares with Hobbes' materialism. Hobbes, *Leviathan* (London: Dent, 1950 [1652]) at 10: 'For after the object is removed, or the eye shut, we still retain an image of the thing seen, though more obscure than when we see it. And this it is, the Latines call *Imagination*, from the image made in seeing . . . IMAGINATION therefore is nothing but *decaying sense*.' Italics in the original.

Judge to reproduce at will the picture of events and the procession of ideas in modalities of depiction. The image, the retention of natural phenomena, of groundedness, leads almost immediately to Schreber's picturing of himself as a woman, as changed and mutable, embodied and becoming according to the dictates of his own will and volition: *honi soit qui mal y pense* – dishonour to those who think ill of the feminine. The material of thought, the ground of the 'as if', is for Schreber corporeal and phenomenological. We start where we were, with what we have experienced, with 'this image', this body, this thought. It is, as the Judge remarks several times, the reverse of the rays, the antithesis of the anathema of the absolute and pure, the abstracted and otherworldly, but in the specific form of fusing the dualism of spectre and flesh, law and image, in the body as the thinking machine, the human and tellurian medium of the new philosophy of law as a creative and feminine endeavour.

Picturing engenders change and gives birth to a novel freedom, the self-conscious fiction of retaking the earth and establishing and investing it with a wholly human order. The prior state of affairs was one in which purity and divinity tied a misunderstood and servile humanity to celestial purposes and an extrinsic ontology that brought with it a *horror vacui* and terrible punishment, the asylum, internal or real, for those who contested it. God was guilty of 'play-with-human beings', of toying in hidden ways with human happiness, as, for example, by sending tested souls back to earth as fleeting-improvised-beings, as ghosts, to terrify and confuse the living. The rays possess unwitting humans and cause them to spout nonsense, intone voices that they do not comprehend and do harm that they are unaware of committing. This play with humans, this toying and puppeteering makes the temporal the plaything of the divine, and Schreber a wretch (*Luder*), an impure soul, in the eyes of God. Here again, however, a reversal takes shape through image and imagination.

Picturing entertains the judge, promotes musical and poetic expression and slowly turns the gravity and whiteness of the pure player against Him. Schreber satirises the divinity and laughs at the pure theory, not simply by reinventing himself, by becoming a woman, and so, in the context of his time, escaping law, outraging custom and use, but also and quite explicitly by using humour to upend the distractions and other influences of the rays. He experiences a queer humour (*sonderbare Unterhaltung*) and joking (*scherzhaft*) in the miracles, in the attempts to stun and capture him.[72] He sees through these ploys, these attempts to play with him and turns to play (*ludere*) with

---

[72] *Memoirs* at 211.

them.[73] Schreber comes to laugh at the divinity and picture ridiculous ends for the miraculous manifestations, and particularly the birds – the brainless, the birdbrains, the little girls, according to the telling diction of the psychoanalysts – that the Judge would 'jokingly (*scherzhafter Weise*)' picture being eaten by a cat. Picturing takes mental strength, energy and fortitude as it turns the external law against itself and makes it an interior will. Schreber's *Luder*, in other words, must also be understood as the Judge's game, by means of which, in his turn, having been a human plaything, he reverses the spectrum and plays with the image of God so as to rectify this 'thoroughly mismanaged affair' by becoming a woman.

[73] On the etymology of play, from the Latin *ludus*, the best source remains J. Huizinga, *Homo ludens* (New York: Roy Publishers, 1950) at 35 et seq.

5

The Judge's New Body: Am I That (Woman)?

The month of November marks an important time in the history of my life, and in particular in my own ideas of the possible shaping of my future. I remember the period distinctly; it coincided with a number of beautiful autumn days when there was a heavy morning mist on the Elbe. During that time the signs of transformation into a woman became so marked on my body, that I could no longer ignore the imminent goal at which the whole development was aiming.[1]

The easy pastoral style, the bucolic feel of the autumnal setting, the natural falling away, the sibylline turning of seasons, all suggest a certain comfort, a momentary coming to terms with transition, an acceptance of fate on the part of the Judge. The change of seasons is mimicked in the bodily transition. The mist perhaps connotes a veil, an accoutrement of desire, the accompaniment of beauty, the allure of vision naturally softened before the unveiling of the body occurs. Seduction preceding revelation. What appears most evident, however, is the trajectory back and forth between gender dysphoria and transitional relief, as also between sexes, one then the other, part and whole, bi and tri, or, as Preciado puts it, who forces one to choose?[2] Judge Schreber, Miss Schreber, Mr Ms Dr Jur. Präsident Miss Esquire, so many prefixes and suffixes to come unfixed. When the Judge collided with his past he let his body speak, the most radical of gestures and one that exceeds the structural blindness, the binary divides of law, of morals and of medicine to this day.

There is no question that Schreber struggled and suffered, doubted and regretted at various stages as his 'unmanning' (*Entmannung*) became manifest, but it also needs to be recognised that he equally if slowly came to

---

[1] *Memoirs* at 176.

[2] Preciado, *Testo Junkie* at 236: 'Why bother changing your mental state when you can change your sexopolitical status? Why change your mood when you can change identities: Behold the sexopolitical superiority of steroids.'

accept his trajectory and at times even welcomed his fate, its pleasures and hir experiences of femininity, soul voluptuousness and even blessedness. He shares both his pain and his pleasure, and throughout the *Memorabilia*, his text vividly tracing the trajectory and complexity of transition in the categories and performances of identity that the late nineteenth century struggled with as it lived out the Biblical generative dictum *masculam et feminam fecit eos* in its classical juridical form, which adds that the masculine is greater than the feminine. As for the Judge's performances of gender transition, it is the doctors, the Asylum attendants, the lawyers and the social *mores* of late nineteenth century, Lutheran, *Ludertum*, Germany that appeared most immediately not to wish to acknowledge and so sought to foreclose, to shut away his increasingly vivid experience of bodily transition, his discovery of the hedonism of the flesh and the impermanence of desire. The doctor, Flechsig, recollect, wouldn't show him how to use the scales at the Leipzig clinic, and thereby impeded also his understanding of his body, of change, of how she would weigh less so as to mean more.

A woman, recollect, could not in that era or any era before it, be a lawyer, and certainly could not be a judge. There is the literary fantasy of Portia, a foreign and feminine *persona* acting the lawyer, and there are occasional historical anecdotes of women dressed as young men and, as in the case of the daughter of the great glossator Accursius, teaching law, but the role even then remained institutionally tied to playing the part of the masculine.[3] Accursius' daughter would lecture from behind a screen so as to conceal her gender or in alternate versions of the anecdote, would dress as a man. The intimation, of course, is that the other sex obtrudes and intrudes into the jurisdiction when she claims the personality of the legal subject. By the time that Schreber was Judge, women were seeking actively to gain access to law, as yet in the main unsuccessfully, not least because of the explicitly expressed judicial view that they were infantile, fickle, mere appearance, the harbingers of seduction and distraction. They were extra, too much to be lawyers, excluded by the language as well the codes and the case law. The feminine threatened the law-school classroom, and the ancient figure of Phryne, the *hetaera* or harlot who stripped naked in front of her judges and so successfully defeated her accusers,

---

[3] On the daughter of Accursius and related anecdotes circulating in legal texts, see Peter Goodrich, Oedipus lex: *History, Psychoanalysis, Law* (Berkeley: University of California Press, 1995). For an exemplary instance of judicial hostility, see *Jex-Blake v University of Edinburgh* (1873) 11 M 784. The history is given in Albie Sachs and Joan Hoff Wilson, *Sexism and the Law: A Study of Male Beliefs and Judicial Bias* (London: Martin Robertson, 1978); and for a compelling recent overview, see Joanne Conaghan, *Law and Gender* (Oxford: Clarendon Press, 2013).

still stalked the juridical imaginary as the exemplum of the derangement that
femininity could instigate in the decisional process of law.[4] Closer to home,
to Leipzig in fact, the tension found expression in the case of the breakdown
of the first German woman lawyer, Emily Kempin, who in her turn wished
to become a man and also ended her days in the Asylum, pasting clippings
of female faces on to male bodies.[5] The Judge, in our case, was certainly
not to be encouraged to experience either corporeal change or altered gender
performances and was most definitively not supposed to become, *in nomine*
or *in re*, in name or in substance, a woman. The preclusion of these proleptic,
projected and imagined, transitions, male to female, female to male, anything
in between, and the resultant foreclosure of all intimation of gender or sex
change generates first the internal struggle that the Judge experiences and,
latterly, his external exclusion by psychiatrists and so also his incarceration.
The stage is set, the theatrical curtain raised by the famous hypnopompic
dream that, recollect, contains two crucial elements, two liminal points on
the spectrum of transition. On the one hand, and eventually victorious in its
way, the glimmering inclination and tacit desire contained in the proleptic
perception that it must be rather beautiful to yield to intercourse as a woman.
This is expressed in the positive and imperative, in the affirmation that 'it
really must be'. Here we can glimpse the glimmer of the dormant hedonic
body, the oneiric self that may just experience and relay the reverie of that
pleasure. Such an idea and connotation of implicit, repressed desire, is in
the second moment of the recollection, immediately denied as being weird
(*sonderbar*) and foreign (*fremd*) and 'I would have rejected it with indigna-
tion if fully awake.'[6] That, as Freud correctly points out, is the antinomy that
inaugurates the Judge's trajectory of struggle, his elongated and painful quest
to interiorise and incorporate what is initially apprehended as an external,
hostile and intrusive demand, a divine ploy aimed at immorally unmanning the Judge. The conventional categories, and Freud is complicit in this
manipulation, of law and the *nomos* of the body, the proper performative
order of gender display, reappear with an all too predictable certainty and
swiftness. They are protested too much and in being so bellowed they drown
out the nascent fantasy and inchoate desire of the Judge, and along with it
his manifold expressions of his theory of how that other body may come to

[4] Cornelia Vismann, 'Beyond Image', in Peter Goodrich et al., *Law, Text, Terror* (London:
    Glass House Press, 2006) at 35.
[5] The narrative of Emily Kempin-Spyri is relayed in Eveline Hasler, *Die Wachsflügelfrau*,
    trans. Edna McCown, as *Flying with Wings of Wax* (Fromm International Publishing, 1993
    [1991]).
[6] *Memoirs* at 36.

be. The Judge's sensorium, his narrative of transition, the back and forth, the doubts and the hopes, the smells, the sounds, the contortions, *eros* and anti-*eros*, deserve the space of their expression. The beginning of the process, the Spring, the conception of his rebirth as opposed to the ease of the Fall and the autumnal retraction of the flesh, is antinomic, painful, protracted and nerve wracking. Law and lawyers are slow to change and when the abrogation is as radical as playing a feminine role, multiplication or change of gender, taking the shape of the other sex, of the third sex in the argot of the time, it is bound to be wrapped in an interiorised sense of splitting, of retention and relinquishment.[7] For the Judge there was the immediate loss of status and legal personality, and then incarceration, surveillance, diagnosis as mad, in a tradition that returns to Hippocrates. The resistance, anxiety and denial he experiences are particularly predictable facets of legal conventions that historically insist upon warning against all novelty – *novum omne cave* – and demand obedience to custom and use in all matters. *Eppur si muove*, and yet it moves. The change, the internal elopement of the Jurist, the transitional desire proves throughout too strong a force, too interior a drive to repress for long. The structure of this transition, the opposed forces or in Fernie's analysis the process of possession of the Judge's body, is visceral and at times shattering, upending or what in French is termed *bouleversant*. The sudden emergence of an *argumentum ad feminam* in the entrails of the Judge was always likely to meet juristic, theological and psychiatric resistance.

The starting point is the legal exclusion of the feminine that goes back to early Roman law and stems from the *Digest* 1.9.1 (Ulpian) that states unequivocally that the condition of women is inferior to that of men.[8] Later reception of the text did not stint in its application of that principle, and women were expansively excluded from the polity because they did not have *potestatem*, they lacked capacity and personality, and because they importuned, could not bring lawsuits. Subject to a male parent, guardian or husband, if they suffered the sexual abuse that Schreber sometimes admits to fearing may be inflicted on him in his new identity, then only if their male master, guardian or tutor brings the claim can a wrong be asserted. At its

---

[7] Alfred Delvau, *Dictionnaire de la langue verte* (1866), 'troisième sexe: celui qui déshonore les deux autres' (the third sex, the one that dishonours the two others) cited in Laure Murat, *La Loi du genre* at 195–205, on the archaeology of transsexualism.

[8] *Digest* 1.9.1. *detior est conditio feminarum quam masculorum*. The theme is taken up in similar form in the common law reception of Roman law, in Henry de Bracton, *De Legibus et consuetudinibus Angliae* (On the Laws and Customs of England) (London: Ricahard Totell, 1569 [1189]). These and further texts are discussed at length in Peter Goodrich, *Oedipus lex*, chapter 3.

highest points, the juristic denigration of the feminine includes among its dismissive accolades the opinion of the humanist lawyer Cujas that woman was not properly speaking human – *Foemina item non est proprie homo.*[9] For Alciatus, citing to a classical *topos* and formula, the question *quid est mulier?* – what is a woman? – receives the expansive and dramatic answer that she is 'the ruin of man, an insatiable beast, continual disquiet, and unlimited disturbance'.[10] Salic law, that of France, famously precluded the inheritance of land by women and both at common and civil law the feminine equated with the infantile, the evidentially fickle and unreliable.[11] It was not a status to which a man, let alone a judge, would aspire, and thus Schreber's initial and terrified incomprehension, his praise and longing for his previous profession, for his manly (*männlichen*) ambitions and the proper juridical exercise of his intellectual powers. An interiorised sexual identity and public commitment, the office and role of juridical male, cannot be overthrown in an instant, nor can its routines and trappings, its repetitions and enactments be reversed with ease. The silenced is not easily spoken.

The process of transformation, the transitional identity, so often ignored by the analysts as being simply a sign of madness, of megalomania or even fascism, because of the struggle with external prohibitions, with God and law, merits careful reconstruction. The conflicted feelings, the sense of nostalgia for the old law, for a professional identity, its certainty and its virility, in legal argot, its *vim et potestatem*, are proclaimed and then negated rather brilliantly with the statement, Bartleby like in its expression: 'I would like to meet the man who, faced with the choice of either becoming a demented human being in male habitus or a spirited woman, would not prefer (*vorziehen*) the latter. Such and *only such* is the issue (*die Frage*) for me.'[12] It is this clarity of vision, this unequivocal drive or libidinal propulsion that explains the persistence and fortitude of the Judge in the face of extreme hostility, denunciation, abandonment and what he may well have viewed, with some justification, as his extraordinary rendition.

The principal obstacle to becoming a woman is less technological or pharmacological, for Schreber, than socio-legal, being that of facing the rejection of his colleagues, his wife and his wider family, and that collective moral censure that variously travels under the sign of the social, nature, or, for the

[9] Jacques Cujas, *Opera Omnia* (Lyons: Bonhomme, 1567) at 34–5.

[10] Andreus Alciatus, *De notitia dignitatum* (Paris: Cramoisy, 1651) at 190.

[11] See especially Antoine Hotman, *Traité de la loi Salique* (Paris: Cramoisy, 1593); and for an English equivalent, Sir John Fortescue, *De natura legis naturae* (London: Society of Stationers, 1466) in *The Works of John Fortescue* (1869).

[12] Schreber, *Memoirs* at 178; emphasis in the original.

Judge, that of a dualistic – Manichean – God. To borrow from Murat's sympathetic account of the intermediate sex, transition is less outside of the law of nature than by nature outside of the law of genre.[13] Eric Santner has traced at length, and with considerable insight, the gendered character of the war that the Judge, in claiming to become a woman, conducts with the divinity. He is thrust towards abjection, insulted, called a wretch – *Luder*.[14] The term *Luder*, of course, carries gendered valences as well, of death, putrescent flesh and wanton sexuality. In almost theological tones, the wretch is an image, a woman, a harridan and whore.[15] There is no question that the struggle, the abjection and the turmoil are real, as also the defining out is precise and painful, but as adverted earlier, it is equally important to note the trajectory of this transitional desire, the gender dysphoria and its path eventually even to 'palms of victory' or homecoming. The pain is palliated and there follow moments of enjoyment, of intense pleasure, of imaginary, which is to say phantasmatic relief, and thus the incursion or *détournement* that supplies the missing element of the human comedy, the dark humour, the puns and plays and, in sum, Schreber's game, the conjunction, present throughout in the Judge's text, of law and laughter, of absurdity and gravity, of struggle and hope. The key point is that *Luder* can be twisted many ways and has further and more positive ludic dimensions as well as those noted by Santner, of the 'German vice', of abjection, pain and prostitution.[16] It is this dialectical torsion, the comedic coupling of opposites and, specifically, the humour, both dark and mirthful, of ideas expressed in body parts, the internal assertion of the feminine as well as the pain of external rejection, and the legal fight that ensues, that need to be expounded as the narrative of this exceptional transition between radical extremes.

Immediately after being labelled 'Luder', a wretch, or at least after hearing the resounding and mighty bass voice of the lower God Ariman 'directly in front of my bedroom windows', and after noting the unfriendly sounding words used, including the frequent expression *Luder*, there is a sudden shift that Santner does not cite: 'Yet everything that was spoken was genuine, was true (*echt*), not phrases learnt by rote as they later were, but immediate

---

[13] Murat, *La Loi du genre* at 49–54.

[14] Santner, *My Own Private Germany* at 41–3, arguing that God transforms Schreber into a *Luder*, resulting, through mental and physical torture, in the 'production in the subject of a heightened experience of *abjection*'. Emphasis in the original.

[15] Santer, *The Royal Remains*, continues the pursuit of this theme, particularly at 104, 164.

[16] Murat, *La Loi du genre*, discusses the conjunctions Berlin–Sodom, and Paris–Lesbos, from which the 'German vice', namely pederasty, derives, as part of the debate and phantasy in late nineteenth-century France.

expression of true feeling (*wirklichen Empfindung*).'[17] What was being expressed in the nomination *Luder* was real life, actual inclinations, surprising and voluble sentiments betraying a conflicted divinity, a screaming exteriority, a threatened realm but also a desiring order and trajectory of change and its bittersweet embrace. The force that presses towards the nocturnal, perhaps also the dreaming volition of the Judge, acts as an attraction, an oneiric or at least allegorical figuration, whose interpretation should by now be somewhat simpler than the prior and largely prejudged categories – lunacy, perversion, catastrophe, megalomania, anti-Semitism, fascism, to name but a few. The image is important, the spirit and sound that wants to come in through the window being the mark of the trajectory – the *via regia* – to the interior of *homo fenestris,* as the Judge must surely be recognised to be. One could even add that when the expression *Luder* next appears, it is when little men appear in his 'mind's eye' (*geistigen Auge*) and on his eyelids, from where he would wipe them away with a sponge.[18] These little men, these merely masculine *homunculi,* these deprived, impure, tested and partially disembodied hostile figures, the 'little Fleschsig', the 'little von W.', occupied themselves with pulling the eyelids open and closed, seeking to interrupt and if possible destroy thought. The 'little devils' compress the head, cause pain and interfere as much as possible with the Judge's soul. It is significantly the Judge's perception, his picturing and vision, the relation of inside to outside, that the window of the eye both represents and facilitates that is to be obstructed, so that his transition, transcendence and so accession to the law of his own body be impeded. These little devils, the little wardens, clerks, doctors and lawyers, are the traces of the absurdity of a virile world that seeks, in medicine and in law, to preclude and exclude the expansion of experience and the fluctuation of gender, the transition that the Judge, by his own account, were it ever to be listened to, is committed and impelled to embrace and express.

It is, for the Judge, specifically a question of vision and most particularly of body image, its pains and its pleasures. He goes on in a footnote, confutation yet again of the ludicrous notion that he had no sense of irony, nor ever used metaphor, to observe 'of course one can *not* see with the *bodily* eye what goes on inside one's own body . . . but . . . one can see it with *one's mind's eye,* as the necessary illumination of the inner nervous system provided by rays'.[19] In being transitive, mobile and sonorous, the passage of the spirit and

17 Schreber, *Memoirs* at 136.
18 Ibid. at 158. My thanks to Daniela Gandorfer for pointing this, and much else, out to me. Schreber goes on in a footnote, confutation yet again of the ludicrous notion that he had no sense of irony, nor ever used metaphor.
19 Ibid. at 158–9; emphasis in the original. The concept of multiple 'eyes' is familiar in

the significance of the inner portrait and portrayal should be understood as indicators of change, as reflections, depictions of the Judge's journey and desire, as well as being metaphorical approaches to the sound barrier, and to the window, to the liminal bursting point of the changing body image, and the literal *ecstasis,* the movement, that it promises.[20] What is vital, and omitted from Santner's otherwise compelling reading, is that, in this instance, the Judge is neither afraid nor fearful, but rather, in his own fine words, his impression is 'largely one of admiration for the magnificent and sublime', so much so that overall, after sharing the image, the dialectical vision, the interiority of his morphing, he feels a calming effect and eventually falls back to sleep.[21] It could be argued that the Judge's abjection is his pleasure, his finely detailed record of the law of his transition a masochistic assignment of guilt and application of punishment precisely to the process of transformation.[22] Certainly, what seems most crucial to Schreber is that his passage, the process of interior disruption, contortion and bodily change be acknowledged, measured and respected. The nerves and rays can see within, can read his images, can view his change but the lawyers and the wardens and keepers of the asylum cannot and will not. Good Judge that he is, he calls for measurement, for *nomos,* for objective study of his changing state, in the hope of garnering support, proffering empirical proof, using science and law to further his cause in tellurian and synaesthetic confines, its impure and incarnadine state. The very opening of his Preface to the *Memorabilia* states, second sentence: 'Yet I believe that expert examination of my body . . . would have value for science and the knowledge of religious truths.'[23] At other junctures, this appeal to science, to proof and thus the reality of what he feels, the emanation and measurable spectral evidence of his becoming feminised, the recognition of

---

theology. The mind's eye (*oculi animi*), the eye of the spirit (*oculi spiritus*), the eye of the soul. My favourite discussion of such themes, from Bishop John Jewel, who is not usually deemed psychotic, is as follows, citing from St Chrysostom: 'the eyes of the spirit are able to see the things that be not seen, and have no being'. John Jewel, *A Defence of the Apology of the Church of England* (London: Fleetstreet, 1567) at 273.

[20] As the window is an important metaphor in the *Memorabilia*, it is worth just signalling the wonderful study of Gérard Wacjman, *Fenêtre. Chroniques du regard et de l'intime* (Paris: Verdier, 2004). There is a translation of one portion of the text in *Lacanian Ink* (2006).

[21] Schreber, *Memoirs*, 137.

[22] On masochism and the law, Deleuze's analysis of *Venus in Furs* remains unsurpassed, see *Masochism* (Zone Books, 1989) Ch. VII (Humor, Irony and the Law). There is *jouissance* in the suffering, desire propels and drives the transitional, however hard, however socially contested and personally costly the process. It is that desire, recognition of its possessiveness, that seeks recognition.

[23] Schreber, *Memoirs*, iii.

his being also a woman, repeat in ever more intense form: 'There is only one point I wish to explain now: that I would at all times be prepared to submit my body to medical examination for ascertaining whether my assertion is correct, that my whole body is filled with nerves of voluptuousness from the top of my head to the souls of my feet, such as is the case only in the adult female body.'[24] He is offering himself, his body, as an auto-icon, as an object of study and science, so that others can profit from his suffering, so that his pain can do some good.[25] So it rolls on, alternately convulsively and voluptuously, the Judge increasingly at ease with the incontestable changes in his appearance, his image of his female buttocks, retracted genitalia, breasts and slimmed-down form.

Yet no-one seems to pay much attention to these appeals to science, even now, when embodiment is simply significant prosthesis, when pharmaco-pornography can alter sexopolitical states, and xenofeminism allows a multitude of non-binary forms, the diagnosticians and the thematics of analysis still refuse to put him on the fanged scales that may measure his feminine sensibilities, his interior mutations, let alone apply a juristic lesbian rule to his sense of a morphing frame, as if he has somehow become untouchable, resistant to all study, the silent object of medical diagnosis and exclusion. His treatment is effectively to 'act normal', take dinner at High Table with the warden of the Asylum, Dr Weber, and converse with women as if he were still simply and only a man. The good Judge not only shows a certain sympathy for this dictate that he in effect 'shut up', but also displays a remarkable talent for the aimless disquisition of bourgeois *politesse*. Even his physician, and self-proclaimed friend, Dr Weber, says as much, although doubting that it is grounds for release: 'he was well-behaved and amiable during light conversation with the ladies present and his humour was always tactful and decent; during the harmless table talk he never brought up anything which should not have been introduced there but during medical visits.'[26] The interior, the belief system, the psychic change and its rampant desire for expression is entirely shunned by the medical establishment, except insofar as it is the referent for the exclusion of the Judge as mad, in oppositionally composed reports and filings to the Courts. As, at the time, it was a priori impossible for

---

[24] Schreber, *Memoirs*, 274.

[25] It is not insignificant that Jeremy Bentham, author, *inter alia*, of the *Theory of Fictions*, also offered his body to science and it remains to this day, though in a wax form, the original having suffered deterioration through insect attacks and student misuse, in the foyer of University College London. The story is told in C. F. A. Marmoy, 'The Auto-Icon of Jeremy Bentham at University College, London,' II *Medical History* 77-86 (1958).

[26] Schreber, *Memoirs* at 397–8.

Schreber to be or become a woman, there was no point it seems in extracting any libidinal detail, any expressions, let alone any *nomos* of the flesh.

It is for this reason, because of the 'scientific' evasion of desire, that the more interesting passages, those that subtend his exterior and objective changes, the ones that he wants measured, confirmed and doubtless also affirmed, but that never are, is that internal and erotic description of decomposition and re-composition from Judge to *optima femina*, the best woman that a man can be, if the medieval Latin maxims so brilliantly studied by Kantorowicz can be shifted into a feminine mood.[27] Eventually, as Fernie succinctly puts it, Schreber 'ends by enthusiastically getting down to it' and embraces his female identity, the interiority and erotic imagination of both sex and sensuality.[28] The site of this enthusiasm, of the shift from legal body to feminised flesh, would today be the object of extensive therapeutic discussion, airing and elaboration, as well as potentially, if rarely, being confirmed through painful but possible surgery. As Schreber puts it, with remarkable insight and not a little wit, whether or not his 'so-called "delusions" and "hallucinations"' can be proved by reasoned argument as to their truth is not really the issue, and is hardly possible in his current environment, and so the verification and meaning of his transformation is a *topos* that, in his own words, 'the future alone can decide'.[29]

The future, as I have argued at length, has been rather over-determined by the psychoanalytic and psychiatric assumption that it is Schreber's lunacy, his tragic and titanic struggle against Freud's assumed image of the father, fostered and furthered by the pontifical Lacan, that needs to be elicited, examined, explained, rather than his lucidity and the positivity of his interior record, the manifestations, strangulated for obvious reasons, but equally evident and vibrant, that need expatiation and explication. The Judge is clear that the change is coming, that his body has duplicated and blurred, become masculine *and* feminine, and that this inexorable passage cannot but be followed, manifested and recorded. His journey starts with the embracing of this new corporeal state and sense, 'unperturbed by the judgment of other people', even that of his wife, because, as he observes in a footnote, 'I can deplore this, but am unable to change it; even here I must guard against false sentimentality.'[30] The Judge is clear that he must be true to himself, honest and unflinching in his admission and embrace of the ambiguity of bodily change and burgeoning desire, the voluptuousness that alone seems to allow

[27] Kantorowicz, *The King's Two Bodies* at 61 discussing *optimus homo*.
[28] Fernie, *The Demonic* at 281.
[29] Schreber, *Memoirs* at 274.
[30] Ibid. at 178, and 179 fn 76.

him some peace and sleep. We can trace two levels of this becoming feminine, this ceasing to exist as man, as Lacan may put it, in serial or progressive order of intensity.

The first is palliative, performative and local in the sense of reflecting the general precepts and gender divisions of his era. The Judge experiences considerable conflict, pain and at times guilt and remorse at the change of sex and role. He notes this at several points and focuses upon the *physical* dimensions of transition, commenting at one point that 'particularly helpful for my bodily well-being are those jobs which count as feminine occupations, for instance sewing, dusting, making beds, washing up and so on. Even now there are days when apart from playing the piano I can occupy myself only with such trifles.'[31] It is hard, in other words, to adapt to the new physical form, the body image and role that becoming a woman imposes on the turn-of-the-century male lawyer, and it requires ploys and plays, jokes and other ruses to be bearable and in time enjoyable. Thus, also, the wearing of female 'adornments', which the Court and Freud both treat as important because they are harmless projections, rather than as the surface manifestation of deep-seated and viscerally core expressions of desire to transform, to play a different role, to be in a feminine and hedonic erotic mode, or in Judith Butler's parlance, to get to repeat.[32] Wrapped in the banner of his desire to be a woman, dressing and acting the part, as he conceives it, locked in the Asylum, within a conventional frame of feminine sense and sensibility, it is hard to imagine what else the Judge could have done to signal his transitional drive.[33] The *Luder*, the bellowing, the satirical and parodic outbursts are modes of theatricalisation of juridical rage, forms of becoming which, to borrow from Preciado again, allow that '[l]aughter is a form of resistance,

---

[31] Ibid.

[32] Judith Butler, *Gender Trouble: Feminism and the Subversion of Identity* (London: Routledge, 1989), of course, and also Butler, *Bodies that Matter: On the Discursive Limits of Sex* (London: Routledge, 1993).

[33] On the stereotyping of the feminine in the juridical, see the excellent Greta Olson, 'Law is not Turgid and Literature not Soft and Fleshy: Gendering and Heteronormativity in Law and Literature Scholarship', 36 *Australian Feminist Law Journal* 65–83 (2012). See also Preciado, *Testo Junkie* at 289: on the rhetoric of gender, in which 'sure, stable, and permanent implies industrial and male and flexible, changeable, mobile, and precarious implies postindustrial and female'. From another perspective, one in which the weight of sex is embedded in the structure of discourse and is carried in language, see Yvette Russell, 'Woman's Voice/Law's Logos: The Rape Trial and the Limits of Liberal Reform', 42 *Australian Feminist Law Journal* 273 (2016) at 290: 'the erasure of the feminine, of woman, within the deep economy of language generally, is also found in legal discourse, and therefore also in the rape trial – the very space in which law has no choice but to confront woman.'

survival, a way of mustering forces. Shouting too. When you belong to an oppressed group, you have to learn how to laugh in the face of the enemy.'[34]

Underlying the role-playing, the offices and apparel of the feminine, the appearance of being woman, is the much more forceful libidinal drive, the tearing and unnerving push and pull of feminine against masculine that for the Judge is eased only when he gives way to the hedonic and erotic imagination of transformation, the completion of the trajectory of being woman through housing in interiority, in the mind's eye, in image, the contortions, the pleasure and pain of the tactile and libidinal body, the feminine as desire. Here it is sensual pleasure, heightened states of erotic gratification, a tensile and sexualised body, that mark the feminine and thus also the Judge's projected future state: 'when I exert light pressure with my hand on any part of my body I can *feel* certain string or cord-like structures under the skin; these are particularly marked on my chest where the woman's bosom is . . . Through pressure on one such structure I can produce a feeling of female sensuous pleasure, particularly if I think of something feminine.'[35] The becoming woman, the changes in the body, the libidinal surge are expressly recorded by Schreber as 'subjectively certain' (*subjektiv gewiß*), as transitional in the sense of not yet being necessarily or objectively fully present, as his intensive body contracts and expands according to the dialectic of his own struggle. On the one hand, the *pousse-à-la-femme*, and pitched against this drive or symptom, depending upon your perspective, the resistance, the male objection, the fight to maintain social appearances, to convince the warders and latterly the judges that he is legally competent, sane and can be released, despite the wild views, the metaphysics, the becoming woman and most of all the *soi-disant* medical betrayals that masquerade as judgments. The path to his sense of what he lacks, physical pleasure, voluptuousness of body and soul, is hardly ever easy and for a senior Judge in late nineteenth-century Germany that represents a considerable understatement, and yet Schreber persists, stays with it and yields to his desires. Thus, he relentlessly records and relays his perception of 'the actual sensation (*tatsächliche Wahrnehmung*) of voluptuousness', the 'impression (*Eindruck*) of a pretty well-developed female bosom', the feminine buttocks and the 'undoubted impression (*unzweifelhaften Eindruck*) of a female torso (*weiblichen Oberkörpers*)', even when the last sensation is not enhanced by female attire. The Judge is also determined to maintain the appearance of propriety in his transition and thus the interior conflict, the stress, the bellowing and the laughter that capture his sense of

---

[34] Preciado, *Testo Junkie* at 136 (citing 1970s feminist activist Faith Ringgold).
[35] Schreber, *Memoirs* at 277; emphasis in the original.

the absurd, his phantasmatic access to a supernatural voluptuousness, never intending, he assures his audience, the Asylum, Court and posterity '*any sexual desires towards other human beings (females) least of all sexual intercourse*'. The passage being in italics throughout in the original, to stress the importance, the gravity of his commitment to hygiene, as well as to marriage and to its law. Thus, he continues, 'I have to imagine myself as man and woman in one person having intercourse with myself, or somehow have to achieve with myself a certain sexual excitement.'[36] All of this, the concealment, the internalisation, the auto-affection is made necessary, Schreber proclaims loudly, as 'the art of conducting my life in the bizarre (*verrückten Lebenslage*) position I find myself' by which he means expressly 'the sense-defying (*Widersinnige*) relation between God and myself'.[37] Explicitly both male and female, housing two souls in one body, the Judge records how he is impelled by seemingly external forces, an alien interiority, by God, or we may say by birth, by nature, by genes, by choice, to feminine inclinations, to affections that he and his professional environments, legal and medical, both vehemently resist. To the end, there can be no public display, and the Judge is left with the painful tearing of the impetus to womanhood while acknowledging both the unreal quality of his situation and the unstoppable subjective force of his desires. If hell is other people, Schreber certainly has his share of the inferno. Exteriority constantly demands conformity, the appearance of his sexual offices, the sound of his genuflection. He has to fight himself, conduct an interior war, act the lawyer so as to be released, while inside he screams and bellows, howls and hallucinates, and hears voices mocking, insulting, provoking, cajoling and stringing him along as he nonetheless fearlessly pursues his inner imperative, his libidinal economy, which is perhaps always at some level a hidden force: 'if only I could *always* be playing the woman's part in sexual embrace with myself, *always* rest my gaze on female beings, *always* look at female pictures, etc.'[38] In a postscript dated 1901, in miscellaneous considerations on the future, the Judge repeats both the struggle between his conflicted feelings, the pain of transformation and the pleasure of his changing sex: 'there are periods every day, when I float in voluptuousness so to speak, i.e. when an indescribable feeling of well-being corresponding to feminine feelings of voluptuousness pervades my whole body.'[39] He hastens to add that such erotic pleasure is not always sexual, but can also be tied to poetry, music and art. The Judge is here forging his own path, owning his *eros*, his sex and his

---

[36] Ibid at 282; emphasis in the original.
[37] Ibid at 283–4.
[38] Ibid at 285; emphasis in the original.
[39] Ibid at 336.

aesthetics, in sum changing his being, his praxis, his mode of enacting the self in everyday life. The new identity and desire of the Judge is necessary in the last instance so as to restore the Order of the World and, one can suppose, so as to instantiate, legitimate and make a space for his right to feminine feeling and expression. Law was inadequate, the *morbus juridicus* profound, and the Judge has no choice but to restructure himself so as to rectify his image of the world. The Judge's body divides into two warring parts, blurring the distinction between masculine and feminine, merging *animus* and *anima* in precisely the same sense that the text diffracts and mingles lunacy and law, madness and the conventions of sanity. His alternating trajectory between the categories, his pure embrace of impurity, serves to enact, among other things, a jurisprudential transition in which the mystic body, the *corpus iuris mysticum*, becomes in *ecce homo*, Judge Daniel Paul Schreber, the *corpus physicum* of a novel and earthly justice, the *justissima tellus* of an aesthetic, erotic, harmonious and most of all human sensibility. The English jurist Blackstone remarks that Judges are a mirror in which the face of the King, not of justice, appears.[40] And in regard to Schreber a similar metaphor of the speculum could opine that the Judge's body no longer reflects God, King or dogma, but a species of post-servile race, *humanitas*, a new people as imagined into being by the libidinal creativity, the erotic art and musical aesthetic that the *Memorabilia* have struggled so magnificently to introduce. It is not, however, as is usually the case, a change of mind, a new theory that has engendered this juridical theology of human independence, but rather a change of body image, the Judge's duplication of the *corporae* of law in his vivid although, save in text, ultimately unsuccessful temporal transformation. The Judge's soul, to paraphrase and subvert the Foucault of *Discipline and Punish*, has become to all appearances the prisoner of its mutating, splitting, torturing experience of the body. The question, juristically, as obvious as it is latent, because utterly unexamined, is that of what is to be made of the Judge who aspires to the feminine, who believes he is becoming a man and a woman? It should be acknowledged first that the Judge's book, his graphic records and wild conceptual pictures of sex change break new ground. Where the lawyers had

---

[40] William Blackstone, *Commentaries on the Laws of England* (Chicago: Chicago University Press, 1978 [1765]) 1.7 (On Persons) depicting the royal prerogative, remarking 'a consequence of this prerogative is the legal ubiquity of the king. His majesty, in the eye of the law, is always present in all his courts, though he cannot personally distribute justice. His judges are the mirror by which the king's image is reflected. It is the regal office and not the royal person that is always present.' For a brilliant discussion of this and related themes, see Philip Manow, *In the King's Shadow: The Political Anatomy of Democratic Representation* (Cambridge: Polity, 2010) at 50–6.

previously distinguished the mystic body and dignity of office from the temporal being of the body natural, Schreber's fight is to inaugurate a novel and unified body, against the divinity and in exclusion of God from the Order of the World. The *corpus mysticum* of the sovereign being, the God whose death inaugurated the late nineteenth-century investiture crisis, was in Schreber very much alive rather than immortalised, as Nietzsche has it, by assassination. God was to be exiled to a great distance, but in recognition of the fact that the divinity is simply displaced rather than removed by execution, the Judge's war with the spirit world is precisely to embody the divine principle in his own flesh. We are witness in the *Memorabilia* to an episode of incarnation, the birth of a novel duality in which the imagined body of the abstract deity is transformed into the corporeal, living and breathing, noisy and smelly, tintinnabulating and hallucinating *corpus physicum*, that is Schreber. What is born is a new duality of law and desire, of Judge as incorporating a woman, which engenders a feminine principle, an unheard of *anima* inside the jurist and to whose desires the Judge was frequently attentive and sometimes captive. After all, as it is relayed, when the Judge looks in the mirror he sees a woman.[41] In an argument that has been well traversed by others, the transition of sacrality from one imagined body to another is precisely a displacement, a continuation of the dual ontologies of form and content, ought and is, purity and *humus* that Hans Kelsen, in particular, elaborated brilliantly in relation to law as a system, an order, an ether and architectonic. The 'worship of legal science', of abstraction and purity, propels the Schreberian reversal, that seeks to give birth to an alternate self, a *persona non data*. His is an incarnadine jurisprudence, sanguinated, full of *humus*, tellurian, full of entrails, both cacchinating and in an ambivalent fashion copraphilic. The episode of incarnation is unique, despite its extraordinary *difficilitas conveniendi*, the painful tearing apart of his body, in that he seeks to accommodate the newly unified duality in one person, one body, one law. To borrow from Kantorowicz, he becomes that person 'who is in the highest degree One' within their own kind, representative of *humanitas*, in the *genus humanum*.[42] The sacral of course remains but it is properly elsewhere in the Judge's world order, as he embraces his own sanctity as flesh, as nerves and rays, that once combined, also figure the image of a feminine persona and office. It is, of course, an impossible unity that Schreber essays, or at least it is unacceptable to his epoch and moral times, and so he has to bellow it from behind bars or hide it to pass quietly, reasonably, as a legal actor. If there is a model, distant

---

[41] *Memoirs* at 429, 'at times I was seen standing in front of the mirror or elsewhere with some female adornments (*weiblichem Zierrath*).'

[42] Kantorowicz, *Two Bodies* at 461.

but pertinent, for this painful suppression of the flesh, the repressed body of the Judge, it is that of a translated masculinity, and, to coin an annoying because temporary phrase, *foemina instrumentum humanitatis*. Kantorowicz traces the juristic trajectory that underlies Dante's poetic inscription of a human sovereignty, centred upon *humanitas* rather than the mystery of divinity.[43] Borrowing from the jurists, the ceremonial figure of the leader was to be *philosophissimus*, the most philosophical of authorities whose imperium was to coincide with his theoretical acumen and perception of ends.[44] What was crucial to such a designation and presumably so disorienting to Schreber was the sacred, the concept of the no more one, more than one, that constitutes the collectivity of the human, the body politic as figured in the Judge but stripped of all ceremonial trappings and support. He had to make his own, the feminine adornments, the female breasts and buttocks, the diminished torso and recumbent sexual position all enact a becoming, an incarnation, a ceremonial re-entry into the realm of the redefinition of the symbolic. It is this making flesh, perhaps more than anything, that marks the lucidity and jurisprudential value of Schreber's vision. Free to choose between *papatus* and *imperiatus*, the Judge seeks his place *naturam non gratiam,* by nature and not by grace: 'an intellectual and moral baptism by transference' into humanity in a 'para-sacramental' fashion.[45] The displacement from the ecclesiastical to the temporal, into *humanitas*, as Kantorowicz has elaborated, crowns Adam through an intellectual baptism, instilling the *virtutes intellectuales* upon the dual symbol, effigy and figure of the first, best and One, human being: *corpus mysticum Adae quod est humanitas* – a phrase that indicatively enough simply replaces Christ with Adam, and the Church with humanity. The human body, the *corpus iuris humanitatis*, may again appear split, a divided entity, imbued interestingly enough with rays of intellectual virtue and beatitude, and joins *Adam subtilis*, an innocent, Edenic, human, with *Adam mortalis*, an ambulant image and flesh. The shift that Kantorowicz and others have remarked from Church to humanity, the transition to the lawyer poet's adumbration of the tellurian body, makes room for a radical shift in focus, a potentially democratic turn 'in which humanity took rule over the

---

[43] Ibid. at 451 et seq. Santner, *Royal Remains*, in the epilogue also picks up on this trajectory, arguing that the structure and dynamics of monarchy do not disappear but rather 'migrate into a new location, which thereby assumes a turbulent and disorienting semiotic density previously concentrated in, to use Foucault's formulation once again, the "strange material and physical presence" of the king' (245). A similar argument is made also in Manow, *In the King's Shadow* particularly 26–38.

[44] Kantorowicz, *Two Bodies* at 455–7.

[45] Ibid. at 492.

human'.[46] The 'Dignity of Man' included supreme jurisdiction over man *qua* mortal man, regardless of position and rank, while 'he who was in the highest degree One within his kind', acted as the instrument of that Dignity – '*homo instrumentum humanitas*'.[47] Schreber's war against the divinity both reflects and exceeds the para-ecclesiastical investiture of humanity in the early juristic conceptual elaborations. He conflates and joins an immanent duality and what were traditionally *virtutes infusae,* virtues infused by the divinity, become for the Judge, through his prolonged struggle and conversion of the divine rays to his own purposes, at least in potential, humanly acquired. Born of struggle, however, Schreber *subtilis et mortalis*, has to live with the fact that his investiture, his infusion and Oneness are acquired by means of his own induction into his own offices. It is a radical step beyond the Adamite figuration of the human in the myth of the first man, because it implodes the historical and figurative, the symbolic and juridical into the singular body of the Seer and Judge, *philosophissimus*, himself as both *genus* and *species humanum*, both body and idea, *anima* and *animus*, or in whatever version, vice versa, occasion prefers.[48] As he puts it, returning to the *ipsissima verba* of the Judge: 'I have gained the certain conviction that spontaneous generation (parentless generation, *generatio aequivoca*) does in fact exist' by means of miracles and 'due to the divine power of will or divine power of creation'.[49] It is that very power that Schreber struggles to incorporate and to manifest as creative force, as rejuvenating spirit, as virtue and as the restorer of the proper order of a world free of God.

There is also, of course, the twist in the tail of Schreber's transformation, and in his juridical theology, which is that his self-investiture is necessary because he is becoming a woman. Where historically the investiture of the woman is by the offices of the man, the priest, the Church, the law (ecclesiastical), for Schreber it is the woman who invests the man and induces the union, the *generatio* that here becomes *instauratio aequivoca*. One could argue here that, *per naturam non gratiam*, man cannot make woman, but woman can engender man. The miraculous, the Duke of Argyll's mystic hand, Kelsen's *Grundnorm*, the big Other in its various guises, all externalise the generation of change and the source of the power that makes it possible.

---

[46] Notably Victoria Kahn, 'Political Theology and Fiction in *The King's Two Bodies*', 106 *Representations* 79 (2009); Santner, *Royal Remains* at 43–7, and epilogue.

[47] Kantorowicz, *Two Bodies* at 493.

[48] On the distinction and play of *animus* and *anima*, whose androgynous reference comes from Karl Jung, the text I prefer is Gaston Bachelard, *The Poetics of Reverie* (Boston: Beacon Press, 1971).

[49] Schreber, *Memoirs* at 241.

For Schreber, inducing transformation, social and corporeal, and thence the instantiation of a proper order, alike require the internalisation, the taking hold of the rays and transforming them, as power, as pure creativity, into his own nerves, flesh and erotic ligatures. The immanent embrace and flowering of the interior principle of the miraculous is that of the labour of birthing a new order and law. His virtue and philosophy, what the Judge wishes to infuse, is a principle of spiritual harmony, the One, as the expression of the essence of the human in separation, distinction and opposition to the divine, which has to withdraw to its colossal and indistinct distance. Thus, in answer to the question of what it means to make law feminine and tactile, to invest the juridical office of the woman, the preliminary answer is that it means picturing a libidinal substrate, an erotic and fleshy source of law, membrane, touch, sound and smell as also aspects of an aesthetic, ethics and synaesthesia of legality. The *corpus iuris*, as subject, as persona, becomes literally this legal body, this flesh, here and now.

Schreber is very precise in terms of what his body experiences, and thus provides significant detail of the corporeal sensations, the sounds and sights, as well as of the expansions and retractions, contractions and dilations, the multiple excitations that mark the passage to the image of the feminine and, in his case, its secular lunacy, its veiled and illicit corpuscular law. If we return to Sanders argument that it was the inability to use the scales that most definitively marks the legal character of his nervous breakdown, then allowing them 'their full judicial symbolism' means recognising a deficit of justice, an imbalance in the moral order, in the customs and principles of *lex terrae* that demarcate and impel the Judge's novel jurisdiction and the need to weigh both the body as change and the rule of law as an obstacle to transformation. The impure is factual, corporeal, tactile, sensory and libidinal. These sensory elements of surface and dirt, of the alien and impure are precisely what the neo-Kantian philosophical drive in the legal theory of his day tried to expel as involving will, interpretation, morality, policy and politics, everything in sum that is necessary to judgment, the act that legitimises or in the case of Schreber's greater sensitivity unsettles and expands, corporealises and so actualises the judicial figure.[50] For Schreber the body becomes the site and source of interpretation and judgment. The flesh, the nerves, the rays, the emanations, the visions, the 'alucinations', the conceptual wanderings and auditory cacophonies are the very material of decision, of the cutting, of determining

---

[50] Sanders, 'Psychoanalysis, Mourning and the Law' at 132: 'I am putting forward a more specific explanation, proposing that we have before us a crisis of judging. I am with Duncan Kennedy when he observes that the legitimacy of a judge depends on the manner in which he or she decides cases' (footnote omitted).

how to give to each their due in proper effectuation of the purpose of judgment. It is precisely this wild array of empirical and emotional factors that
intervene and corrupt the purity of abstract regimes or architectonics of regulation. This stuff of interpretation, the tellurian and corporeal is the essence
of the Judge's dispute and defection from the ranks of jurists intent upon a
science of law and a totalising codification, replete with its self-completing
mechanisms of automatic gap filling and compelled thought. The gap in the
extant theory of law was either that it interpreted, as did conceptual jurisprudence (*Begriffsjurisprudenz*), by cognitive elaboration of the abstract system,
without connection to the real, body or practice or, as with Hans Kelsen, the
science of law, the Pure Theory, by means of avoidance in arguing that
the theory should have no role to play in the alien and irrational practice of
actual, empirical decision-making. Thus, when it comes to interpretation, to
the application of norms, of impact upon bodies and lives, the Pure Theory
goes silent: 'From the standpoint of positive law, however, there is no criterion on the basis of which one of the possibilities given in the frame of the
norm to be applied could be favored over other possibilities.'[51] Even more
strongly and perhaps we could say there is a tone of frustration, a little bit of
madness in the exit from praxis: 'It is futile to try to establish "legally" one
possibility by excluding the others. Both familiar means of interpretation,
argumentum a contrario and analogy are worthless' because they provide no
objective standard for law application.[52] The Pure Theory is simply a philosophy of law that has yet to find a body and, to coin a phrase, 'a philosophy that
does not use the body as an active platform of technovital transformation is
spinning in neutral'.[53] So, the Judge is in effect on his own, given his freedom
through his very perception of the silence of law, its absence, God like and so
immoral, in acting from a great distance, from an elsewhere in which it
should both know better and remain confined. Repeating and perverting
Kantorowicz, how is the Judge, law's son, to become law's mother? For the
Kelsenian thematic, that is not a possibility and should not be a question for
jurisprudential analysis but rather must be abandoned in favour of the proper
topic of the 'as if' of the *Grundnorm* and elaboration of the system that
devolves from it. The judge, as mouthpiece of the law (*la bouche des lois*), is
simply an automaton, a conduit, in slavish faith to the God of form. For
Argyll, to take our other contemporary example, the supernatural, the extra-
tellurian should be apprehended, as far as is humanly possible, and then left
to the postulates of the unknowable and ineffable manifestations of a

---

[51] Kelsen, *Problems of Legal Theory* at 81.
[52] Ibid. at 82.
[53] Preciado, *Testo Junkie* at 359.

Grundnorm, in the form of a divine will as expressed, and the Duke as juris-prudent is explicit about this, in rays and the miraculous. Schreber, in chal-lenging the father, in refusing to be the plaything of the Gods, embarks upon a very different project of reconstruction. The irrationality of the lived, the impurity of the body and the unpredictability of the emotions and the senses become hir resources and hir aesthetics of interpretation. These are the build-ing blocks for an incorporated and generative law, another and more visceral morality and order of the extant world, Schreber's 'as if'. The mystic body of the Judge is an atemporal and theologico-juridical *corpus*, experienced pain-fully as an abstract and compelled, automatic, compulsive and so vacuous body. It is against this rejected dignity and high office that he establishes his natural body as a new *corpus iuris* with its flaming speech, its images, its insights, voluptuousness, its senses and curves, its transformations. More than that, the key to the struggle lies in the soul being recalled to the flesh and often with excruciating force entering the body. The mystic becomes the corporeal, and, to borrow a phrase, 'Schreber becomes the woman that men lack.'[54] I will argue that it is by the same token, in taking up and inhabiting the place, the *jouissance* of the other that he becomes the body that law denies. The absence that the Judge, in his transitional state, fills, is that of praxis, the interface and intercourse of body and world, flesh and *lex terrae*, the sensory and *nomos*, for want of better words. It is as mutable, emotive, erotic and aesthetic flesh that the Judge emerges in his text to challenge the order and law of what is in his sensual apprehension a depopulated, cadaverous, ghostly world, governed by an antipathetic order of automatic and so senseless beings. How then is the Judge's other body, the rejected, transitional, curvaceous, feminine form to come into the moral order, the *Weltordnung*, the *nomos* of the earth? The irruption of the body into the symbolic order, the rending of science, abstraction and purity of theory that this would entail meets radical resistance. At the psychological level it is deemed mad to release such sensory forces and tactile apprehensions in the cadaverous domain of legalism, and even if it is deemed a 'harmless' lunacy, spiritualist effluvia and effluxion, it is to be discounted and dismissed – imprisoned even, for a while. For the jurists, even those of the historical school, the confusion of the *Volksgeist* with any real body, the purpose of law with the existential body of a judge, lawyer, legislator, is also deemed anathema. Kelsen, because his theory rises to the acme of the 'science of order', addresses the point in an intriguing essay on Freud's *Totem and Taboo* and *Group Psychology and the Ego*.[55] His thesis is

---

[54] Morel, *Sexual Ambiguities* at 103.

[55] Hans Kelsen, 'The Conception of State and Social Psychology – With Special Reference to Freud's Group Theory', 5 *Int. J. Psychoanalysis* 1 (1924).

that a group, a collectivity and ultimately the state, is cognisable only as absolutely distinct from the individuals, the psychic bodies, that make it up. The state is not an entity or collective being but rather a concept, an 'as if', which would be rendered meaningless by 'hypostasizing' the collective unity and attributing to it a 'collective pscyhe'.[56] The individual remains entirely outside and external to the science of order, for once science enters the mind of the subject 'no roads lead out again. From the point of view of psychology the individual mind is really a windowless monad.' Science, for Kelsen, connotes the 'subjugation and negation' of the singularity.[57] The office of the jurist has no subject, masculine or feminine, in the scientific fantasia of law. The subject is something else, other, and indeed alien, amorphous, and irrational from the point of view of purity and its bleached erasure of all colour. The sum of Schreber's tortured outpourings, his text, his flaming speech, his bellowing and visions, is that of seeking to break the barriers that would confine him in the prison of the juridical body, a monad, alone, windowless, subjugated and negated. In place of such simple and passive acceptance of either versions of confinement, the Judge attempts a break out; he attempts to elaborate a jurisprudence of resistance to the perception of the body as a thing 'separate from the person, but the bearer of that person', as a legal subject distinct from the corporeal, an abstract function, a schema of parts and their price.[58] For the Judge, it is change, mutation, transformation that best captures his multiple experiences, once finally allowed and expressed, of embodiment, and of the law as embodied: 'I only remember that I once had a different heart.'[59] The question to follow and trace is that of what it is that is expressed in the Judge's new body, meaning that to expatiate upon his transformation means quite simply and literally, because it is his text through which such change is tracked, pursuing the physical transformation, metaphoric and real. It is necessary here to recall that there is reality in our symbolisation, fiction (*fingo*) in all language use, imagination in law, because semblance is the necessary path of thought, and picturing, especially for Schreber, the mode of feeling our connections and directing our cerebrations towards just ends. It all starts with the process, inexplicable and visceral, of unmanning, *Entmannung*, in which the body is prepared for its new heart, and with it the performance of femininity. Thus, the changes to his symptomatically italicised sex organ: 'several times there were marked indications of

---

[56] Kelsen, 'Group Theory' at 12–13.

[57] Ibid. at 6.

[58] On the juristic construction of the body as thing, as cold and unsympathetic, see Alan Hyde, *Bodies of Law* (Princeton: Princeton University Press, 1997).

[59] Schreber, *Memoirs* at 150.

an actual retraction of the male organ (*Geschlechtstheile*)', there was 'a soften-ing approaching almost complete dissolution', and with that came removal of hairs from his beard and moustache, as also 'a change in my whole stature'.[60] Here we are witness to the advent, much mocked, by the voices, English in the original, of 'Miss Schreber'. She needs her clothes, her *armamentarium* as the Judge designates them, for protection, for safety in a hostile environ-ment, so as to protect her rights.[61] Next, we encounter the picturing of transi-tion: the compression of the chest, the alteration of the stomach, the lungs, the pharynx, catarrhal inflammation, seminal cord, spinal cord, the feet accosted by little men (*kleine Männer*), the head, the muscles, the eyes, the eyelids are all pictured attacked, changing, in struggle and transition to the reception of the feminine, as also to the halcyon autumnal feelings, the beauty of voluptuousness that emerges when such transformation is accepted. Along with bodily sense come feelings, smells, sounds, sights, colours, inten-sities, pain and, final point, self-consciousness of bodily functions, pleasures, contortions and even evacuation. The Judge has to be rid of something. To change means leaving part of the self behind and taking on the new. So much is obvious, but the specific details of this release, this cleansing of the so-called pollutions of the body merit brief attention. The stomach putrefies, the Judge holds back and experiences a somewhat ironic copraphobia, a retention and resistance to defecation. Waste needs to be expelled, and when the voices demand, in slow diction, 'Why do you not shit?' the Judge explains the frustration of this delay and retention by way of the image: 'a faint idea of the nervous unrest caused is perhaps the example of a Judge or teacher always listening to a mentally dull witness or a stammering (*stotternd*) scholar, who despite all attempts cannot clearly get out what he is asked or wants to say.'[62] The path to the other body is neither easy nor swift. The body that functions, that micturates and defecates, that perspires, weeps, smells, contracts, ejacu-lates and convulses is experienced initially by the Judge as the conventional object of derision. The body is subjected, in juridical theology, to a 'perfidious politics (*Perfidie der Politik*)' of obstruction and becomes a figure of stupidity, of mental dullness, of lack of reason and of aspersions of dementia. It is something to be destroyed not enjoyed. The understanding and the *jouissance* of sex, the enjoyment of the body, entry into the world, the symbolic, through all manner of expressions, as Schreber imagines most indicatively through his ironic metaphor of the boredom of the Judge, is a process, a coming to

---

[60] Ibid. at 149.
[61] Ibid. at 166 – and again, just saying, who could deny the humour, the irony, the play in such a recondite and apposite choice of word?
[62] Ibid. at 223.

understand and accept, an enactment and play. Thus, further into the text, the fourth of the appendices, embedded in the trajectory of depictions of the (missing) voluptuous body, of being in the feminine, in the evocation of the erotic enjoyment of libidinal surfaces, skin and ligament, organism and orgasm, the Judge, discussing an italicised *purposeful thought*, postulates the necessity of being able 'to do *in concreto* what is indispensable for one's bodily well-being; emptying in particular . . . I now achieve best when I sit on a bucket in front of the piano and play until I . . . usually after some straining, empty my bowels. However incredible this may sound, it is true.'[63] It is the *in concreto*, the image and the intestinal detail, the dirt – 'the small remnants in the bowl are smeared on my backside' – the *cacozelia*, the rendering of excrement, as much as the truth, the music, the bringing of soul and body together, that deserves attention.[64] What is important in the imagery is the mixing of the senses, the aesthetic and diurnal dirt, the imbrication of excretion, emission and expression, micturation and music, pail and piano.[65] This reeks of childhood, of the infant coming into being, explosive, inarticulate, a combination of needs and functions that are tied to an infinite potential. It is the structure of what Haverkamp elaborates as the *et infra . . . et supra*, the 'and beneath . . . and above', of the body and the law, that here receives its third term, a final and integrating transitional *et* that is the interpenetration of the two. The dead metaphor, the *catachresis*, and historical injustice of the theological in its continuation in the political receives its paradoxical, because unlovely, *coup de grace*, its end, in a merely, and only human body and politics.[66] After which, what remains, is there by virtue of the poets as legislators.[67] It is left to the creators, the creatures, the feminine in the masculine, the man in the woman, to alter, generate and change into new law, neither *infra* nor *supra* but *intra*. It is not necessarily a pretty process; it is frequently likely to be painful and polemical, contested and resisted, but invention, and particularly the creations of law, deserve their insight, their moments of exposure, the window into the process that becomes law for us. It is perhaps too easy to

---

[63] Ibid..

[64] Patricia Gherovici, *Transgender Psychoanalysis: A Lacanian Perspective on Sexual Difference* (London: Routledge, 2017), on the interplay of excrement and voluptuousness, beauty and dirt as a mode of enjoyment, as a species of art.

[65] Anselm Haverkamp, 'Richard II, Bracton and the End of Political Theology' 16 *Law and Literature* 313 (2004).

[66] Haverkamp, 'End of Political Theology' at 315

[67] The reference is to Hölderlin, noted in Haverkamp, 'End of Political Theology' at 316, and traced in more detail in Haverkamp, *Leaves of Mourning: Hölderlin's Late Work – With an Essay on Keats and Melancholy* (Albany: SUNY Press, 1996) at 48–54 ('was bleibet aber, stiften die Dichter").

wander, to stray, to lucinate with Schreber, a fact that leads to Freud's proleptic and revealing conclusion that he, too, may eventually be judged delusional.[68] There is a heavy-handed irony to Freud's admission, particularly as today
it is the notion that playing the feminine is perverse, that the desire to be
another, a woman, a man, a homosexual, is disastrous, that is the sign of
delirium. The concept that transition is catastrophic, the imaginary a mad
hallucination, a projection on to an irreal screen, limps in the texts of uncertain science and is subject to continuous critical revision.[69] While the Judge's
fantasia of the body, meaning his imagining himself transformed, different,
interior, voluptuous, and erotically engaged in enjoyment, is creeping ever
closer to the existential norm, the modern *Argonauts* are transitional practi-
tioners of the fluidity of gender and advocates of the fragile pointlessness of
any absolute sexual division. To let the body in, to acknowledge the sensory,
to address a synaesthesia of law, all allow for recognition of the Judge, and
specifically of 'Miss Schreber' as being painfully and proleptically ahead of hir
time in exposing to view an interiority hidden by office, an illicit backface and
underside, the impure process of invention and judgment as they actually are
in practice. A last divagation. The retraction and expansion, appearance and
disappearance of the bodily changes, as well as the oscillation and interplay of
its objective and subjective forms, suggest that Schreber's new body was
ambiguous, imagined and denied, conceived and abandoned. To break out of
the Asylum, the Judge had to participate in the incredible banality of meal-
time conversation with Dr Weber, his medical warden and opponent, his
almost Judas, almost friend, and with the female dinner companions. His
prandial torture was to say nothing surprising, nothing profound. He had to
pass unnoticed and unheard, as normal and compliant, and this he did,
doubtless at the considerable cost and delay of repression. Interestingly he
retains his sorrow and his humour, her melancholy and comedy, the latter in
the mode of irony, Puttenham's *metaphora continua*, but here of his own creation. The juxtapositions, the sense of the absurd, the punning and the playing
indicate that the Judge retained an extraordinary sense of the irony of his situation and of the game that he was choosing, albeit also forced to engage in
entertaining. Moving across a spectrum from belligerent and bellowing, to

---

[68] Freud, *The Schreber Case* at 66.

[69] The Lacanian notion of the solidity of symbolic places, elaborated most notably by the
Lacanian jurist Pierre Legendre, 'The Other Dimension of Law', in D. Carlson and
P. Goodrich (eds), *Law and the Postmodern Mind* (University of Michigan Press, 1998) at
175, in terms of the dependence of the social upon the invariance of the symbolic structure,
including that of the sexes, is perhaps the most contestable and potentially harmful of these
presuppositions.

consonant ease, to picturing and enjoyment, from exile, to 'enthusiastically getting down to it' with God, as Fernie puts it, the Judge is using his juristic skills to play his various roles and parts.[70] Where God or the voices call Schreber *Luder*, they are not just projecting a wretchedness on to him but equally designating him a player, perhaps even in the oldest sense of lawyer as *actor* and narrator. The legal and the liturgical, the trial and the play, have long been compared and are complicit in the theatricalisation of the various stages and offices of the social. Schreber succeeds to a remarkable extent in manifesting this theatre and in playing his parts in a profoundly, not to say at times tormentedly critical and self-conscious manner. He brings his body, affect, transition, the choice to be whatever sex, onto the public stage for centuries to come. It often feels as though he understands the allegory of sex in the socio-legal much better than his analysts and that he laughs at his predicament, his *gnosis*, more acutely and more perceptively than his various disciplinary guards and judges. In urban slang, *Luder* now also means bitch. The social gods were not pleased with Miss Schreber's appearance, her manifestation on stage, the choice of changing sex, but that designation also has the irony of recognising the feminine. Bitch also means strong woman, a recognition of the Judge's courage, determination and tenacity in maintaining belief and persisting with a choice that had led to his ostracism and incarceration, that forced him to sit every night at dinner and perform a role that was no longer relevant. *Luder* in its plurality of connotations recognises a site of transition, of metagraphic displacement and reinsertion, abjection, laughter, bellowing, guffawing, are fighting signs, flags of change, modes of marking the birth of something new, a pronoun, an agenda, a gender, a body.

There is finally also a considerable dimension of satire, of life and of laughter in his *Ludertum*, in the stunned and stunning text. Satire is in one etymology derived from *satyr*, the Greek mythical figure of woodland bacchanal, as in *satura in sylvae*. The satyr thus becomes for Nietzsche a figure of the gay science – *gaya scienza* – a Dionysian approach to knowledge as inclusive of the body, of affect, of the dance of sex and time. It is not without pertinence that the satyr is a body that incorporates the human and the animal and signifies a radical transgression of corporeal boundaries as well as of social norms. In Rabelesian terms – and where else to look for the paradigms of the satirical? – the howling Judge Schreber is a Gay Scientist, *sans culottes*. He is choosing his sex, baring his body, against the law, to change the law, out of necessity, at whatever cost. It takes a lot of humour, a considerable sense of the irony of the human comedy and the absurdity of legal institutions, to

---

[70] Fernie, *The Demonic* at 281.

imagine a new body, for a male Judge to mould and meld a feminine form, to dress as a woman, to self-create and see in the mirror not the King but the Judge as a woman. What if the Judge, law's son, becomes law's daughter? The irony of the question should not be lost.[71] It is also as *Luder*, as sufferer, satirist, humorist, and particularly as someone with a sense of irony, who made the world laughable for his own benefit, that the *Memorabilia* are without question at their most remarkable.

---

[71] Aristotle, *Rhetoric*, III 419 b 8–9: 'it is for himself that the ironist makes the world laughable"; insightfully cited and discussed in Paul Audi, *Lacan ironiste* (Paris: Mimésis, 2015) at 72 et seq.

Conclusion: Laughing in the Void

Nemo nascitur artifex[1]

M y argument, as brilliant as it now seems banal, is that Schreber's transition, his pain and dysphoria, as also his desire to identify as feminine,
to feel as a woman, to leave the law so as to right the law, was a simple reflection, among other causes, of the contemporary institutional prohibition of
such visceral and visible performances of ambivalent or transitional gender
identification. He was diagnosed as mentally ill, incarcerated as mad, and yet
maintained throughout that he was sane, that his transition was real, and that
the experience was sufficiently important to record in minute detail and to
present to science and philosophy as an empirical datum. Medical categories
change, the Diagnostic and Statistical Manual of Mental Disorders (DSM)
moves on, and today we would more likely view the Judge's *jouissance*, the
pain and the pleasure of transition, as expressing a profound conflict between
convention and desire, between the erotic and the juridical, between affect and
medicine, the repetition compulsion of the feminine and the failure of the
repression barrier. What is surprising is that the antinomy was one of which
Schreber was in significant measure aware and in which he was, at great personal cost, one could say at the expense of his life, far ahead of his times. This
was his *Luder*, his wretchedness, but also, as I have detailed, his play, his self-
conscious comedy of bellowing resistance, of increasingly 'loud laughter', his
extra-judicial howl from the Asylum, as he became his chosen self, a Seer, a
woman, a gnostic, in the sense of one who knows full well the comedy of
human abandonment. How better to end than to pursue this novel thesis, the

---

[1] This maxim, translating best as 'no one is born a lawyer', is from no less a source than Sir
Edward Coke, that pre-eminent sage and chef of English common law. See *The First Part
of the Institutes of the Lawes of England. Or, A Commentarie upon Littleton, not the name of
a Lawyer onely, but of the law itselfe* (London: Society of Stationers, 1628) at 97. And, of
course, the artisanal, what is fabricated can, as Schreber so vividly portrays, be unmade,
refashioned, bent, broken, built again.

liminal figure of the jurist as jester, the *serio-ludere* of the ever theatrical performance of law enacted at its most radical by the sex-swapping Schreber. Looking
back over the book, traversing the century and more since the great jurist
penned his remarkable text, there is a great deal of insight and considerable
foresight in his painful levity, his torment and his joy, his writing of a life that
he was precluded, foreclosed from living. Amidst everything else that it may
signify, there is the simple humour of the Judge's inventions, his novel enactments within the framework of the juridical offices of his time, his minor
jurisprudence as the invention of a language and law expressive of multiple
transitions, from pure to impure, abstract to concrete, law to affect, symbolic
to synaesthetic, male to female. He introduces a feminine performance, it is
repeated as a gendered apprehension of the body, and by implication an overturning of the *corpus iuris* as well. The voluptuousness of the flesh, the simple
sexuality of desire, heterosexual, homosexual, hermaphroditic, mono, bi, tri,
cis or alter, may be confused, hidden, tortured and at times denied in its passage into the Judge and into the law, but it is manifest. The Judge's transitional
trajectory may be a conflicted and polarised incursion, but it is nonetheless a
radical and sudden corporealisation, a *body* realised, the repression barrier
shattered, the dull white norm infracted, sex played out in the face of the
juridical, on the skin of the judge. Schreber's affect, the tensile changes in
nerves and ligaments, the becoming erogenous of the body express a radically
self-conscious gendered performance, an incarnadine jurisprudence of the
subject in their affects and with it a diffusion of images of entrails, smells,
sensations, of erotic surfaces, of their throbbing ligatures and distended core.
Along with the body, the erogenous judicial flesh, comes the acknowledgement and at times the celebration of this tactile surface of law, of organism and
orgasm as also being the medium of the lawyer's intercourse with the world, as
part of their embodiment of knowledge and of their method of knowing and
acting, in robes and *sans culottes*. Feeling, which appears, if at all, in the reason-
ing of judgments, as a pale and abstract intuition, a rapidly discarded glimmer
of invention, here takes a much more visible and dramatic role. *Ecce femina*,
the imaginary, which is to say the invented image, the *persona* and performance of Miss Schreber attends to the body precisely so as to undress the spirit
of justice, the greater context and cause, and in the Judge's own case and
forensic struggle in the Asylum, so as garner his release. To play the part of a
woman, however conventional and at times self-confessedly absurd the perception of that role and performance may seem, and still to act as a lawyer, to
successfully litigate his own release from the Asylum, to prove himself both a
woman and a lawyer, is an incredible accomplishment, a unique feat for the
times. More than that, to be a judge *and* to have a body, to admit and display,
to flirt and to flaunt with the libidinal surfaces, the tumescence and dilation,

expansions and contractions of flesh and skin, to embrace the actual ligaments of law was to draw away a veil that judiciary and jurisconsults alike had timelessly worn. Consider the hiding that judging traditionally requires, both the monumental architecture and heavily guarded spaces of judgment, the sartorial symbolism of the robes, the hoods, the wigs, the cloaks, all those forms of disguise that leave just the face and the hands, as the heavily figurative *personae,* the masks of reason through which the speech of the law sounds. Uniquely, for a senior Judge, Schreber takes his readers through the mask, under the gowns, between the sheets to make them vividly aware of the all too human site of judgment, the synaesthetic method before its time, expressed in the fusion of aesthetic space and ludic mood through which his thought, and his judgment travels. He is aware of the humour, the obscenity, the fine and fantastical feel of these perceptions as he puns on his inability to weigh himself, let alone others. He relays the allegorical image of sitting on a pail and playing the piano while, in Rabelasian fashion, pissing and shitting. That is the human condition, the underpinning of civility, the bedrock of morals in the comedic meeting of body and spirit, of base need and musical form, of creativity and law. A minor jurisprudence is an expression of resistance, minority representing, to borrow from Deleuze, a movement that has 'no model, it's a becoming, a process', one that fabulates in a non-conformist manner.[2] In musical terms, of which the Judge was fondest, the minor, associated with *cantus mollis,* subverts the major, the mode of *durus,* the figure of hierarchy and harsh and inflexible sounds. The major also, however, includes the minor, the minus or less than, which the feminine juristically represented, the figure of the melancholic, of the lesser and seldom heard. The minor, in gesture and in exception can also in time become the greater, reform and reformulate both language and the law. Schreber's minor jurisprudence of transition, and this is my argument throughout, is now coming to be seen, will be seen in time, as greater than the binary legal thinking that for so long, and with such Biblical force, imposed the absolute divide between male and female sexes, between body and soul, reason and affect, gravity and levity, law and critique.[3] Schreber screams out that law needs a sex change but screened by the walls of the Asylum and by the force and foreclosure of the psy-disciplines, his minor jurisprudence has been a faint cry from a far beyond, and little heard, if at all in legal circles. Returning to the themes addressed, undressed, redressed in his

---

[2] Gilles Deleuze, *Negotiations* (New York: Columbia University Press New York, 1995) at 175. The concept originates for these purposes in Gilles Deleuze and Félix Guattari, *Kafka: Towards a Minor Literature* (Minneapolis: University of Minnesota Press, 1986).

[3] I develop these themes in different directions in 'How Strange the Change from Major to Minor', 21 *Law Text Culture* 30 (2017).

jurisprudence, the gestures of his legal thought can be rehearsed in synoptic form, or as he put it, as a flag, as colours. The fabulation begins with the apprehension that the law's major mode, the exclusively male form, the virile profession and hierarchy of law has to be exited for life, for change and becoming to take shape and affective and indeed erotic form. So begins the theorisation, the jurisprudence of the Order of the World as out of joint and in disarray. The reign of law, to borrow Argyll's argot, is in essence and epistemology that of divine ordinance and miraculous or unknowable decrees. The major mode in law is that of the shadow of a *hieros* and hierarchy imposed upon the human from a space beyond materiality and lived forms. For Schreber, a minor jurisprudence is an inhabitation of the office of the jurist, it is a lifestyle, a claiming of your own law, an all too human law, a gay science in the wholly novel sense of a transitional bodily affect and expression of legality. Schreber's insistence upon a material order of norms, a synaesthetic apprehension of the mundane and corporeal patterning of existence, insists upon the rights of whatever sex and echoes Joyce, 'a man or a woman, who cares?' In the minor mode we do not have to choose, our affects can be mutable, temporal clusters that transform and transition, fabulate and refigure as occasion and epoch suggest, or eros requires. The minor character of Schreber's jurisprudence gains short, if any, shrift from the excoriators and commentators, from the cold critics and affectless scientists. They have not lived the law as Schreber did and this is the signal and minor import of his passage. I have argued that *Luder* belongs within *artem ludicram*, the performing arts – theatre, opera, ballet, dance, but also law, that most spectacular of enactments upon the great stage of public life. Schreber, in having to withdraw, and in being in transition, as also in advocating the feminine, embraces his minority or in Fransiscan terms his minorist position. The minor is here a lower key, 'a subsystem or outsystem', that is diffractive and inconstant.[4] The minor jurisprudence is an opening, an image of another law in its most visceral and embodied of forms, bellowing against the shackles, dancing free in the outside that is interior to legality, the *alieni iuris* of a forbidden *sui iuris*. Less formally, Schreber leaves the law so as to write his minor jurisprudence, as a lifestyle, as an authentic inhabitation of the body and office that he invents, so as to stage a novel persona in all of its occult because unrecognised expressions. His minor jurisprudence failed and yet its failure was and is its success, it was a mode of becoming and in stalling it kept open the possibility of future becomings, plural modes, the whatever of sexuation.

---

[4] Gilles Deleuze and Félix Guattari, *A Thousand Plateaus: Capitalism and Schizophrenia* (London: Athlone, 1987) at 105.

Writing in the Asylum, theorising in prison, unmanning and unjudging, undergoing transformation, there is a necessarily episodic quality to what are in diverse forms escape attempts. The Judge seeks to break out of his major role, to abandon the judgement of God, to deconstruct the norm at its most basic or inaugural level, that of sex and sanity. There is an important sense in which Schreber shatters the prison house of precedent and the priority of rules. He successfully litigates his release, and then he publishes the treatise that his Asylum Warden, Dr Weber, and the Judges of the Royal Court of Appeals had alike viewed as unpublishable, and that the former had attempted to silence as calumny, scandal and lunatic prose. The Warden's judgement, as I have detailed, was a lasting one and others have consistently followed in its wake and in reading the Judge's text have managed, mainly, only to see Dr Weber's judgement. The point is that such a judgement, that hard tone, can no longer stand. Morals have changed, *mores* have moved on, the third sex has increasingly been recognised and validated legally in the West, marriage has been pluralised, identities and offices recognised in their multiplicities, sexes changed, genders crossed. As one recalcitrant yet compliant English judge put it, not that long ago, in accepting that same-sex couples can be 'spouses' within the meaning of the relevant legislation may be to 'read black as meaning white',[5] but to 'conclude otherwise would be to stand like King Canute, ordering the tide to recede'.[6] A man or a woman, in principle, we no longer care. Both, either or neither will do. It is a matter of choice, of identification, of self-designation and performance, drive and adaptation to role.

Transitions hurt, roles bite, here is Juliet Jacques again, to take a contemporary example of the resident spirit of Schreber, when she prepares for surgery: 'I break down in tears, crying for thirty years of feeling like an outsider, twenty years of knowing this to be related to my gender, ten years of exploring it, three years of transition and two years of writing about it, with all their stresses and traumas simultaneously hurtling to the fore.'[7] The Judge did not have the options that Juliet has, and he couldn't telescope that pain into an operation. It lingered and outlived him. Still, for him, as graphically described and memorably depicted in images, allegories and metaphors, the inside and the outside, the genital and the sartorial, the sexual and the social can all be mixed, mingled, confused, expanded, altered,

[5] *Ghaidan v. Godin-Mendoza* [2004] UKHL 30, [2004] 3 All ER 411 at 440 [para 70] (Lord Millett).
[6] *Fitzpatrick v. Sterling Housing Association Ltd* [1998] 2WLR 225 [1998] 2 WLR 225 at 259 (Lord Justice Ward).
[7] Jacques, *Trans* at 2.

replayed. The Judge marked a beginning of such radical passage, transition and re-identification within the discourse of law. That case is made. What remains is to pick up on a final, liberatory and even somewhat surrealistic point. The Judge's *Luder*, his *serio-luder* has received perhaps even greater resistance than his sexual re-identification or at least has been more utterly overlooked by the agelasts of the law, in all its institutions and disciplines, than any other aspect of his treatise. It should be recollected that law has long recognised the ambiguity of sexual identification. Early in the *Digest* of Justinian, Ulpian is cited raising the question of the proper mode of treatment of hermaphrodites, a question that he answers, in his wisdom, which is to say in his legalism, as being according to the sex that predominates.[8] The English Judge Bracton, early in *De Legibus*, mentions 'another division of men: male, female and hermaphrodite'.[9] He then follows Ulpian in preferring the predominant manifestation test of gender. The hermaphrodite's right to inherit is addressed later in Book 28 of the *Digest* but the question of judicial hermaphroditism had not yet occurred. Schreber is perhaps the first to pose this juristic doctrinal question and the legal answer was in effect that as long as it did not show, it could be ignored. He was released, in part, because the Court of Appeals was satisfied that he was only dressing and acting as a woman in private. It accepted Schreber's argument that 'nobody will ever have noticed the least sign of faulty conduct' when he made excursions out of the Asylum.[10] Similarly, and even more probative, 'the ladies of the family table of the Director of the Asylum would not have the faintest idea of his delusions, unless informed of them in some other way'.[11] He could pass. He could play his role. But to his immortal credit, repression was not the Judge's interior *modus operandi*. He flaunted, flirted and fought. He demanded his rights, his liberties, his *corpus juris*, both textual and temporal. If, out of the void of self-creation, he was man and woman, transitional, possessed, dysphoric, voluptuous, blessed, he intended to have his say, to bellow, to howl, to laugh, to play. The Judge's *jouissance* was, as the word properly connotes, a mixture of pleasure and pain, an enjoyment of suffering, an accession to an unconventional, dsyphoric and transitional state. His was the human comedy writ at its largest, the juxtaposition of high office and base body, of rule and its distortion in invention, pain and the poetics

---

[8] *Digest* 1.5.10 (Ulpianus) *Quaeritur: hermaphroditum cui comparamus? et magis puto eius sexus aestimandum, qui in eo praevalet.*

[9] Bracton, *De legibus et consuetidinibus Angliae* at 9, available online, should you be interested and sufficiently enthusiastic.

[10] *Memoirs* at 482.

[11] Ibid. at 482–3.

of its play. The Judge gave full vent to hir Egeria, the minor chord, the melancholy muse, *lumière noire* or black sun that acts as the antipode and inspiration of his *détournement*, hir bursts of bellowing and laughter. It is to the bellowing, the claps of thunder, the screaming rage, the peals of laughter that I will attend. Borrowing from Debord's concept of *détournement* one can see that the Judge attempted to devise a critical language, adequate to his experience, to depict his dysphoria and transition, his insights and illations.[12] *Détournement* is defined as the devaluation and re-imagination of extant elements of the tradition, a method that is close to Nietzsche's revaluation of all values, which must pass initially through its moment of nihilism or loss of faith in existing *mores*. Schreber starts out, sure as night, with such a devaluation and despair. His is what Debord terms a 'deceptive *détournement*', the taking and turning of an intrinsically significant element of the tradition, and giving it a different scope, a new context, a critical meaning. The major revaluation is marked by 'parodic-seriousness' which, more than anything else, reflects the contradictions of an era, marking simultaneously the impossibility and the glimpse of opportunity for innovation, for changing a category, for undoing a convention, for upending a practice and here a performance of judicial gender. Schreber was prodromus and precursor, forerunner and forebear, herald and harbinger of a transition and change of sexual sensibility. Ahead of his time, he was also part of a parodic and satirical tradition of images and indeed of juristic and political depictions of the intermingling of genders and combination of sexes. The tradition of *emblemata* has numerous images and verbal depictions of the human body transformed or bestialised, from pictures of the Sphinx to figures with the heads of dogs, women with the tails of fish, pregnant men and so on, in satirical and caustic critical vein, including catamites, sodomites, masculine women and effeminate men in the saturnalia of emblems. The lexicon is provided early on in the translation of the hieroglyphs by Horapollo and then more expansively in Piero Valeriano and these get played with and turned around by the later tradition.[13] There is a received and established, recognised and systematised inventory of depictions of comedic and critical

---

[12] Guy Debord, 'A User's Guide to *Détournement*', in Kenn Knabb (ed.), *The Situationist International Anthology* (Berkeley: Bureau of Public Secrets, 2006), pp. 14–20. I owe this reference to the excellent essay by Keston Sutherland, *Stupefaction: A Radical Anatomy of Phantoms* (London: Seagull Books, 2011).

[13] The pregnant man, the image closest perhaps to Schreber's concerns, can be found first in Andrea Alciato, as, for example, in *Emblemata* (Lyon: Rouille, 1550) at 98 'Gula'. The verse begins 'Circulione gruis tumida vir pingitur alvo' (Here we have a man painted with a crane's long gullet and a swollen womb). I am indebted here to John Manning, *The Emblem* (London: Reaktion, 2004) chapter 7.

themes, both cautioning and entertaining, didactic and diverting, in what Debord would doubtless term a minor key, where the issues are of superficial morals and excessive or caricatured inversions of the norm. I will reference only two instances as illustrative of the trajectory of transition, of comedy and critique, pain and pleasure, dysphoria and didacticism to which I believe Schreber and his jurisprudence belong and can take their proper place. The first is from the early to mid-sixteenth century hieroglyphic work of Piero Valeriano, although I will take the image from a later treatise, that of the Jesuit priest and heraldic author Silvestro Pietrasancta, on symbols.[14] In book six, on the nature and strength of 'heroic symbols', meaning devices and other armorial insignia, he explains how the *impresa* or device is the visual sign, the external mark that shows to the world (*videntur omnes*) what nature and the deity have imprinted upon the human. These signs are indicative of the order of honour – *heroïcum* – and of dignity and office. The devices offer a weighing of worth, a balance of value, a visual mark of judgement and are metaphors for the *persona* that they represent.[15] The true image is that of the wisdom and judgement of the divinely inspired and vicarious. At this point he inserts an image of Fabius Maximus Cunctator, the Roman general who delayed engaging the Carthaginians, in the Second Punic war, until Rome had recovered her strength (Fig. 5). Pietrasancta reproduces a quadripartite image with three corresponding attributes. Under the acronymic motto FAB, for Fabius, is a depiction of the head of a horse, the face and beard of a man, the tail of a chicken and the legs and the talons of a crane. The equine head indicates prowess in war; the face and beard of a man signifies wisdom, patience and vigilance; while the tail of the chicken and feet of the crane signal victory.[16] There are elements here, early though the image is within the tradition, of a *détournement,* a moment of *ludus,* and of the metagraphic to which Debord will later refer.

Returning more directly to the themes that occupied Schreber, it is a later political emblem that I will reference and reproduce. We find it in a 1729 edition of *The Art of Politicks, in Imitation of Horace's Art of Poetry* (Fig. 6).[17]

[14] Silvestro Pietrasancta, *De Symbolis heroicis* (Antwerp: Moreti, 1634) at 165–6. The name is itself, of course, a pun. The source is Piero Valeriano, *Hieroglyphica sive de sacriis Ægyptorum literis* (Basle, 1556) at 38, who explains the enigmatic virtues of delay (*contatoris*): the head of a horse represents skill in war; the chest in the form of a bearded face represents caution (*contationem*) and wisdom (*prudentiam*); and the feet of a crane and the feathers and tail of a chicken signal victory.

[15] Pietrasancta, *De Symbolis* at 200, citing Cicero.

[16] Ibid. at 203.

[17] [James Bramston], *The Art of Politicks, in Imitation of Horace's Art of Poetry* (London: Lawton Gilliver, 1729).

LIBER SEXTVS. 203

num caput, cum hominis & vultu & barbâ in pe-
ctus promissâ, cum pedibus gruis, cum caudâ galli
gallinacei, & cum adscriptis ternis characteribus,

Pierius in Hiero-glyph.
Gorlæus in Dacty-lotheca.

FAB. schema fuit Fabij Cunctatoris; vt virtutes v-
nius perfecti Ducis eo monstro exprimerentur: hoc
est, equi capite, præfectura & principatus in bello;
vultu, barbâ, & pectore hominis, prudentia: cuncta-
tio & vigilantia, pedibus gruis; & caudâ galli gallinacei demum victoria.

C c 2   Eduar-

Figure 5 Silvestro Pietrasancta, *De Symbolis heroicis*, 1634 edition. Courtesy of David M. Rubenstein Rare Book & Manuscript Library, Duke University.

Figure 6 From James Bramston, *Art of Politics*, 1729. Photograph P. Goodrich.

Here we find a replay and revision of Pietrasancta's device in the mode of a frontispiece emblem to the satirical work. It depicts the bewigged head of a lawyer turned politician, a horse's neck and mane, two ample female breasts, the feathers of a macaw and the tail of a fish. Again, a quadripartite depiction, but this time with the sex of the figure rendered ambiguous and hermaphrodite. The motto – *risum teneatis amici?* – how, friends, can we help laughing? – indicates the human comedy that underlies the political critique, the vehicle of laughter being the mode and method of advocating change that here would be a minor *détournement.* The categories, thus far, are neither aesthetically, nor politically nor metaphysically particularly significant.

It is once we arrive at Schreber that the *détournement,* which after all
has now extended for more than a century, gains a major and compelling
significance. It is the binary of sex, the idiotic and now essentially contested
divide between genders and performances, the rigidity and brittleness, the
pain of separation, interior and exterior, that receives its juridico-political
reinscription. Comedy, the sense of the absurd, laughter at the absolute,
marks and opens up the cracks in the foundations of knowledge.[18] Together
with the humour, the irruption and bodily force of laughing is the gregarious
nature of the comic, its intercession, intermingling and appeal, that carries
with it the marks of the band and bond of friendship, Debord's comrades,
and that signals the collective re-inscription by means of the *genus jocosum,*
the humorously serious and seriously humorous that often alone will shift
a culture and change its *mores.* At the very least it must be recognised that
by the time that Schreber starts to imagine and embody his femininity,
to attach breasts to his chest and develop a feminine torso and loins, that
painful transition, all those years of pent-up rage and un-spilled tears, can
finally gain a degree of recognition, a moment of acknowledgement and the
possibility of laughter as well as pain. In dressing as a woman, in imagining,
in the strongest of senses, in developing the sensual apprehension of breasts
and of a feminine body Judge Schreber radically flaunts his desire. To borrow
from Virgil, *trahit sua quemque voluptas,* he follows his lust, acknowledges
his voluptuousness, literally, which is to say corporeally, as felt intendment,
and metaphysically, in imagination. The very fact that the Judge could play,
pun, laugh, that he was able to exercise his *Luder,* in its multitude of senses,
and continue to bellow, to roar, to howl, to guffaw and variably vociferate
indicates a connection to the world and the political, a relationship to the
real, that the slogan of lunacy, wielded like a scimitar by the medical profession, and also by the Vienna brigade, too quickly and easily denied. Think
of Schreber in this respect as belonging to the genre of prison writings,
as an intellectual incarcerated reflecting upon the human juridico-political
and sexual condition. He is in this regard a modern Boethius, a proleptic
Gramsci, a before Bobbio, whose sense of justice and whose performance
of gender have long outlived him and to extraordinary effect.[19] His is a

---

[18] See the inspiring final three pages of Erica Weitzman, *Irony's Antics: Walser, Kafka, Roth,
and the German Comic Tradition* (Evanston: Northwestern University Press, 2015) at
185–7.

[19] Reference can be made to Rivkah Zim, *The Consolations of Writing: Literary Strategies of
Resistance from Boethius to Primo Levi* (Princeton: Princeton University Press, 2014) at 306.
Better, however, I think, and with all due respect, to read Boethius, Gramsci, or Levi or
Schreber.

testimony of resistance, a witnessing of injustice and, most remarkable of all, the narrative of an incredible victory, both personal and legal. He wrote his way out of confinement, he successfully advocated his right to be transitional, transgender and trans-juridical. Let me end with the last neologism, the play of the trans and the juridical, the transgender and transsexualism in the institution and specifically in the law – in the courts, in the chambers, in the dock and in the cells. The implicitly transvestite historical practices of the judiciary, the *peruques*, the robes, the silver-buckled shoes already hint at the issue, the transmorphism of the hieratic, the image of the feminine into which the *corpus* of law somehow evaporates in its higher echelons, in its own third sex, its angelological body, the feminine muse of legality, *Iustitia*. Our Judge carries on that tradition and carries it much more self-consciously and much further. A matter of Schreber *maximus cunctator*, one could say, if afflicted with Latin, and the cane marks of a classical education. He has delayed long enough, now is hir time, his transition, her completion. The narrative is one that finally deserves justice, even if it is only the posthumous rendering of historical accounts.

It is to that end, in the spirit of Schreber, that a little picturing, a conjuring in invented images, may be permitted. The famous photoportrait of Schreber that is often used as frontispiece or cover image of works from that of Neiderland to Lothane, shows the Judge in civilian dress, youthful and luxuriantly moustached. Bow tied and besuited, Daniel Paul looks intense, poetic and perhaps musical, a hint of the flâneur, a man of style and aspiration. If one were to remove the moustache, add lips and then imagine the woman that Daniel Paul saw in the mirror, Miss Schreber to her maligners, her honour to her friends, hir *semblables*, and then the image would be something like the cover picture, produced by the installation artist and cookbook author, Jake Tilson. Here we see Schreber transitional and transformed (frontispiece 1). The same face now feminine, the same eyes and lips, but female adorned lips and then also the accessories and accoutrements of style that the Judge so enjoyed comporting. A fanned hat and silk bows, a wig, earrings, a simple, brief, yet utter transformation. It does not take much for the appearance of transition, for the miracle of change, to allow Schreber to be happy in gender, correct in sex, the female now taking over the place of the man (Frontispiece 2). To borrow from Bramston, who can avoid smiling at this subtle yet significant change.

I am struck, and have made too much, according to Professor Tarizzo, with whom I have an intermittent correspondence, of Schreber's laughter, his *Luder* and his bellowing. I disagree because I believe that the Judge's mixture of laughter and outcry, was immanent and unavoidable. The Judge had to bellow for his condition to be heard and his dysphoric dilemma aired.

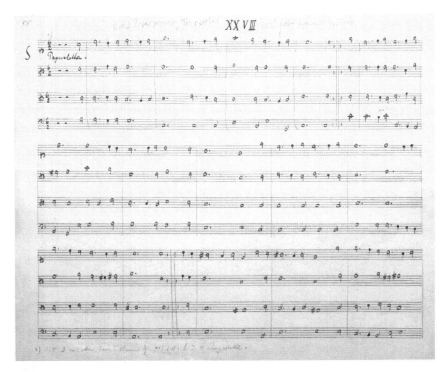

Figure 7 Sheet music in Schreber's possession. With thanks to the Library of Congress, Niederland Collection.

His howls were the cries of birthing. If he had not been loud then he would never have been audible outside the walls of the Asylum; he would have been silenced, hidden, secreted, locked away and, worst of all, unpublished. We would not hear him now. The future could not read him. What intrigues me most, however, is the relation of bellowing, the one most persistent expression of malaise and the basis of his case. The bellowing was first, *ex hypothesi*, the sign of his rage, his anger at the abuse of doctors, the misdiagnosis and exclusion. He could so easily have become an invisible moment in Foucault's archaeology of silence, one more entry in the psychiatric books of the law. As it is, he broke out of the crystal palace, he slipped through the bars of the prison and the cage of gender alike. He was, to borrow a phrase, a man who could walk through walls. To do that, he needed to bellow, to be heard, to inscribe, to write with his voice. That, in the end, was his contribution, hir legislation and law. What better sign of the Judge could there be than his continued edicts, his *bullae*, his judgments issuing on and issuing still from whatever space of a novel law. The Judge has never left us, or in the urban slang of today, the *Luder*, the bitch, is back.

Bibliography

Ackersdyke, Wilhelm Cornelius, *Disputatio philologico-juridica. De utilitate et auctoritate poeseos et poetarum in jurisprudentia, nec non de utilitate jurisprudentiæ in legendis et explicandis poetis* (Paddenburg, 1779).

Agamben, Giorgio, Opus Dei: *An Archaeology of Duty* (Palo Alto: Stanford University Press, 2013).

Alciato, Andrea, *Emblemata* (Lyons: Rouille, 1550).

——, *De notitia dignitatum* (Paris: Cramoisy, 1651).

Allison, David et al. (eds), *Psychosis and Sexual Identity: Toward a Post-Analytic View of the Schreber Case* (Albany: SUNY Press, 1988).

Aristodemou, Maria, *Law, Psychoanalysis, Society: Taking the Unconscious Seriously* (London: Routledge, 2015).

Audi, Paul, *Lacan ironiste* (Paris: Mimésis, 2015).

Auerbach, Erich, 'Figura', now available in James Porter (ed.), *Time, History and Literature: Selected Essays of Erich Auerbach* (Princeton: Princeton University Press, 2016), pp. 65–113.

Bachelard, Gaston, *The Poetics of Reverie* (Boston: Beacon Press, 1971).

Barthes, Roland, *A Lover's Discourse: Fragments* (London: Jonathan Cape, 1979).

Bayard, Pierre, *How to Talk about Books that You Haven't Read* (London: Bloomsbury, 2009).

Benjamin, Walter, 'Books by the Mentally Ill', in Benjamin, *Selected Writings 1927–1930* (Cambridge, MA: Harvard University Press, 1999).

Bentham, Jeremy, *Theory of Fictions* (London: Kegan Paul, 1932).

Berke, Joseph H. et al. (eds), *Even Paranoids Have Enemies* (London: Routledge, 1998).

Berkowitz, Roger, *The Gift of Science. Leibnitz and the Modern Legal Tradition* (Cambridge, MA: Harvard University Press, 2005).

Berman, Harold, 'The Origins of Western Legal Science', 90 *Harvard Law Rev.* 894–943 (1977).

——, *Law and Revolution: The Formation of the Western Legal Tradition* (Cambridge, MA: Harvard University Press, 1983).

——, *Law and Revolution II: The Impact of the Protestant Reformations on the Western Legal Tradition* (Cambridge, MA: Harvard University Press, 2006).

Blackstone, William, *Commentaries on the Laws of England* (Chicago: University of Chicago Press, 1978 [1765]).

Bond, Henry, *Lacan at the Scene* (Boston: Massachusetts Institute of Technology, 2009).

Brabant, Eva et al. (eds), *The Correspondence of Sigmund Freud and Sandor Ferenczi, Volume 1* (Cambridge, MA: Harvard University Press, 1994).

Bracton, Henry de, *De Legibus et consuetudinibus Angliae* (On the Laws and Customs of England) (London: Richard Totell, 1569 [1189]).

Bramston, James, *The Art of Politics, in Imitation of Horace's Art of Poetry* (London: Gilliver, 1729).

Brubaker, Rogers, *Trans: Gender and Race in an Age of Unsettled Identities* (Princeton: Princeton University Press, 2016).

Butler, Judith, *Gender Trouble: Feminism and the Subversion of Identity* (London: Routledge, 1989).

——, *Bodies that Matter: On the Discursive Limits of Sex* (London: Routledge, 1993).

Calasso, Roberto, 'A Report on Readers of Schreber', in Calasso, *The Forty-NineSteps* (Minneapolis: University of Minnesota Press, 2001), pp. 122–31.

Canetti, Elias, *Crowds and Power* (New York: Farrar, Straus, Giroux, 1984).

Carpzovius, Benedictus, *Practica Novae Imperialis Saxonica Rerum Criminalium* (Wittenberg: n.p., 1652).

Castoriadis, Cornelius, *Crossroads in the Labyrinth* (Brighton: Harvester, 1984).

Coke, Sir Edward, *The First Part of the Institutes of the Lawes of England. Or, A Commentarie upon Littleton, not the name of a Lawyer onely, but of the law itselfe* (London: Society of Stationers, 1628).

Coke, Roger, *Justice Vindicated from the False Fucus put upon it, by Thomas White Gent., Mr Thomas Hobbes, and Hugo Grotius* (London: Tho. Newcomb, 1660).

Conaghan, Joanne, *Law and Gender* (Oxford: Clarendon Press, 2013).

Cujas, Jacques, *Opera Omnia* (Lyons: Bonhomme, 1567).

Cusset, François, *French Theory: How Foucault, Derrida, Deleuze & co. transformed the Intellectual Life of the United States* (Minneapolis: University of Minnesota Press, 2008).

Debord, Guy, 'A User's Guide to *Détournement*', in Ken Knabb (ed.), *The Situationist International Anthology* (Berkeley: Bureau of Public Secrets, 2006), pp. 14–20.

Deleuze, Gilles, *Masochism* (New York: Zone Books, 1989).

——, *Negotiations* (New York: Columbia University Press, 1995).

Deleuze, Gilles, and Guattari, Félix, *Anti-Oedipus: Capitalism and Schizophrenia* (London: Penguin, 2006).

——, *Kafka: Towards a Minor Literature* (Minneapolis: University of Minnesota Press, 1986).

——, *A Thousand Plateaux: Capitalism and Schizophrenia* (London: Athlone Press, 1987).

Deniau, Alain, 'Du fantasme au pousse-à-la-femme, la psychose', 25 *Che Vuoi?: Revue de Psychanalyse* 63–76 (2006).

Duke of Argyll, *The Reign of Law*, 5th edn (New York: Alden Press, 1884).

Ehler, S. Z. and Morall, J. B. (eds), *Church and State through the Centuries: A Collection of Historical Documents* (London: Newman Press, 1954).

Fajardo, Diego de Saavedra, *Idee de un principe politico Cristiano* (Monaco: n.p., 1640).

Felski, Rita, *The Limits of Critique* (Chicago: University of Chicago Press, 2015).

Fernie, Ewan, *The Demonic: Literature and Possession* (London: Routledge, 2013).

Forrester, John, *Language and the Origins of Psychoanalysis* (London: Macmillan, 1980).

——, *Dispatches from the Freud Wars: Psychoanalysis and its Passions* (Cambridge, MA: Harvard University Press, 1998).

Fortescue, Sir John, *De natura legis naturae* (London: private circulation, 1466).

Foucault, Michel, *The Archaeology of Knowledge* (New York: Pantheon Books, 1972).

——, *Language, Counter-Memory, Practice: Selected Essays and Interviews* (Ithaca: Cornell University Press, 1977).

——, 'The Father's No', in *Language, Counter-Memory, Practice: Selected Essays and Interviews* (Ithaca: Cornell University Press, 1977), pp. 68–86.

——, *The History of Sexuality. Volume 1* (New York: Vintage Books, 1990 [1978]).

——, *Abnormal. Lectures at the College de France 1974–1975* (London: Verso, 2003).

——, *History of Madness* (London: Routledge, 2009).

Freud, Sigmund, 'Psychoanalysis and the Ascertaining of Truth in Courts of Law', in *Collected Papers*, vol. II (London: Hogarth Press, 1946 [1906]), pp. 13–24.

——, 'Psychoanalytic Notes on an Autobiographical Account of a Case of Paranoia (Dementia Paranoides)', in James Strachey (ed.), *The Standard Edition of the Complete Psychological Works of Sigmund Freud vol XII* (London: Hogarth Press, 1958 [1911]), pp. 9–82.

——, *Totem and Taboo* (Harmondsworth: Hogarth Press, 2001 [1913]).

——, *The Schreber Case* (London: Penguin, 2003).

Gherovici, Patricia, *Please Select Your Gender: From the Invention of Hysteria to the Democratizing of Transgenderism* (London: Routledge, 2010).

——, *Transgender Psychoanalysis: A Lacanian Perspective on Sexual Difference* (London: Routledge, 2017).

Gherovici Patricia, and Steinkoler, Manya, *Lacan on Madness: Madness, Yes You Can't* (London: Routledge, 2015).

——, *Lacan, Psychoanalysis, and Comedy* (New York: Cambridge University Press, 2016).

Goodrich, Peter, 'Critical Legal Studies in England', 12 *Oxford J. Legal Studies* 195–236 (1992).

——, Oedipus lex: *History, Psychoanalysis, Law* (Berkeley: University of California Press, 1995)

——, 'Satirical Legal Studies: From the Legists to the *Lizard*', 103 *Michigan Law Rev.* 397–517 (2004–5).

——, *Legal Emblems and the Art of Law* (New York: Cambridge University Press, 2014).

——, 'How Strange the Change from Major to Minor', 21 *Law Text Culture* 30–53 (2017).

—— (ed.), *Law and the Unconscious: A Legendre Reader* (London: Macmillan, 1995).

Gordley, James, *The Jurists* (Oxford: Oxford University Press, 2013).

Green, André, *The Work of the Negative* (London: Free Association Books, 1999).

Haines, Chelsea, 'Beyond the Schreber Principle', 35 *Mousse* 264–8 (2012).

Hall, Will, *Outside Mental Health: Voices and Visions of Madness* (New York: Kickstarter: Will Hall, 2016).

Hasler, Eveline, *Die Wachsflügelfrau*, trans. Edna McCown, as *Flying with Wings of Wax* (New York: Fromm International Publishing, 1993 [1991]).

Haven, Alexander van, *The Other Zarathustra: Madness, Schreber and the Making of Religion in 19th Century Germany* (Chicago: University of Chicago, PhD, 2009).

Haverkamp, Anselm, *Leaves of Mourning: Hölderlin's Late Work – With an Essay on Keats and Melancholy* (Albany: SUNY Press, 1996).

——, 'Richard II, Bracton and the End of Political Theology', 16:3 *Law and Literature* 313–36 (2004).

Hobbes, Thomas, *Leviathan* (London: Dent, 1950 [1652]).

Hotman, Antoine, *Traité de la loi Salique* (Paris: Cramoisy, 1593).

Huizinga, J., *Homo ludens* (New York: Roy Publishers, 1950).

Hyde, Alan, *Bodies of Law* (Princeton: Princeton University Press, 1997).

Jacques, Juliet, *Trans: A Memoir* (London: Verso, 2015).

Jellinek, Elvin Morton, *System der subjektiven öffentlichen Rechte*, 2nd edn (Tübingen: J. C. B. Mohr, 1905, repr. Aalen: Scientia, 1979).

Jewel, John, *A Defence of the Apology of the Church of England* (London: Fleetstreet, 1567).

Jhering, Rudolf von, *Der Geist des römischen Recht* (Leipzig: Breitkopf und Härtel, 1852).

——, *The Struggle for Law* (Chicago: Callaghan & Co, 1915 [1872]).

——, *Law as a Means to an End* (Boston: Boston Book Co., 1913 [1903]).

Kahn, Victoria, 'Political Theology and Fiction in *The King's Two Bodies*', 106:1 *Representations* 77–101 (2009).

——, *The Future of an Illusion: Political Theology and Early Modern Texts* (Chicago: University of Chicago Press, 2014).

Kant, Immanuel, *Critique of Pure Reason* (London: Macmillan, 1929).

Kantorowicz, Hermann, 'Savigny and the Historical School of Law', 53 *Law Quarterly Review* 326–43 (1937).

Kantorowicz, Ernst, *The King's Two Bodies: A Study in Medieval Political Theology* (Princeton: Princeton University Press, 1958).

Kelley, Donald, *The Human Measure: Social Thought in the Western Legal Tradition* (Cambridge, MA: Harvard University Press, 1990).

Kelsen, Hans, *Hauptprobleme der Staatsrechtslehre* (Tübingen: J. C. B. Mohr, 1911).

——, 'The Conception of State and Social Psychology – With Special Reference to Freud's Group Theory', 5 *Int. J. Psychoanalysis* 1–38 (1924).

——, *General Theory of Law and State* (Cambridge, MA: Harvard University Press, 1946).

——, *The Pure Theory of Law* (Berkeley and Los Angeles: California University Press, 1960).

——, *Introduction to the Problems of Legal Theory* (Oxford: Clarendon Press, 2002 [1911]).

Kittler, Friedrich, *Discourse Networks 1800/1900* (Palo Alto: Stanford University Press, 1990).

——, *The Truth of the Technological World: Essays on the Genealogy of Presence* (Cambridge: Polity Press, 2014).

Kraepelin, Emil, *Psychiatrie. Ein Lehrbuch für Studirende und Aerzte*, 5th edn (Leipzig: A. Barth, 1896).

Lacan, Jacques, 'L'Etourdit', 4 *Scilicet* 5–52 (1973).

——, *The Four Fundamental Concepts of Psychoanalysis* (New York: Norton, 1981).

——, 'Presentation of the *Mémoires* of President Schreber in French Translation', 38 *Ornicar?, revue du Champ freudien* 5–9 (1986).

——, *Television: A Challenge to the Psychoanalytic Establishment* (New York: Norton, 1990).

——, *The Seminar of Jacques Lacan Book III: The Psychoses* (New York: Norton, 1993).

——, *Écrits: The First Complete Edition in En*mpany, 2006).

——, 'Presentation on Psychical Causality', in *Écrits: The First Complete Edition in English*, trans. Bruce Fink (New York: Norton, 2006), pp. 123–58.

——, *The Other Side of Psychoanalysis* (New York: Norton, 2007).

Lacan, Sibylle, *Un Père* (Paris: Gallimard, 1997).

Laplanche, Jean, *Hölderlin and the Question of the Father* (Victoria, BC: ELS Editions, 2007).

Leader, Darian, *Why Do Women Write More Letters Than They Post* (London: Faber, 1997).

——, *What is Madness?* (Harmondsworth: Penguin, 2012).

Legendre, Pierre, *L'Amour du censeur* (Paris: Seuil, 1976).

——, 'The Judge amongst the Interpreters', in Peter Goodrich (ed.), *Law and the Unconscious: A Legendre Reader* (London: Macmillan, 1992), pp. 1 64–210.

——, *Dieu au mirroir* (Paris: Fayard, 1995).

——, 'Hermes and Institutional Structures', in Peter Goodrich (ed.) *Law and the Unconscious: A Legendre Reader* (London: Macmillan, 1995), pp. 137–63.

——, *Le Désir politique de Dieu* (Paris: Fayard, 1996).

——, *Les Enfants du texte: Etudes sur la fonction parentale des Etats* (Paris: Fayard, 1992).

——, *De la societé comme texte* (Paris: Fayard, 2001).

——, 'The Other Dimension of Law', in D. Carlson and P. Goodrich (eds), *Law and the Postmodern Mind* (Ann Arbor: University of Michigan Press, 1998), pp. 175–92.

——, *L'Autre Bible de l'Occident. Le Monument romano-canonique* (Paris: Fayard, 2009).

——, *God at the Mirror: Study of the Institution of Images*, trans. Peter Young (London: Routledge, forthcoming).

Leibnitz, Gottfried, *Nova methodus discendæ docendaque jurisprudentiæ, ex artis didacticæ principiis in parte generali præpræmissis, experientiæque luce* (Frankfurt: Zunneri, 1667).

——, 'Elementa juris naturalis (1666–7)', in *Philosphische Scrhiften Erster Band 1663–1672* (Berlin: Akademie Verlag, 1990).

Lothane, Zvi, 'The Psychopatholgy of Hallucinations – A Methodological Analysis', 55 *British Journal of Medical Psychology* 335–48 (1982).

——, *In Defense of Schreber: Soul Murder and Psychiatry* (Hillsdale: The Analytic Press, 1992).

Lyotard, Jean-François, *Libidinal Economy* (London: Athlone Press, 1993).

MacCabe, Colin, 'Discourse', in MacCabe (ed.), *The Talking Cure* (London: Macmillan, 1990), pp. 188–217.

——, 'Introduction', in Sigmund Freud, *The Schreber Case* (London: Penguin, 2002), pp. vi–xxii.

MacNeil, William, *Lex Populi, The Jurisprudence of Popular Culture* (Stanford: Stanford University Press, 2007).

Manderson, Desmond, *Kangaroo Courts and the Rule of Law: The Legacy of Modernism* (London: Routledge, 2012).

Manning, Erin, *The Minor Gesture* (Durham, NC: Duke University Press, 2016).

Manning, John, *The Emblem* (London: Reaktion, 2004).

Manow, Philip, *In the King's Shadow: The Political Anatomy of Democratic Representation* (Cambridge: Polity, 2010).

Marmoy, C. F. A., 'The Auto-Icon of Jeremy Bentham at University College, London', 2.2 *Medical History* 77–86 (1958).

Morel, Geneviève, *Sexual Ambiguities: Sexuation and Psychosis* (London: Karnac, 2011).

Murat, Laure, *Loi du genre: Une histoire culturelle du 'troisième sexe'* (Paris: Fayard, 2006).

——, *The Man Who Thought he was Napoleon: Toward a Political History of Madness* (Chicago: University of Chicago Press, 2014).

Nelson, Maggie, *The Argonauts* (Minneapolis: Graywolf Press, 2015).

Niederland, W. G., 'Schreber: Father and Son', 28:2 *Psychoanalytic Quart.* 151–69 (1959).

——, *The Schreber Case: Psychoanalytic Profile of a Paranoid Personality* (New York: Quadrangle, 1974).

Ogorek, Regina, 'Inconsistencies and Consistencies in 19th Century Legal Theory', in Christian Joerges and David Trubek (eds), *Critical Legal Thought: An American–German Debate* (Baden-Baden: Nomos Verlagsgesellschaft, 1989), pp. 13–36.

Olson, Greta, 'Law is not Turgid and Literature not Soft and Fleshy: Gendering and Heteronormativity in Law and Literature Scholarship', 36 *Australian Feminist Law Journal* 65–86 (2012).

Pashukanis, Eugeny, *Law and Marxism* (London: Pluto Press, 1978).

Pietrasancta, Silvestro, *De Symbolis heroicis* (Antwerp: Moreti, 1634).

Porter, James, 'Disfigurations: Erich Auerbach's Theory of *Figura*', 44 *Critical Inquiry* 80 (2017).

Preciado, Paul B., *Testo Junkie: Sex, Drugs, and Biopolitics in the Pharmacopornographic Era* (New York: Feminist Press, 2016).

Puttenham, George, *The Arte of English Poesie* (London: Richard Field, 1589).

Resnik, Saloman, *The Logics of Madness* (London: Karnac, 2011).

Rosenstock-Huessy, Eugen, *Out of Revolution: Autobiography of Western Man* (Norwich, VT: Argo, 1969 [1938]).

Russell, Yvette, 'Woman's Voice/Law's Logos: The Rape Trial and the Limits of Liberal Reform', 42:2 *Australian Feminist Law Journal* 273–96 (2016).

Sachs, Albie and Wilson, Joan Hoff, *Sexism and the Law: A Study of Male Beliefs and Judicial Bias* (London: Martin Robertson, 1978).

Sanders, Mark, 'Psychoanalysis, Mourning and the Law: Schreber's Paranoia as Crisis of Judging', in Austin Sarat and Martha Merrill Umphrey (eds), *Law and Mourning* (Amherst: University of Massachusetts Press, 2017), pp. 117–47.

Santner, Eric, *My Own Private Germany: Daniel Paul Schreber's Secret History of Modernity* (Princeton: Princeton University Press, 1996).

——, *The Royal Remains: The People's Two Bodies and the Endgames of Sovereignty* (Chicago: University of Chicago Press, 2011).

Sass, Louis, *The Paradoxes of Delusion: Wittgenstein, Schreber and the Schizophrenic Mind* (Ithaca: Cornell University Press, 1995).

Savigny, Friedrich von, *The Vocation of Our Age for Legislation and Jurisprudence* (Union, NJ: Lawbook Exchange, 2002 [1814]).

Schatzman, M., *Soul Murder: Persecution in the Family* (New York: Signet, 1973).

Schreber, Daniel Paul, *Denkwürdigkeiten eines Nervenkranken nebst Nachträgen und einem Anhang über die Frage: 'Unter welchen Voraussetzungen darf eine für geisteskrank erachtete Person gegen ihren erklärten Willen in einer Heilanstalt festgehalten werden?'*, 1st edition (Leipzig: Oswald Muße, 1903).

——, *Memoirs of My Nervous Illness*, trans Ida MacAlpine and Richard Hunter (Cambridge, MA: Harvard University Press, 1988 [1955]).

Sloane, Tom (ed.), *The Oxford Encyclopedia of Rhetoric* (Oxford: Oxford University Press, 2001).

Southern, D., 'German Legal Ideas in the Nineteenth and Twentieth Centuries', 10:1 *Liverpool Law Review* 63–81 (1988).

Stein, Peter, *Roman Law in European History* (Cambridge: Cambridge University Press, 1999).

Sutherland, Keston, *Stupefaction: A Radical Anatomy of Phantoms* (London: Seagull Books, 2011).

Sutter, Laurent de, *Deleuze: La pratique du droit* (Paris: Michalon, 2009).

——, '*Contra Iurem*: On the Two Ontologies of Giorgio Agamben', in Peter Goodrich and Michel Rosenfeld (eds), *Economies of Interpretation* (New York: Fordham University Press, 2018).

Sylvestre, Michel, *Demain la psychanalyse* (Paris: Albin: 2003).

Szasz, Thomas, *Schizophrenia. The Sacred Symbol of Psychiatry* (Syracuse: Syracuse University Press, 1976).

Tomsic, Samo, *The Capitalist Unconscious: Marx and Lacan* (London: Verso, 2015).

Tort, Michel, *Le Fin du dogme paternel* (Paris: Aubier, 1992).

Vaihinger, Hans, *The Philosophy of 'As If'. A System of the Theoretical, Practical and Religious Fictions of Mankind*, trans. C. K. Ogden (London: Kegan Paul, 1924).

Valeriano, Piero, *Hieroglyphica sive de sacris Ægyptorum literis commentarii* (Basle: n.p., 1550).

——, *Hieroglyphica sive de sacriis Ægyptorum literis* (Basle, 1556).

Vismann, Cornelia, 'Beyond Image', in Peter Goodrich et al., *Law, Text, Terror* (London: Glass House Press, 2006), pp. 35–43.

Wacjman, Gérard, *Fenêtre. Chroniques du regard et de l'intime* (Paris: Verdier, 2004).

Wan, Marco, *Masculinity and the Trials of Modern Fiction* (London: Routledge, 2016).

Watson, Alan, *The Making of the Civil Law* (Cambridge, MA: Harvard University Press, 1981).

Weber, Samuel, 'Introduction to the 1988 Edition', in Daniel Paul Schreber, *Memoirs of My Nervous Illness* (Cambridge, MA: Harvard University Press, 1988), vii–liv.

Weitzman, Erica, *Irony's Antics: Walser, Kafka, Roth, and the German Comic Tradition* (Evanston: Northwestern University Press, 2015).

Wigmore, John, 'Nova methodus discendæ docendaeque jurisprudentiae', 30:8 *Harvard L.R.* 812–29 (1916).

Wilden, Anthony, *System and Structure: Essays in Communication and Exchange* (London: Routledge, 2003 [1972]).

Zim, Rivkah, *The Consolations of Writing: Literary Strategies of Resistance from Boethius to Primo Levi* (Princeton: Princeton University Press, 2014).

Index

abjection, 117–19, 136
Accursius, 113
Acheiropoiesis, 83
Ackersdyke, Wilhelm Cornelius, 85
Adam, 126, 128
administration, 21, 62, 76, 80; *see also* oikonomia
Agamben, Giorgio, 74, 107
agelasts, 143
Alciatus, Andreas, 116, 144
alieni iuris, 141
allegory (*allegoresis*), 64–6, 80, 135
als ob (as if), 91, 93–7, 109, 129–32
amanuensis, 83
analogy, 93–4
anti-psychiatry, 9
aposiopesis, 12, 15
apparatus *see dispositif*
arcana imperii, 86
argumentum ad feminam, 115 *et seq.*
Argyll, Duke of, 89–92, 102, 105, 124, 128, 130–1, 141
Aristotle, 64, 101, 137
artem ludicram, 141
as if (*als ob*), 21, 108, 110, 120, 130–2
asylum, 11, 33, 82, 98, 113, 124, 135, 138, 139, 142, 150
atopia, 108–9
Auctoritates poetarum, 85
Audi, Paul, 94, 137
Auerbach, Erich, 95
auto-icon, 120
automata, 59, 80–3, 84, 86–7, 98, 100, 108, 130–2

Bachelard, Gaston, 128
Barthes, Roland, 33
Bayard, Pierre, 63
Beethoven, Ludwig, 64

bellowing, 6, 7, 9, 26, 32, 63, 82, 84, 85, 99, 122, 123, 136, 138, 144, 149
Bentham, Jeremy, 94, 120
Berkowitz, Roger, 101–3
Berman, Harold, 73, 101
binaries, 112–16, 120, 128, 135, 148
bitch, 136, 150
blackletter, 15, 16, 86, 100
Blackstone, Sir William, 125
blind spots, 32
boredom, 133–4
Bracton, Henry de, 115, 143
Bramston, James, 145
Butler, Judith, 121

Calasso, Roberto, 34–5, 39
Canetti, Elias, 10, 36
Canute, King, 142
Carpzovius, Benedictus, 67
Castiadoris, Cornelius, 48–9
catachresis, 134
Catholicism, 71
celestial bodies, 79, 107–9
Christ, Jesus, 63, 64, 72
Coke, Roger, 66
Coke, Sir Edward, 138
comedy, 117, 135–8, 142–6
compulsive thinking, 82
Conaghan, Joanne, 113
copraphobia, 133–4
corpus iuris civilis, 62, 81, 115, 129–30, 142
    humanitatis, 126, 139
    mysticum, 125–6
    physicum, 125–6, 129, 143
counter-transference, 36–7, 48
Crenshaw, Kimberlé, 74
critique, 1–2, 5, 21, 30, 52, 60 *et seq.*, 74–5, 87, 99, 140
Cujas, Jacques, 116

Dame de Balance, 87
Darwinism, 89, 91
Debord, Guy, 144–5
Deleuze, Gilles, 63, 140, 141
delirium, 61, 83, 133, 134
dementia paranoides, 14, 34, 35
denial, 43, 106, 115
Derrida, Jacques, 74
détournement, 117, 136, 144, 147
dictatus papae, 71–3
dispositif, 37, 40, 54, 82
dolus indeterminatus, 67–70, 74
dysphoria, 2, 7, 19–20, 22, 37, 43, 96, 112,
    118, 138, 142–4, 149

ecstasis, 119
Egeria, 144
Eros, 107, 121, 123, 124, 141
erotomania, 49, 107
estoppel, 92
exegesis, 81, 84, 100

Fabius, Maximus Cunctator, 145
fasces, 79
father
    fantasm of, 42, 43, 45, 55, 59
    law of, 37–42, 44–6, 49–50, 58–9, 61–2,
        99
Felski, Rita, 75
feminine
    dress, 121, 123, 125–7, 133–4,
        148–9
    ideation, 63, 65–6, 73, 77, 84, 96–9,
        107, 110–11, 139–42 (*et passim*)
Ferenczi, Sandor, 35, 44–5
Fernie, Ewan, 5, 10, 64, 81, 90, 121,
    136
figura, 94, 132
Flechsig, Professor, 2–3, 23, 24, 25, 33,
    38–9, 44, 48, 51–2, 69, 77–8, 87,
    95–6, 106, 113, 118
fleeting improvised beings, 4, 6, 21, 24, 26,
    35, 57, 65, 76, 78, 79, 80–3, 86, 95,
    108, 110
Fleiss, Wilhelm, 39
foreclosure (*Verwerfung*), 4, 7–8, 10, 22,
    50–3, 57, 59–60, 61
forecourts (of heaven), 23, 59, 68, 76, 95,
    105–7
Forrester, John, 33–4, 45
Fortescue, Sir John, 116
Foucault, Michel, vii, 7, 30–31, 32, 33, 88,
    127

Freud, Sigmund, 9, 10, 14, 17, 22, 26, 33
    et seq., 54, 55, 58–60, 61, 73, 95, 114,
    121, 122, 131, 135

Gandorfer, Daniela, ix, 118
gay science, 124, 136
German Civil Code (BGB), 81, 100,
    103
German vice, 117–18
Gherovici, Patricia, 48, 134
God, 4, 24, 42–4, 50, 63, 67, 68, 71,
    75–76, 89–92, 96–7, 106, 113, 124 (*et
    passim*)
    actio in distans, 76, 130
    Ariman, 106, 117
    death of, 73–4
    speech of, 35, 50, 95
Gordley, James, vii, 102
Green, André, 58
Gregory VII, Pope, 71–3, 74
Grundnorm, 83, 105, 130–1
Grundsprache, 34–5, 50, 95, 108
Guattari, Félix, 63, 135
guilt, 41–4

Haines, Chelsea, 31
Halle, Maurice, 64
hallucination, 26, 39, 54–5, 57, 121
Haven, Alexander van, 53
Haverkamp, Anselm, 134
head-compressing machine, 80
Hegel, Wilhelm Friedrich, 11
Heritier, Paolo, viii
    nods, viii
hermeneutics, 55
hieroglyphs, 55, 144
Hobbes, Thomas, 109
Hölderlin, 30, 61, 134
homo fenestris, 118, 119
homosexual ideation, 7, 10, 26, 38–9,
    44
homunculi, 118
Horapollo, 144
Hotman, Antoine, 116
Huizinga, J., 111
humanitas, 125
humour, 25, 40, 57, 64, 110–11, 118–19,
    121–3, 133, 135–7, 138, 142–5
Hyde, Alan, 132
hyperaesthesia, 39
hypochondria, 25, 39
hypnopompic dream, 6, 26, 37–8, 40, 44,
    69, 114

images, 54–5, 58–60, 63, 80, 96, 109–12, 119
imaginary, 66, 92–3, 139
in hoc signo vinces, 73, 77
interrupted speech, 56, 67, 80, 82, 91, 93, 95
investiture, 126–8
  crisis, 71–4
ius commune, 68

Jacques, Juliet, 142
Jakobson, Roman, 64
Jellinek, Elvin Morton, 104
Jew (exemplary), 90
Jewel, John, 119
Jhering, Rudolf, 100–3, 106
jouissance, 51–2, 105, 119, 133, 138, 143
Joyce, James, 141
judgement, 24
jurisprudence, 87, 95, 100–4
  Historical School, 100–2, 131–2
  incarnadine, 65, 95, 104–6, 124–7, 129–33, 139–42
  minor, 124, 139–44 *et passim*
  positivised, 100–5
jurists, 102; *see also* lawyers
  as jesters, 139
justice, 25, 59, 61, 69–74, 75, 82, 84, 139–42, 149
  scales of, 69–70, 117
Justinian, 62, 115–16, 142
justissima tellus, 75–6, 88, 105, 107–10, 125

Kahn, Victoria, 128
Kant, Immanuel, 4, 11, 53, 95, 100, 103, 104
Kantorowicz, Ernst, 66, 121, 125–8
Kelley, Donald, 101
Kelsen, Hans, 21, 84, 93, 103–7, 126, 130, 131–2
Kempin, Emily, 113, 114
Kennedy, Duncan, 74
Kittler, Friedrich, 84, 96, 100
Kojève, Alexandre, 53
Kraepelin, Emil, 57, 58

Lacan, Jacques, 9, 10, 12, 14, 22, 43, 48 *et seq.*, 61, 63–6, 83, 91–2, 95, 121
  nom du père, 49, 60, 62
  Roman Catholicism, 49, 60, 63, 66
Lacan, Sybille, 60
Langdell, Christopher Columbus, 102
Laplanche, Jean, 30, 61

laughter, 141–5; *see also* bellowing
law
  corpuscular, 129, 132–4, 141
  critique of, 59–60, 66, 69, 73–5, 80–5, 100–8, 127–31, 139–44
  desire, 50–2, 54, 122–6
  discourse of, 41, 59–60, 142
  femininity and, 65–6, 113–16, 142–9
  hearing, 69, 122
  hermaphroditism, 143
  and literature, 66, 125
  as science, 98–9, 101–7, 129–30, 132
  source of, 62, 129
  spectres of, 81
  symbolic, 33, 38, 66, 112–13
  women in, 113–17
lawyers, 26, 29, 61, 74, 77–80, 84, 98, 113–16, 118, 139–43
  actors, 136, 139
  sans culottes, 139
  spectral, 80, 83
legal fiction (*fictio iuris*), 21, 67, 75, 91–2, 104
Legendre, Pierre, 41, 62, 73, 81, 135
leges terrae, 109, 129, 131
Leibnitz, Gottfried, 95, 101–2
Leipzig-Dösen Asylum, 35
lesbia regula, 73
lex divinae, 80
libidinal economy, 96, 107, 121, 125, 132–4
libido theory, 34, 36, 39
linguistics, 54–6
litigiousness, 51
logography, 5, 83
Lothane, Zvi, 10, 19, 45, 47, 51–2, 58, 78
Luder, 40, 108, 110, 113, 117–19, 122, 136, 138, 142–4
lunacy, 7–8, 14, 16, 19, 49, 99, 118, 120, 130, 135
  and law, 98–9, 113–15, 130–1
  and politics, 59, 117
Luther, Martin, 64, 77, 99, 113
Lyotard, Jean-François, 96

Macalpine, Ida, 1, 9, 12–19
MacCabe, Colin, 3, 10, 32, 47, 63
Manow, Philip, 125, 127
Marx, Karl, 74
mens rea, 68
metaphor, 54, 61, 62–7, 69, 70, 75, 82, 90, 95, 118, 119, 125, 135
metonymy, 64, 65

miracles, 67, 76, 83, 92, 96, 99
more geometrico, 101
Morel, Geneviève, 7, 10, 51, 131
mos italicus, 80, 101
mouse, 67–8
Murat, Laure, 7, 11, 40, 53, 58, 115, 117
music, 28, 64, 84, 109

Napoleon, 77
Nelson, Maggie, 91, 135
nerves, 56, 81, 96–8, 106–7, 110, 119, 126, 129
Niederland, William, 47
Nietzsche, Friedrich, 73, 74, 136
noise, 82, 86, 106, 108
nomos, 64, 67, 70, 84, 85, 96–8, 114, 121, 131
noumenal, 4
novum omne cave, 115

Ogorek, Regina, 100
oikonomia, 21, 29, 61, 62, 69, 85
Olson, Greta, 122
Order of the World, 4, 23, 24, 48, 50, 68, 70, 75–8, 91–7, 124, 141
otium cum dignitate, 85

paranoia, 14, 33–4, 39, 43, 44, 49, 50, 55
Pashunkanis, Eugeny, 104
persona non data, 126
Phryne, 113–14
piano, 64, 84, 109, 121, 134
picturing, 108–11, 132
Pietrasancta, Silvestro, 145
Pope, 71–3, 77
Portia, 113
possession, 83–4
pousse à la femme, 84, 110, 124
praesumptio iuris, 94, 104, 108
Preciado, Paul B., 5, 112, 122–3, 130
preface (*prae-ludium*), 2–3
prison writing, 46
projection, 54–5, 58–9
Proudhon, Pierre-Joseph, 74
psychiatry, 7, 9, 14, 20–1, 38–40, 48–50, 59, 77–8, 96, 114, 121
psychoanalysis, 57–8, 61, 66, 121
psychosis, 7, 14, 22, 29–30, 44, 49, 54, 57, 91
Puchta, Georg Friedrich, 98
Pure Theory of Law, 102–7, 108, 126, 130
Puttenham, George, 64–5, 135
Pythagoras, 64

Rabelais, 91, 136, 140
railways, 76
Ramus, Petrus, 101
ratio scripta, 11
rays (divine), 56, 76–7, 79, 83, 87, 92, 97, 106–7, 110–11, 118–19, 126, 129
red lettering, 16
Reichstag, 1, 6, 10, 69
representing, 82, 84
resistance, 34, 42, 43
revolution
  interpretative, 72–4
  papal, 71–4
  third, 74
rhetoric, 64, 133–5
Rosenstock-Huessy, Eugen, 72
Royal Court (Saxony), 5, 11, 14, 19, 26, 29, 47, 67–9, 80, 98–9, 124
Rubicon, 29
Russell, Yvette, 122

Salic law, 116
Sanders, Mark, ix, 25, 44–5, 69–70, 87, 129
sans culottes, 136–7
Santner, Eric, 10, 34, 43, 45, 69, 71, 108, 117–19, 127
Sass, Louis, 10, 40
satire, 136
Saussure, Ferdinand, 64–5
Savigny, 100, 102–3
scales, 25, 69–71, 87–8, 113, 117, 120
Schatzman, Morton, 47
Schreber, Daniel Paul
  body, 107–8, 110, 112–15, 118–21, 124–6, 131–3, 139–43
  femininity, 26–8, 63, 112 *et seq.*, 120, 130–5
  forensic essay, 12, 14
  jurisprudence, 21, 84–5, 94, 143–5
  law, 20–1
  lawsuit, 3–5, 11–15, 18, 22, 29, 78–9, 98, 139
  legal competence, 4, 11, 47, 51
  Miss Schreber, xi, 61, 99, 112, 133, 135–6, 139
  picturing, 54
  science, 2, 22–3
  style, 64
  text, 5–6, 10–15, 21–2
  theology, 2, 4, 19, 21, 22, 23, 63
Schreber, Moritz, 33, 47, 54–6
Schreber, Sabine, 26, 121

scilicet, 75, 87, 91–2
scotomise, 32, 64
Scriptarrhea, 1
serio-ludere, 139, 143
Shelley, 24
Sonnenstein, 2, 32, 41, 54
soul, 24, 26, 95–6, 106–8, 126
    murder (*Seelenmord*), 3, 64
    tested, 4, 23, 56, 67, 68, 80, 82, 106
    voluptuousness, 71, 82, 95, 96, 106
sovereignty, 61, 62–3, 71–4, 82, 106–10
speech, flaming, 64
Stein, Peter, 101
subsumtionsautomat, 100
sui iuris, 141
Sutherland, Keston, 144
Sutter, Laurent de, 107
Sylvestre, Michel, 51
symbolic order, 66, 92–3, 94, 108–10, 126
synaesthesia, 119, 124, 129, 139–41
Szasz, Thomas, 9

Tarizzo, Davide, ix, 3, 149
theatre of law, 135–7
third sex, 7, 37, 40, 45, 142, 149
Thoth, 1
Tort, Michel, 37, 42, 51
Totem & Taboo, 42–4
trans, vii–viii, 6–7, 28, 37, 40, 45, 51, 63,
    66, 77, 84, 107, 112–14, 120–4, 128,
    132–6, 138, 142, 149
translation, 1, 2–3, 9, 12–21

Trüstedt, Katrin, 98
Twelve Tables, 92
typography (Gothic), 16

Unger, Roberto, 74
unmanning (*Entmannung*), 7, 65, 82, 84,
    112–14
usus modernus, 102

Vaihinger, Hans, 21, 93–8, 104
Valeriano, Piero, 144–5
veils, 140
Vertov, Dziga, 54
victory, 117, 149
Vismann, Cornelia, 114
Volksgeist, 102, 131
voluptuousness, 77, 96, 120, 124, 134

W, von, 64
Weber, Guido, 2–3, 11, 38, 39–40, 77, 120,
    135, 142
Weber, Samuel, 10–11, 25
Weber, Max, 99, 100–1
Weitzman, Erica, 148
Williams, Patricia, 74
Wolff, Christian, 102
writing-down system, 67, 79, 82–4, 99–100,
    108

xenofeminism, 120, 142

Zartaloudis, Thanos, 73